E. F. Codd and

Relational Theory

A Detailed Review and Analysis

of Codd's Major Database Writings

C. J. Date

ISBN: 978-1-6847-0527-6 (sc)
ISBN: 978-1-6847-0528-3 (e)

Library of Congress Control Number: 2019907105

Lulu Publishing Services rev. date: 07/15/2019

The paragraph below describes a situation that, it seems to me, exactly parallels the one that arises in connection with Codd's invention of the relational model, on the one hand, vs. the many subsequent contributions to that model (also to other aspects of relational theory) made by later researchers, on the other. Accordingly, I'd like to make it as clear as possible that the analysis, comments, and criticisms in the chapters that follow are all offered in, and should all be construed in, the spirit of this paragraph:

Jakob Bernoulli's productive years coincided with Leibniz's discovery of calculus, and [he] was one of the chief popularizers of this immensely fruitful subject. As with any developing theory, calculus benefited from those who followed in its creator's footsteps, scholars whose brilliance may have fallen short of Leibniz's but whose contributions toward tidying up the subject were indispensable. Jakob Bernoulli was one such contributor.

—William Dunham:
The Mathematical Universe (1974)

This next quote summarizes, for me, the essence of Codd's contribution. Hilbert was talking about Cantor, of course, not Codd, but I've taken a small liberty in translation here:

Aus dem Paradies, das Cantor uns geschaffen, soll uns niemand vertreiben können.
(No one shall expel us from the paradise that Codd has created.)

—David Hilbert:
On the Infinite (1926)

My apologies to all concerned, but I was so delighted when I discovered the following definition and explanation that I simply couldn't resist quoting it here:

Codswallop. A lot, or **a load of codswallop**. Simply nonsense or rubbish; said of something silly, far-fetched or fanciful when advanced as serious information or explanation. In 1875 Hiram Codd patented a mineral water bottle with a marble stopper. *Wallop* is a slang term for beer. Thus *Codd's wallop* is said to have become a disparaging term among beer drinkers for mineral waters and weak drinks and in due course the term gained a more general application.

—*Brewer's Dictionary of Phrase and Fable* (14th edition, 1989)

———— ◆◆◆◆◆ ————

*Dedicated to the memory of Ted Codd
and all keepers of the true relational flame*

About the Author

C. J. Date is an independent author, lecturer, researcher, and consultant, specializing in relational database technology. He is best known for his book *An Introduction to Database Systems* (8th edition, Addison-Wesley, 2004), which has sold some 900,000 copies at the time of writing and is used by several hundred colleges and universities worldwide. He is also the author of numerous other books on database management, including most recently:

- From Ventus: *Go Faster! The TransRelational^{TM} Approach to DBMS Implementation* (2002, 2011)

- From Addison-Wesley: *Databases, Types, and the Relational Model: The Third Manifesto* (3rd edition, with Hugh Darwen, 2007)

- From Trafford: *Logic and Databases: The Roots of Relational Theory* (2007) and *Database Explorations: Essays on The Third Manifesto and Related Topics* (with Hugh Darwen, 2010)

- From Apress: *Date on Database: Writings 2000-2006* (2007)

- From Morgan Kaufmann: *Time and Relational Theory: Temporal Databases in the Relational Model and SQL* (with Hugh Darwen and Nikos A. Lorentzos, 2014)

- From O'Reilly: *Database Design and Relational Theory: Normal Forms and All That Jazz* (2012); *View Updating and Relational Theory: Solving the View Update Problem* (2013); *Relational Theory for Computer Professionals: What Relational Databases Are Really All About* (2013); *SQL and Relational Theory: How to Write Accurate SQL Code* (3rd edition, 2015); *The **New** Relational Database Dictionary* (2016); and *Type Inheritance and Relational Theory: Subtypes, Supertypes, and Substitutability* (2016)

Mr Date was inducted into the Computing Industry Hall of Fame in 2004. He enjoys a reputation that is second to none for his ability to explain complex technical subjects in a clear and understandable fashion.

Contents

Preface

I'm a relational advocate. Forgive the lack of modesty, but I'm *known* as a relational advocate. I've spent almost the entirety of my professional career—which is to say almost half a century, at the time of writing—researching, writing about, and teaching relational theory and relational technology. It's my very firm belief that the relational model of data is a hugely beneficial and beautiful invention, and I'm grateful, as indeed all of us should be, to E. F. ("Ted") Codd for having presented it to the world. As I'm sure you know, Codd was awarded the 1981 ACM Turing Award for his contribution, and in my opinion he richly deserved that recognition.

In connection with that award, in 2018 I was invited to edit a book "celebrating Codd's accomplishment, explaining the research that led to the award, and discussing the impact of that research." After careful consideration, I decided, for reasons there's no need to go into here, to decline the invitation. However, it did get me thinking; more specifically, it got me thinking about an itch I'd been meaning to scratch for at least the past 25 years. Let me elaborate.

Beginning in the year 1969, Codd produced a lengthy series of writings (over 50 of them by my count) dealing with the relational model and various aspects of relational theory and relational systems. Of those numerous writings, the ones that seem to me far and away the most significant for one reason or another are as follows:

- "Derivability, Redundancy, and Consistency of Relations Stored in Large Data Banks" (August 19th, 1969)[1]

- "A Relational Model of Data for Large Shared Data Banks" (June 1970)

- "Relational Completeness of Data Base Sublanguages" (March 6th, 1972)[2]

- "A Data Base Sublanguage Founded on the Relational Calculus" (July 26th, 1971)

- "Further Normalization of the Data Base Relational Model" (August 31st, 1971)

- "Interactive Support for Nonprogrammers: The Relational and Network Approaches" (June 6th, 1974)

- A two-part paper, "Is Your DBMS Really Relational?" (October 14th, 1985) and "Does Your DBMS Run By The Rules?" (October 21st, 1985)

---

[1] *Data bank* was an early term for what subsequently, and much more commonly, came to be called a database.

[2] At the time *database* was usually written (as in the title of this paper) as two words, thus: *data base*.

■ A book, *The Relational Model for Database Management Version 2* (1990)

(The dates shown in the foregoing list are the dates of first publication; however, all of the writings in question have since been republished, some of them several times. Full citations can be found in Appendix C.)

The itch I wanted to scratch was this: Of course, I read most of these documents when they first appeared,[3] but I'd been meaning for years to reread them in the light of all that's happened in the field since. In particular, I had a feeling that there might be aspects of them that didn't hold up all that well to modern critical analysis, and I wanted to see if that feeling on my part was justified. In other words, I wanted to analyze the publications as carefully as I could, and I wanted to write a detailed critique of them accordingly. And that's basically what this book is: It's my analysis of, and commentary on, the publications listed above. The first six are discussed in Part II of the book and the others in Part III.[4] (Part I is a purely introductory part—it serves to lay some necessary groundwork to pave the way for a proper understanding of the other two parts.)

There's one thing I'd like to make very clear right up front, though: My analysis and commentary are *not* meant as an attack. Certainly not! It's true that portions of the text are quite critical—even severely so, in some places—but my overall aim is to be constructive. Basically, what I want to do is (a) to highlight the many fundamental things that Codd got right, but at the same time (b) to identify aspects (some of them of lesser importance, perhaps) on which Codd wasn't as clear as he might have been or was, in a few cases, almost certainly wrong.

There's another point, too. Those publications of Codd's—the first six of them, at any rate—are the foundation texts on which our field (the entire relational database field, that is) is based. Yet I know from personal experience that very few of those who work in that field have actually read all of those texts, or even have much awareness of what they contain. And I'd like to do something about this somewhat sorry state of affairs. In a nutshell, I'd like to explain, for each publication in the foregoing list, just what the contribution was, how and why it was important, and to some extent also what it wasn't.

In the interest of full disclosure, I must explain that I knew Codd well. We worked together as colleagues for many years, first in IBM[5] and subsequently in a series of companies (Codd & Date International and various subsidiaries of that company) that, along with Sharon

---

[3] The only one I didn't read as soon as it first appeared was the 1969 paper (my own database career didn't really get under way until 1970). As for the rest, however, I actually read most of them, at least in draft form, *before* they were formally published.

[4] And here's as good a place as any to note that if you have access to any of those publications of Codd's, it would be a good idea to keep them with you and read them alongside the pertinent chapter(s) of the present book.

[5] Regarding our time in IBM, though, I should also make it clear that we were always in different divisions of the company (Codd was in Research and I was in a series of development divisions). For the first few years of our acquaintance (1970-1974), we were even on different sides of the Atlantic—Codd was in California and I was in England—and our collaboration during that period was hardly very extensive, being conducted mostly by telex (!) and regular mail. But from 1974 on, although we were in different divisions, our workplaces were just a few miles apart in Silicon Valley, and we worked together much more closely, and saw each other socially too. However, I should add that my part in this joint professional activity, at any rate up until 1979 or so, consisted primarily though not exclusively in interpreting Codd's ideas and explaining them to other people.

Weinberg (later Sharon Codd), Codd and I formed in 1983. We were friends, too, for my part. And I want to say this, too: Codd was undoubtedly a genius. He was, I think, one of just three people I've known well to whom I believe that epithet might reasonably be applied. The insights that led to his relational model were, in my opinion, absolutely brilliant, and his early papers (despite any shortcomings I might be identifying subsequently in this book) were brilliant also.

All of that said, however, I do have to say as well that he could be rather stubborn on occasion—and in later life he became (in my view) perhaps a little too sensitive to criticism and a little too defensive regarding such criticism. In fact I have in my possession a letter from him, written sometime in 1992 and addressing the question of such criticism, in which he admits to being aware of "only two mistakes ... in all of [his] work of [the past] two decades" (work, that is, on relational matters). And he goes on in that letter to identify and describe the mistakes in question, as follows (paraphrasing very slightly):

1. "[There] was a boundary error in the [1972] proof of the reducibility of a relational request from a version expressed in predicate logic to a version expressed in the *n*-ary relational algebra ... This error did not invalidate the theorem. Only the proof needed to be corrected." *Note:* See Chapter 3 for a detailed discussion of the reducibility theorem and related matters.

2. "In the 1985 set of twelve rules for comparing DBMS products claimed to be relational, Rule 6 required that the DBMS should be capable of determining the updatability for all views that are theoretically updatable. This rule has been changed to reflect the logical undecidability of the general theoretical problem." *Note:* See Chapter 7 for a detailed discussion of the twelve rules and related matters.

I'll leave it for you to decide, after reading this book, to what extent you feel the foregoing remarks are accurate, or justified, or sufficient.

There are a couple of further preliminary matters that need to be addressed:

■ Throughout the book there are numerous references to something called *The Third Manifesto*. *The Third Manifesto* (the *Manifesto* for short) is an attempt by Hugh Darwen and myself to pin down as precisely as possible exactly what the relational model is and what some of its implications are.

■ Throughout the book there are also coding examples written in a language called **Tutorial D**. **Tutorial D** is a concrete language, designed by Hugh Darwen and myself, intended to illustrate the abstract ideas of *The Third Manifesto* (and intended also to be more or less self-explanatory).

See the website *www.thethirdmanifesto.com*, also our book *Databases, Types, and the Relational Model: The Third Manifesto* (3rd edition, Addison-Wesley, 2007), for detailed information concerning both *The Third Manifesto* and **Tutorial D**.

    Finally, the book also contains three appendixes: one containing the text of the piece I wrote in connection with Codd's Turing Award for the pertinent section of the ACM website (*amturing.acm.org*); one containing a set of formal definitions; and the last consisting of a consolidated list of references for the entire book.

Prerequisites

I assume you have a professional interest in the theory of relational databases. Ideally, you should be familiar with that theory at least to the level discussed in one or other of the following books by myself (though Chapter 1 of the present book does provide a brief overview of the material in question):

- *Relational Theory for Computer Professionals: What Relational Databases Are Really All About* (O'Reilly, 2013)

- *SQL and Relational Theory: How to Write Accurate SQL Code* (3rd edition, O'Reilly, 2015)

For Chapter 5 some elementary knowledge of dependency theory is also desirable. That theory is discussed (briefly) in the first of the two books just mentioned but not the second.

Publishing History

- Chapter 1 was previously published, in somewhat different form, on the website *www.thethirdmanifesto.com*.

- Portions of Chapter 6 were previously published, in considerably different form, in the book C. J. Date, *Relational Database: Selected Writings*, 1st edition, © 1986. Reprinted by permission of Pearson Education, Inc., New York, New York. *Note:* The same material was originally included in Randall J. Rustin (ed.), Proc. ACM SIGMOD Workshop on Data Description, Access, and Control, Vol. II, Ann Arbor, Michigan (May 1974), © ACM 1975. Reprinted by permission of ACM.

- Other portions of Chapter 6 were previously published, in considerably different form, in the book C. J. Date, *Relational Database Writings 1991-1994*, 1st edition, © 1995. Reprinted by permission of Pearson Education, Inc., New York, New York.

- Portions of Chapters 7 and 8 were previously published, in considerably different form, in the book C. J. Date, *Relational Database Writings 1989-1991*, 1st edition, © 1992. Reprinted by permission of Pearson Education, Inc., New York, New York.

- Appendix A was previously published on the ACM website *amturing.acm.org*, © 2012. Reprinted by permission of ACM.

Acknowledgments

First and foremost, of course, I'd like to thank Ted Codd for writing the material on which this book is based, and more generally just for inventing his wonderful relational model. We all of us owe him a tremendous debt of gratitude. Thus, as I've already said, the chapters that follow, critical though they certainly are in places, are categorically not meant as an attack. Rather, they're offered in the spirit of honest scientific inquiry and analysis, in an attempt to achieve a "more perfect" statement of what relational theory is, or should be, really all about.

Second, I'd like to thank the many people in addition to Ted Codd himself who have helped shape my database thinking over the years. There are far too many of you to name individually, but among those I'd especially like to mention are (in alphabetical order) Charley Bontempo, Hugh Darwen, Ron Fagin, Adrian Larner, and David McGoveran.

Third, I'd like to thank my reviewers Declan Brady, Hugh Darwen, François de Sainte Marie, and Lauri Pietarinen for their thorough and meticulous reviews of early drafts of just about everything in the body of the book. Of course, it goes without saying that any remaining errors of fact and infelicities of phrasing are mine.

C. J. Date
Healdsburg, California
2019

Part I

SETTING THE SCENE

This part of the book consists of a single chapter, viz., "What's a Relational DBMS?" Unlike later chapters, it isn't directly tied to any of Codd's relational writings. Rather, it's the "prerequisites" chapter—it provides an overview of material you'll be expected to be familiar with when you read those later chapters. Now, much of what it covers will doubtless be familiar to you already (in fact I sincerely hope it is); however, I'd like to suggest that you at least skim it even so, because (a) it's always good to know what it is you're supposed to know, and (b) in any case, you might find there are certain aspects of the material that you're not all that familiar with after all. For example, do you know what a relvar is?

Chapter 1

What's a Relational DBMS?

Ignorance is an evil weed, which dictators may cultivate among their dupes,
but no democracy can afford among its citizens.

—William Henry Beveridge:
Full Employment in a Free Society (1944)

This chapter was originally intended to serve as an informal introduction to the IEEE Annals of the History of Computing, Vol. 34, No. 4 (October-December 2012, "Relational Database Management Systems: The Formative Years") and Vol. 35, No. 2 (April-June 2013, "Relational Database Management Systems: The Business Explosion"). It was rejected for that purpose, however, possibly because it assumed too much technical background on the part of the reader, but more probably because of its somewhat critical tone. It's based in part on various published books by myself, including in particular SQL and Relational Theory: How to Write Accurate SQL Code (3rd edition, O'Reilly, 2015). It's meant to be suitable for anyone with an interest in the history of relational database management, including but not limited to anyone who's a current practitioner in the database field and thus has some familiarity with SQL in particular.

"Everyone knows" that relational DBMSs are one of the great success stories in the computing field.[1] What almost no one does know, however, is that there aren't any relational DBMSs!—at least, not if we limit our attention to commercially available mainstream products. Rather, those commercial products are all *SQL* DBMSs. And, sadly, there's a wide gap between relational theory as such, on the one hand, and SQL, considered as an attempt at a concrete realization of that theory, on the other. Now, it's my aim in this chapter to explain what relational, not SQL, DBMSs are all about—but if I'm successful in that aim, then one consequence will inevitably be to show how SQL falls short of that relational ideal.

So what *is* a relational DBMS? Well, first, it's a DBMS, of course, which means it provides all of the usual DBMS functionality: data storage, query and update, recovery and

---

[1] DBMS = database management system. By the way, please note that I don't make the (unfortunately all too common) mistake of referring to the DBMS as a database. The problem with that usage is this: If you call the DBMS a database, then what do you call the database?

concurrency, security and integrity, and so on. But second, it's relational, which means the user interface is based on—better: *is a faithful implementation of*—the relational model. As far as the user is concerned,[2] in other words, (a) the data looks relational, and (b) relational operators such as join are available for operating on that data.

"DATA LOOKS RELATIONAL"

The relational model is founded on a crucial underlying principle, which Codd (the inventor of the model) called *The Information Principle*:

> *At any given time, the entire information content of the database is represented so far as the user is concerned in one and only one way: namely, as relations.*[3]

By way of example, consider Fig. 1.1, which shows sample values for a database concerning suppliers (S), parts (P), and shipments of parts by suppliers (SP):

S

SNO	SNAME	STATUS	CITY
S1	Smith	20	London
S2	Jones	10	Paris
S3	Blake	30	Paris
S4	Clark	20	London
S5	Adams	30	Athens

P

PNO	PNAME	COLOR	WEIGHT	CITY
P1	Nut	Red	12.0	London
P2	Bolt	Green	17.0	Paris
P3	Screw	Blue	17.0	Oslo
P4	Screw	Red	14.0	London
P5	Cam	Blue	12.0	Paris
P6	Cog	Red	19.0	London

SP

SNO	PNO	QTY
S1	P1	300
S1	P2	200
S1	P3	400
S1	P4	200
S1	P5	100
S1	P6	100
S2	P1	300
S2	P2	400
S3	P2	200
S4	P2	200
S4	P4	300
S4	P5	400

Fig. 1.1: The suppliers-and-parts database–sample values

---

[2] Throughout this book I take the term *user* to mean either an interactive user or an application programmer or both, as the context demands.

[3] *Relation* is, of course, the formal term for the relational model counterpart of what SQL would call a table. Likewise, *attribute* and *tuple* are the formal terms for the relational counterparts of what SQL would call a column and a row, respectively. Please note, however, that these correspondences aren't exact—there are some important logical differences (the details of which would be out of place here) between relations, attributes, and tuples, on the one hand, and tables, columns, and rows on the other.

Now, the suppliers-and-parts database—by which I mean, of course, that database as seen by the user—certainly abides by *The Information Principle*, because it quite clearly consists of relations and nothing but relations (three of them, to be precise, and I'll assume for the purposes of this chapter that the meanings of those three relations are all intuitively obvious). But let me now point out that what the figure depicts would more accurately be described as three relation *values*: namely, the three relation values that happen to exist in the database at some particular time. If we were to look at the same database at some different time, we would very likely see three different relation values appearing in their place. Thus, the objects labeled S, P, and SP in the figure are really *variables*—relation variables, to be precise—and what the figure really shows is the current values of those variables at some particular time. For example, suppose that at the time right now the variable S has the value shown in Fig. 1.1, and suppose we delete the set of all tuples for suppliers in London:

```
DELETE S WHERE CITY = 'London' ;
```

Here's the result:

S

SNO	SNAME	STATUS	CITY
S2	Jones	10	Paris
S3	Blake	30	Paris
S5	Adams	30	Athens

In other words, what's happened, conceptually speaking, is that the old value of S has been replaced in its entirety by a new value. Of course, the old value (with five tuples) and the new one (with three) are very similar, in a sense, but they certainly are different values. In fact, the DELETE just shown is logically equivalent to, and indeed shorthand for, the following *relational assignment* operation:

```
S := S MINUS ( S WHERE CITY = 'London' ) ;
```

As with all assignments, the effect here is that (a) the expression on the right side (a relational expression, in this case) is evaluated and then (b) the value that's the result of that evaluation is assigned to the variable (a relation variable, in this case) on the left side, with the result already explained. So DELETE is really shorthand for a certain relational assignment— and, of course, an analogous remark applies to INSERT and UPDATE also: They too are basically just shorthand for certain relational assignments. In fact, relational assignment is fundamentally the only update operator we need, logically speaking (and it's the only one that's included in the relational model).

So there's a logical difference between relation values and relation variables. The trouble is, the database community has historically used the same term, *relation*, to stand for both, and that practice has certainly led to confusion. (SQL makes the same mistake, of course, because it too has just one term, *table*, that has to be understood as sometimes meaning a table value and sometimes a table variable.) In this chapter, therefore, I'll distinguish very carefully between the two from this point forward—I'll talk in terms of relation values when I mean relation values, and relation variables when I mean relation variables. However, I'll also abbreviate *relation value*, most of the time, to just *relation* (just as we abbreviate *integer value* most of the time to just *integer*). And I'll abbreviate *relation variable*, most of the time, to *relvar*; thus, I'll say the suppliers-and-parts database contains three relvars.[4]

So the database consists of relvars, and at any given time each of those relvars has some relation as its value. Now, a relation is a mathematical construct;[5] as such, it has a precise and formal mathematical definition. It wouldn't be appropriate to give that formal definition here, but I do want to mention certain important properties, all of them logical consequences of that definition, that apply to every relation:

- Every relation has a *heading* and a *body*, where the heading is a set of *attributes* (where an attribute in turn is an attribute-name / type-name pair) and the body is a set of *tuples* that conform to that heading. *Note:* Although it's strictly correct to say the heading consists of attribute-name / type-name pairs, it's usual in pictures like Fig. 1.1 to omit the type names, for simplicity.

- Relations never contain duplicate tuples.

- The tuples of a relation are unordered, top to bottom.

- The attributes of a relation are unordered, left to right.

- Relations are always *normalized* (equivalently, they're in *first normal form*, 1NF)—meaning every tuple in every relation contains exactly one value, of the appropriate type, in every attribute position. *Note:* For present purposes, you can take a type to be simply *a named set of values*—e.g., the set of all integers (type INT) or the set of all character strings (type CHAR).

---

[4] More precisely, three real or base relvars, so called to distinguish them from other kinds—for example, views, which are virtual relvars.

[5] As Fig. 1.1 illustrates (and as is well known, of course), relations can conveniently be pictured as tables. However, don't fall into the common trap of thinking that relations *are* tables. To repeat, a relation is a mathematical construct, while a table, in the sense in which I'm using that term here, is merely a picture of that construct (e.g., on paper). And while it's a very nice feature of the relational model that relations can be pictured in such a simple way, it's also true that those simple pictures can be misleading in certain respects. For example, they suggest the tuples of a relation are ordered top to bottom, but they're not. *Note:* The term *table* is thus unfortunately used in the database world with two very different meanings. One is as just described (i.e., as a picture of a relation). But in SQL, of course, it's used to mean the SQL counterpart to either a relation or a relvar or both, depending on the context (and that's not to mention the highly deprecated fact that SQL often uses "table" to mean a base table specifically and thinks that views are somehow not tables at all).

Now, the formulation of *The Information Principle* that I gave earlier is more or less as Codd himself would have given it. But I hope you can now see that the following formulation (which for various reasons I greatly prefer) is logically equivalent the the one I gave earlier:

> *The only kind of variable permitted in a relational database so far as the user is concerned is the relation variable or relvar.*

"RELATIONAL OPERATORS ARE AVAILABLE"

Since the data looks relational, the operators the user is provided with must be relational too. More specifically, those operators must include:

- A relational assignment operator for use in updating relvars (as already discussed), and

- Operators (join, project, restrict, etc.) that derive relations from relations, for use in—among other things—formulating queries. These operators must be *relationally complete*; that is, they must have at least the expressive power of *the relational algebra.*[6]

One important point regarding these operators is that they're all *set level*—that is, they all take entire relations and/or entire relvars as operands, not just individual tuples (a relation contains a *set* of tuples). For example, JOIN joins whole relations together, not just individual tuples; likewise, INSERT inserts a set of tuples into the target relvar, and DELETE deletes a set of tuples from the target relvar. Now, it's true we often talk in terms of, e.g., deleting an individual tuple, but such talk just means the set of tuples we're deleting happens to have cardinality one. There are *no* tuple level operations in the relational model.

And now you can begin to see, if you didn't already, why today's SQL products aren't truly relational. In those products:

a. The basic data object isn't the relation but the SQL table, and

b. The operators provided are ones that operate on SQL tables, not relations.

A list of specific differences between SQL and the relational model can be found in the appendix to this chapter, but some will already be apparent to anyone who knows SQL. For example, no relation ever contains duplicate tuples, but an SQL table can certainly contain duplicate rows.

---

[6] In practice, certain additional ("nonalgebraic") operators are desirable too. An example is ORDER BY, which takes a relation as input but produces an ordered list (of tuples), not a relation, as output (typically for display purposes). Such operators are beyond the purview of the relational model as such, however, and are therefore beyond the scope of the present chapter also.

Of course, an interesting question is: Why did the industry choose to run with SQL instead of the relational model? Especially since (at least as far as I'm concerned) a truly relational DBMS would be vastly superior to a mere SQL DBMS?[7] To spell the matter out:

■ SQL is much more complicated than the relational model, yet it provides no useful additional functionality.

■ In fact, SQL provides strictly less functionality than the relational model, since it isn't relationally complete, implying among other things that there are certain relational queries that can't be done in SQL. (To be specific, no SQL query can ever return a relation of degree zero—and relations of degree zero turn out, perhaps surprisingly, to be crucially important.)

■ No two SQLs are identical. (A standard does exist, but the dialect implemented in any given product is always a proper superset of a proper subset of what's in the standard, and different products implement different supersets of different subsets, and hence different dialects overall.)

Moreover, I can't help adding (though it doesn't have much to do with being truly relational or otherwise) that SQL, considered purely as a formal language, is badly designed by just about any measure.

Now, it would certainly be possible to apply some discipline to (a) the design of SQL tables and (b) the use of SQL operators, thereby making the DBMS behave *almost* as if it were relational. The trouble is, the design of the SQL language and the design of SQL products both militate quite severely, in a variety of different ways, against such a discipline. This state of affairs notwithstanding, however, I do strongly recommend such a discipline myself. For further specifics, see the book mentioned in the preamble to this chapter, viz., *SQL and Relational Theory: How to Write Accurate SQL Code* (3rd edition, O'Reilly, 2015).

A LITTLE HISTORY

The relational model was invented and described by E. F. Codd in a startlingly original series of research papers first published in the late 1960s and early 1970s. Here's a brief summary of some of the most important of them. The very first one was:

■ "Derivability, Redundancy, and Consistency of Relations Stored in Large Data Banks" (August 19th, 1969)

---

[7] I have my own answers to these questions, but this isn't the place to air them; suffice it to say that "for technical reasons" isn't one of them. Also, please note that I'm limiting my attention here to what might be called the relational portions of SQL; I'm not taking into account SQL's various nonrelational features, such as "OLAP" or its so called "window functions."

The next is usually credited with being the seminal paper in the field, though this characterization is a little unfair to its 1969 predecessor:

■ "A Relational Model of Data for Large Shared Data Banks" (June 1970)

Among other things, these two papers proposed an applied form of predicate logic, *the relational calculus*, as a foundation for a database language. In the next paper, Codd described in detail what such a language—he called it ALPHA—might look like:[8]

■ "A Data Base Sublanguage Founded on the Relational Calculus" (July 26th, 1971)

And he subsequently defined both the calculus and the algebra more formally in:

■ "Relational Completeness of Data Base Sublanguages" (March 6th, 1972)

The difference between the calculus and the algebra can be characterized as follows (but please note that this characterization is very loose—in fact, it doesn't really stand up under careful analysis): The calculus provides a notation for *defining* some desired relation (typically the result of some query) in terms of others, while the algebra provides a set of operators for *computing* some desired relation from others. Formally speaking, however, the two are equivalent; that is, for every expression of the algebra there's a logically equivalent expression in the calculus and vice versa.

As its title indicates, the foregoing paper also introduced the notion of *relational completeness* as a basic measure of the expressive power of a database language. Essentially, a language is said to be relationally complete if it's as powerful as the calculus (or the algebra). To quote from the paper:

> A query language ... [that] is claimed to be general purpose should be at least relationally complete ... [Such a language need never resort] to programming loops or any other form of branched execution—an important consideration when interrogating a [database] from a terminal.

In other words, if a language is relationally complete, then any query can be formulated by means of a single expression in the language (speaking a trifle loosely).

The last paper I want to mention here is:

■ "Further Normalization of the Data Base Relational Model" (August 31st, 1971)

---

[8] I'm sorry to have to say that—at least from a present day perspective—one of the most interesting things about ALPHA is that SQL was explicitly designed to be different from it. (Actually, SQL was explicitly designed to be different from the relational algebra also, though perhaps to a lesser extent.)

This was the paper that (a) introduced the notion of *functional dependence*, (b) defined the first three *normal forms* (1NF, 2NF, 3NF), and more generally (c) laid the foundations for the entire field of *dependency theory*, now an important branch of database science in its own right.

Taken together, then, the foregoing papers (along with with others by Codd not mentioned here) proposed **the relational model of data** as a theoretical foundation for a DBMS: in other words, as a kind of abstract specification for the user interface to a DBMS.[9] Nowadays, of course, Codd's ideas are widely accepted (at least, they're widely paid lip service to); for that reason, it can be a little hard to appreciate just how radical his ideas were at the time. In truth, however, the relational model was indeed radically different from all prior approaches (which in fact had no predefined abstract model to be based on anyway). In particular, the notion, or goal, that there should be a rigid distinction between the model and its implementation—i.e., between what the database looked like to the user and what it was "really" like under the covers—was, to say the least, something that earlier DBMSs were a long way from adequately achieving. And I'd like to close this section by elaborating briefly on that notion, because it's the subject of a very common misconception. Here's a typical quote (it's from a well known textbook on database theory and DBMS implementation):

> [It] is important to make a distinction between stored relations, which are *tables*, and virtual relations, which are *views* ... When we want to emphasize that a relation is stored, rather than a view, we shall sometimes use the term *base relation* or *base table*.

I'd like to replace the term *relation* by the term *relvar* throughout this quote, but that's not the main point I want to concentrate on here. Rather, I want to focus on the suggestion that relvars, base or otherwise, might be physically stored. Admittedly the quote doesn't actually say as much, but it does suggest rather strongly that base relvars, at least, are physically stored, in the sense that each such relvar maps to a physical file in secondary storage and each tuple in such a relvar maps to a physical record in the corresponding physical file. Certainly many people believe such a state of affairs to be the case, even today; what's more, it, or something very close to it, certainly *is* the case in most of the best known SQL products. But the relational model deliberately has nothing to say about what's physically stored![10] The idea was that implementers should have the freedom to implement the model in whatever way they chose—in particular, to store and access the data in whatever way seemed likely to yield good performance—without affecting the user interface in any way (this is the well known objective of *physical data independence*). So it's important to understand that the relational model categorically does *not* prescribe any specific data representation in storage; more specifically, it doesn't say tuples have

---

[9] Well, not the "Further Normalization" paper, perhaps. As I've already said, what that paper did was lay the foundations for dependency theory, which is a separate theory in its own right—one that sits on top of, but strictly speaking isn't part of, the relational model as such.

[10] The title of Codd's 1969 paper is perhaps a little unfortunate in this regard.

to be stored as physical records, nor does it say that indexes or other such "fast access paths" have to exist.[11]

WHY DATABASES MUST BE RELATIONAL

In my opinion, there are no serious competitors to the relational model. All of the various other "models" that have been proposed from time to time—inverted lists, IMS-style hierarchies, CODASYL-style networks, the "object model," the XML-style "semistructured model," etc.— are simply ad hoc storage structures that have been elevated above their station and will not endure.[12] Indeed, I seriously question whether they deserve to be called models at all. The hierarchic and network models in particular never really existed in the first place (as abstract models, I mean, prior to any implementations). Instead, they were invented *after the fact*; that is, hierarchic and network products were built first, and the corresponding models were defined afterward by a kind of induction from the products. As for the object and semistructured models, it's possible that the same criticism applies; I suspect it does, but it's hard to be sure. One problem is that there doesn't seem to be any consensus on what those models might consist of;[13] it certainly can't be claimed, for example, that there's a unique, clearly defined, and universally accepted object model, and similar remarks apply to the semistructured model also.

So it's my claim that if you think about the issue at the right level of abstraction, you're inexorably led to the position that *databases must be relational*. Let me immediately justify this very strong claim![14] My argument goes like this:

■ First of all, a database, despite the name, isn't really just a collection of data. Rather, it's a collection of "true facts," or what the logicians call *true propositions*—e.g., the proposition "Joe's salary is 50K." (A proposition in logic is a declarative sentence that's categorically either true or false—e.g., "Joe's salary is 50K," "5 > 7," etc.)

---

[11] It's not the point at issue here, but I really have to comment on another aspect of the quoted text. That text says (paraphrasing) that it's important to make a distinction between base relvars and virtual ones (views). Actually, I would say it's important, at least from the user's point of view, not to make such a distinction at all.

[12] The one possible exception to this claim is the *object/relational* model—but then I would argue that "the object/relational model" is just another name (actually just a marketing name) for "the relational model done right."

[13] My own opinion, for what it's worth, is that the semistructured model is just the old hierarchic model warmed over and the object model is just the old network model warmed over.

[14] One obvious objection to this claim is that nonrelational databases already exist. True enough—but (unlike modern databases) those existing databases were never meant to be general purpose and application neutral; rather, they were typically built to serve some specific application. As a consequence, they don't *and can't* provide all of the functionality we've come to expect from a modern database (ad hoc query, full data independence, flexible security and integrity controls, and so forth). In other words, I regard those older databases as nothing more than *application specific data stores*, and I would frankly prefer not to call them databases at all.

■ Propositions like "Joe's salary is 50K" are easily encoded as *ordered pairs*—e.g., the ordered pair (Joe,50K), in the case at hand (where "Joe" is a value of type NAME, say, and "50K" is a value of type MONEY, say).

■ But we don't want to record just any old propositions; rather, we want to record all propositions that are *true instantiations* of certain *predicates*. In the case of "Joe's salary is 50K," for example, the pertinent predicate is "*x*'s salary is *y*," where *x* is a value of type NAME and *y* is a value of type MONEY. (A predicate in logic is a parameterized proposition—e.g., "*x*'s salary is *y*," "*p* > *q*," etc. And instantiating a predicate involves replacing its parameters by arguments, thereby yielding a proposition.)

■ The set of all true instantiations of some given predicate is the *extension* of that predicate. In the example, therefore, what we want to do is record the extension of the predicate "*x*'s salary is *y*," which we can do in the form of a set of ordered pairs.

■ But a set of ordered pairs is, precisely, a binary relation, in the mathematical sense of that term. Here's the definition: A (mathematical) binary relation over two sets *A* and *B* is a subset of the cartesian product of *A* and *B*; in other words, it's a set of ordered pairs (*a*,*b*), such that the first element *a* is a value from *A* and the second element *b* is a value from *B*.

■ A (mathematical) binary relation can readily be depicted as a *table*. Here's an example:

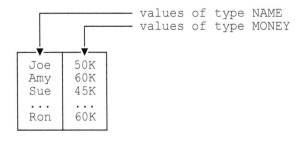

```
                            ──────── values of type NAME
                         ──────── values of type MONEY
                 │   │
                 ▼   ▼
            ┌───────┬───────┐
            │  Joe  │  50K  │
            │  Amy  │  60K  │
            │  Sue  │  45K  │
            │  ...  │  ...  │
            │  Ron  │  60K  │
            └───────┴───────┘
```

So we can regard this table as depicting a subset of the cartesian product of *the set of all names* ("type NAME") and *the set of all money values* ("type MONEY"), in that order.

Given the argument so far, then, we can see we're talking about some fairly humble (but very solid) beginnings. However, back in 1969, Codd realized that:

■ We need to deal with *n-adic*, not just dyadic, predicates and propositions (e.g., the 4-adic proposition "Joe has salary 50K, works in department D4, and was hired in 2008"). So we need to deal with *n-ary* relations, not just binary ones, and *n-tuples* (*tuples* for short), not just ordered pairs.

■ Left to right ordering might be acceptable for pairs but soon gets unwieldy for $n > 2$; so let's replace that ordering concept by the concept of *attributes*, identified by name, and let's revise the relation concept accordingly. The example now looks like this:

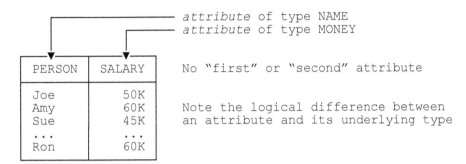

```
                      ┌─────────────────── attribute of type NAME
                      │     ┌───────────── attribute of type MONEY
                      ▼     ▼
            ┌─────────┬─────────┐
            │ PERSON  │ SALARY  │       No "first" or "second" attribute
            ├─────────┼─────────┤
            │   Joe   │   50K   │
            │   Amy   │   60K   │       Note the logical difference between
            │   Sue   │   45K   │       an attribute and its underlying type
            │   ...   │   ...   │
            │   Ron   │   60K   │
            └─────────┴─────────┘
```

Note carefully that—the picture notwithstanding—there's no such thing as the "first" or "second" attribute of a relation in this revised sense. And in the context of the relational model, the term *relation* always means a relation in this revised sense.

■ Data representation alone isn't the end of the story—we need *operators* for deriving further relations from the given ("base") ones, so that we can do queries and the like (e.g., "Get names of all persons with salary 60K"). But since a relation is both a logical construct (the extension of a predicate) and a mathematical one (a special kind of set), we can apply both logical and mathematical operators to it. Thus, Codd was able to define both a *relational calculus* (based on logic) and a *relational algebra* (based on set theory). And the relational model was born.

So now we know what relations are; but what's a database? *Answer:* A database is a container for a set of variables, where the variables in question are, specifically, relation variables or relvars.[15] Each relvar represents a certain predicate ("the relvar predicate"). And if relvar R represents predicate P, then the value of R at time t is a relation r, containing all and only those tuples that represent instantiations of P that are true at time t—i.e., the corresponding true propositions.[16] (In effect, in other words, the heading of R—equivalently, the heading of the current value r of R—corresponds to P as such, and the body of r corresponds to the current extension of P.)

---

[15] These remarks are somewhat oversimplified. The fact is, we ought really to draw a distinction, analogous to the one already drawn between relation values and variables, between *database* values and variables. Then we might say—albeit still not all that precisely—that a database variable is a container for a set of relvars, and a database value is a value of such a variable (in other words, it's a set of relations). But I don't want to get too deeply into such matters here; instead, I'll follow conventional (sloppy) usage and take the term *database* to mean either a database variable or a database value, as the context demands.

[16] Formally, in other words, we adopt *The Closed World Assumption*, which says in essence that (a) if a given tuple appears in r, then the corresponding proposition is true, and (b) if a given tuple could appear in r but doesn't, then the corresponding proposition is false.

THE RELATIONAL MODEL DEFINED

Now I'd like to give a reasonably precise definition—high level, but precise—of just what it is that constitutes the relational model. The trouble is, the definition I'll give is indeed precise: so precise, in fact, that I think it would have been pretty hard to understand if I'd given it earlier. (As Bertrand Russell once memorably said: *Writing can be either readable or precise, but not at the same time.*) Be that as it may, here's the definition:

> **Definition (relational model):** The relational model consists of five components:
>
> 1. An open ended collection of types, including type BOOLEAN in particular
>
> 2. A relation type generator and an intended interpretation for relations of types generated thereby
>
> 3. Facilities for defining relation variables of such generated relation type
>
> 4. A relational assignment operator for assigning relation values to such relation variables
>
> 5. A relationally complete but otherwise open ended collection of generic relational operators for deriving relation values from other relation values

The next five sections elaborate on each of these components in turn.

TYPES

Types are necessary because relations are defined over them—but note carefully that the question of what types are supported is independent of the question of support for the relational model as such. The relational model has never prescribed any specific types (with one exception, type BOOLEAN—see the paragraph immediately following).[17]

Types can be system or user defined. So users must be able to define their own types (this requirement is implied, partly, by the fact that the set of types is open ended). Users must also be

---

[17] It follows from these facts that the relational model requires a supporting theory of types. Such a theory is proposed in *Databases, Types, and the Relational Model: The Third Manifesto* (3rd edition, Addison-Wesley, 2007), by Hugh Darwen and myself, and elaborated on in two further books: *Database Explorations: Essays on The Third Manifesto and Related Topics* (Trafford, 2010), by the same authors, and *Type Inheritance and Relational Theory: Subtypes, Supertypes, and Substitutability* (O'Reilly, 2016), by myself. The present section is based in part on material from these references.

able to define their own operators, since types are useless without operators. The system defined types must include type BOOLEAN—the most fundamental type of all, containing precisely two values (the truth values TRUE and FALSE)—but a real system will surely support others as well (INT, CHAR, etc.). Support for type BOOLEAN implies support for the usual logical operators (NOT, AND, OR, etc). In particular, the equality comparison operator "=" (which is a boolean operator by definition, since it returns a boolean value) *must* be available in connection with every type—for without it we couldn't even say what the values are that constitute the type in question. What's more, the relational model prescribes the semantics of that operator, too. To be specific, if *v1* and *v2* are values of the same type, then *v1* = *v2* returns TRUE if *v1* and *v2* are the very same value and FALSE otherwise.

For each type *T* the model also requires support for at least one *selector* operator,[18] with the properties that (a) every invocation of that operator returns a value of type *T* and (b) every value of type *T* is returned by some invocation of that operator (more specifically, by some corresponding *literal*—note that a literal is a special case of a selector invocation).

THE RELATION TYPE GENERATOR

Conventional programming languages typically support an array type generator, which allows users to specify individual array types. Analogously, the relational model supports a relation type generator, which allows users to specify individual relation types[19] (in particular, as the type for some relvar or some relation valued attribute). By way of illustration, consider the following definition for relvar SP from the suppliers-and-parts database:

```
VAR SP BASE RELATION { SNO CHAR , PNO CHAR , QTY INT }
        KEY { SNO , PNO } ;
```

In this definition, the text

```
RELATION { SNO CHAR , PNO CHAR , QTY INT }
```

(which specifies the type of the variable being defined) is in fact an invocation of the relation type generator. You can think of a type generator as a special kind of operator; it's special because (a) it returns a type instead of a value, and (b) it's invoked at compile time instead of run time.

As for that matter of "intended interpretation" (for a given relation, of a given type, in a given context): That's essentially the business of predicates and propositions as already

---

[18] Nothing to do with the SELECT operator of SQL.

[19] I'd like to call your attention to that phrase *relation types*. Since (a) every value has a type and (b) relations are values, it follows that (c) every relation has a type. Likewise, since every variable has a type and relvars are variables, every relvar also has a type. These simple facts, obvious though they are, are often either forgotten or overlooked! SQL, for example, has no proper understanding of them.

discussed. (Please don't misunderstand me here. I'm not saying the model prescribes the interpretation of every individual relation—that would be absurd. For example, it would be absurd to say the interpretation of the relation that's the current value of relvar SP is prescribed by the model. What the model does say is that every specific relation *has* some such interpretation, as explained earlier in this chapter.)

RELATION VARIABLES

As noted in the previous section, an important use for the relation type generator is in specifying the type of a relvar when that relvar is defined. Relvars are the only kinds of variables permitted in a relational database. That's Codd's *Information Principle*, of course; indeed, I heard Codd refer to it on more than one occasion as *the* fundamental principle underlying the relational model. But why is it so important? There are two main reasons:

1. Along with types, relations are both necessary and sufficient to represent absolutely any data whatsoever at the user (or "logical") level. In other words, the relational model gives us everything we need in this respect, and it doesn't give us anything we don't need.

2. It's axiomatic that if there are n different ways of representing data, we need n different sets of operators. For example, if we had arrays as well as relations, we'd need a full complement of array operators as well as a full complement of relational ones.[20] If n is greater than one, therefore, we have more operators to implement, document, teach, learn, remember, and use (and choose among). But those extra operators add complexity, not power! There's nothing useful that can be done if n is greater than one that can't be done if n equals one (and in the relational model, of course, n does equal one).

What's more, not only does the relational model give us just one construct, the relation itself, for representing data, but that construct is (as Codd himself once put it) *of spartan simplicity*: It has no ordering to its tuples, it has no ordering to its attributes, it has no duplicate tuples, it has no pointers,[21] and (at least as far as I'm concerned) it has no nulls.[22] Any contravention of these properties is tantamount to introducing another way of representing data, and therefore to introducing more operators as well. In fact, SQL is living proof of this

---

[20] We'd also need operators involving a mixture of relations and arrays. And we'd also have to choose which data we wanted to represent as relations and which as arrays, probably without any good guidelines to help us in making such choices. And what about the database catalog? Would it contain relations, or arrays? Or a mixture?

[21] The important fact that—as is well known—pointers are prohibited in the relational model is a logical consequence, though not perhaps an immediately obvious one, of *The Information Principle*.

[22] Here I'm touching on my one major technical disagreement with Codd: He believed in nulls; I—along with numerous other relational theorists—don't. Now, I have strong arguments to support my position, but space doesn't permit their inclusion here. Some of them can be found in the book mentioned earlier, *SQL and Relational Theory: How to Write Accurate SQL Code* (abbreviated in the rest of this chapter to just *SQL and Relational Theory*), and I refer you to that book for further details.

observation—among other things, it has nine different union operators (and ought by rights to have 18, if not 27),[23] while the relational model has just one.

RELATIONAL ASSIGNMENT

Like the equality comparison operator "=", the assignment operator ":=" must be available in connection with every type (for without it we would have no way of assigning values to a variable of the type in question), and of course relation types are no exception to this rule.[24] What's more, support for relational assignment (a) must include support for *multiple* relational assignment in particular and (b) must abide by both *The Assignment Principle* and **The Golden Rule**. To elaborate briefly:

- Multiple assignment is an operator for updating several variables—several relvars in particular—"simultaneously," without any integrity checking being done until all of the individual updates have been completed.

- *The Assignment Principle* states that after assignment of some value v to some variable V, the comparison $v = V$ must evaluate to TRUE.

- **The Golden Rule** states that all integrity constraints must be satisfied at statement boundaries (loosely, "at semicolons").

DERIVING RELATIONS FROM RELATIONS

The operators that "derive relations from relations" are generic, in the sense that they apply to all possible relations, loosely speaking. Exactly which operators must be supported isn't specified, but whichever ones are supported must provide, in their totality, at least the expressive power of the relational algebra—in other words, as noted earlier, they must be relationally complete. Among other things, relational completeness implies *closure*, meaning that (a) the result of every operation is another relation and hence that (b) relational expressions can be nested inside one another.

As I've said, the model doesn't say which operators must be supported, just so long as they include a relationally complete subset. But language designers are free to define any further operators they like, just so long as they're useful and are generally within the spirit of the

---

[23] These claims and numbers are explained and justified in the book I've mentioned several times in this chapter already, *SQL and Relational Theory*.

[24] As previously noted, INSERT, DELETE, and UPDATE shorthands are permitted and indeed useful, but strictly speaking they *are* only shorthands.

algebra. For example, Hugh Darwen and I have defined the following additional operators (as well as several others): RENAME, MATCHING, NOT MATCHING, EXTEND (two forms), XUNION, and something we call the *image relation* operator (IMAGE_IN). I don't want to explain those operators in detail here, but I'd like to illustrate their usefulness in formulating some moderately complex queries on the suppliers-and-parts database. As an exercise, you might like to try giving SQL analogs of these examples.

■ Get all supplier / part combinations:[25]

```
( S RENAME { CITY AS SCITY } ) TIMES ( P RENAME { CITY AS PCITY } )
```

■ Get suppliers who supply at least one part:

```
S MATCHING SP
```

■ Get suppliers who supply no parts at all:

```
S NOT MATCHING SP
```

■ Given that attribute WEIGHT gives weights in pounds, append the gram weight to each part tuple:[26]

```
EXTEND P : { GMWT := WEIGHT * 454 }
```

■ What if parts were all in Nice?

```
EXTEND P : { CITY := 'Nice' }
```

■ Get cities with a supplier or a part but not both:[27]

```
S { CITY } XUNION P { CITY }
```

■ Get suppliers who supply all parts:

```
S WHERE ( IMAGE_IN ( SP ) ) { PNO } = P { PNO }
```

---

[25] As this example suggests, attribute renaming is needed primarily as a preliminary step before invoking an operator such as TIMES (or JOIN or UNION or ...) that imposes some specific requirement on the attributes names of its operands. (TIMES in particular requires its operands to have no attribute names in common. See Chapter 3 for further discussion.)

[26] I don't mean to suggest by this example that I believe the issue of units of measure should be handled in the manner indicated. Rather, I support the approach described in my book *Type Inheritance and Relational Theory: Subtypes, Supertypes, and Substitutability* (O'Reilly, 2016). See also Chapter 4 of the present book.

[27] Expressions of the form $r\{A\}$, like S{CITY} and P{CITY} in this example, denote the projection of relation r on attribute A.

■ Append the corresponding total shipment quantity to each supplier tuple:

```
EXTEND S : { SQ := SUM ( IMAGE_IN ( SP ) , QTY ) }
```

Now I need to add that—the foregoing examples notwithstanding—the algebra is *not* meant just for formulating queries. Rather, it's meant for writing *relational expressions.* Those expressions in turn serve many purposes, including query but certainly not limited to query alone.[28] Here are some other important ones:

■ Defining views and snapshots

■ Defining the set of tuples to be inserted into, deleted from, or updated in some relvar (or, more generally, defining the set of tuples to be assigned to some relvar)

■ Defining integrity constraints (I'll elaborate on this point in the next section)

■ (*Important*) Serving as a basis for investigations into other areas, such as optimization, view updating, and database design

And so on (this isn't an exhaustive list).

INTEGRITY CONSTRAINTS

Although I've had little to say about them so far in this chapter, I believe quite strongly that, in a sense, integrity constraints—constraints for short—are really what database management is all about. The database is supposed to be a representation of some portion of the real world; that representation is supposed to be as accurate as possible, in order to guarantee that decisions made on the basis of what the database says are correct ones; and constraints are the best mechanism we have for ensuring that the representation is indeed as accurate as possible. Constraints are crucial, and proper DBMS support for them is crucial as well.

So what would proper DBMS support for constraints entail? Well, it would certainly include (though it wouldn't be limited to) the ability to state constraints of arbitrary complexity in some declarative form—using, of course, the operators of the relational algebra or equivalent, as discussed in the previous section. Here by way of illustration are a few slightly simplified examples of constraints on the suppliers-and-parts database:

---

[28] Many writers use the terms *query* and *relational expression* interchangeably, but I don't. As far as I'm concerned, a query is a directive to the system that asks for some data to be retrieved. Thus, while it's true (of course) that a query is formulated by means of a relational expression, the point I'm trying to make here is that such expressions have many other uses as well.

■ Supplier status must be in the range 1-100 inclusive:

```
IS_EMPTY ( S WHERE STATUS < 1 OR STATUS > 100 )
```

The expression in parentheses here is a relational expression and thus evaluates to some relation; that relation is then passed as an argument to IS_EMPTY, which is a boolean operator that returns TRUE if its argument relation is empty and FALSE otherwise.

■ Suppliers in London must have status 20:

```
IS_EMPTY ( S WHERE CITY = 'London' AND STATUS ≠ 20 )
```

■ Every supplier has a unique supplier number:

```
S JOIN ( S { SNO } ) = S
```

In practice, constraints like this one would normally be expressed by means of some kind of KEY shorthand, of course (as illustrated earlier in the definition of relvar SP).

■ Suppliers with status less than 20 can't supply part P6:

```
IS_EMPTY ( ( S JOIN SP ) WHERE STATUS < 20 AND PNO = 'P6' )
```

■ Every shipment must be from some known supplier:

```
IS_EMPTY ( SP NOT MATCHING S )
```

In practice, constraints like this one would normally be expressed by means of some kind of FOREIGN KEY shorthand (though that "shorthand" is quite likely to take more keystrokes than the foregoing "longhand" equivalent!).

■ No part can be supplied by suppliers in more than four different cities:

```
IS_EMPTY ( ( EXTEND P { PNO } :
           { NC := COUNT ( ( IMAGE_IN ( SP JOIN S ) ) { CITY } ) } )
                                               WHERE NC > 4 )
```

Not all of the foregoing constraints can be expressed in today's SQL products (some can, but not all); in fact, lack of adequate support for integrity constraints is one of the most glaring weaknesses of those products at the time of writing.

CONCLUDING REMARKS

My aim in this chapter has been to give some idea of what's included—and, to some extent, what's not included—in the relational model, and thereby to give some idea of what a truly relational DBMS would look like. I've also tried to give at least a hint as to how the relational model provides a theoretical framework within which a variety of important practical problems can be attacked in a scientific manner. Needless to say, however, the treatment has been far from complete. Here are some topics that would need consideration, or more detailed consideration, in any more comprehensive examination of the subject:

- The fact that "flat relations" [*sic*] aren't flat at all but *n*-dimensional

- Predicate logic and relational calculus

- Additional algebraic operators

- Aggregate operators such as SUM and AVG

- Views and other derived relvars and operations thereon (especially updates)

- Key and foreign key constraints

- Dependency theory and normal forms

- "Missing information"

- "Recursive queries"

APPENDIX: SQL DEPARTURES FROM THE RELATIONAL MODEL

In this appendix[29] I list, mainly for purposes of reference and with little by way of additional commentary, some of the ways in which SQL—by which I mean, primarily, the standard version of that language—departs from the relational model. Now, I know there are those who will quibble over individual items in the list; it's not easy to compile such a list, especially if it's meant to be orthogonal (i.e., if an attempt is made to keep the various items all independent of one another). But I don't think such quibbling is important. What's important is the cumulative effect, which I frankly think is overwhelming.

---

[29] The appendix is based on Appendix B of the book *SQL and Relational Theory*.

- SQL fails to distinguish adequately between table values and table variables.

- SQL tables aren't the same as either relation values or relation variables, because they either permit or require, as the case may be:

  a. Duplicate rows

  b. Nulls

  c. Left to right column ordering

  d. Anonymous columns

  e. Duplicate column names

  f. Pointers

  g. Hidden columns (at least in some products, though not in the standard as such)

  All of these differences constitute violations of *The Information Principle*, with consequences as mentioned in the body of this chapter (and elaborated in numerous other writings of mine).

- SQL has no proper table literals.

- SQL often seems to think views aren't tables.

- SQL tables (including views) must have at least one column.

- SQL has no support for either empty rows or empty keys. (In fact, SQL suffers from numerous defects in connection with empty sets.)

- SQL has no explicit table assignment operator.

- SQL has no explicit multiple table assignment a fortiori (nor does it have an INSERT / DELETE analog).

- SQL violates *The Assignment Principle* in numerous different ways (some but not all of them having to do with nulls).

■ SQL violates **The Golden Rule** in numerous different ways (some but not all of them having to do with nulls).

■ SQL has no proper "table type" notion. As a consequence, its support for table type inference (i.e., determining the type of the result of some table expression) is very incomplete.

■ SQL has no "=" operator for tables; in fact, it has no proper table comparison operators, as such, at all.

■ SQL supports "reducible keys" (i.e., it allows proper superkeys to be declared as keys).

■ SQL's union, intersection, and join operators aren't commutative.

■ SQL's union, intersection, and join operators aren't idempotent.

■ SQL's intersection operator isn't a special case of SQL's natural join operator.

■ SQL has no proper aggregate operators.

■ Numerous SQL operators are "possibly nondeterministic."

■ SQL supports various row level operators (cursor updates, row level triggers).

■ Although the SQL standard doesn't, the dialects of SQL supported in various commercial products do sometimes refer to certain storage level constructs (e.g., indexes).

■ SQL's view definitions include mapping information as well as structural information.

■ SQL's support for view updating is weak, ad hoc, and incomplete.

■ SQL fails to distinguish properly between types and representations.

■ SQL's "structured types" are sometimes encapsulated and sometimes not.

■ SQL fails to distinguish properly between types and type generators.

■ Although the SQL standard does support type BOOLEAN, commercial SQL products typically don't.

■ SQL's support for "=" is seriously deficient. To be more specific, SQL's "=" operator:

   a. Can give TRUE even when the comparands are clearly distinct[30]

   b. Can fail to give TRUE even when the comparands aren't clearly distinct

   c. Can have user defined, and hence arbitrary, semantics (for user defined types)

   d. Isn't supported at all for the system defined type XML

   e. In some products, isn't supported for certain other types as well

■ SQL is based on three-valued logic (sort of), whereas the relational model is based on two-valued logic.

■ SQL isn't relationally complete.

The foregoing list is not exhaustive.

---

[30] One consequence of this point is that two rows can be duplicates of each other without being identical. A further consequence is that the definition of (e.g.) SQL's UNION operator has to look something like this: Let tables *t1* and *t2* be the union operands; let *r* be a row that's a duplicate of some row in *t1* and a duplicate of some row in *t2*; then the result table contains (a) exactly one duplicate of every such row *r* and (b) no row that's not a duplicate of some such row *r*. (Even this byzantine definition is incomplete, of course—additional rules are needed to specify the column names and types of that result table.) By contrast, the relational definition of union is extremely simple: Let relations *r1* and *r2* be of the same type *T*; then the union of *r1* and *r2* is the relation of type *T* with body the set of all tuples *t* such that *t* appears in at least one of *r1* and *r2*.

    Another consequence of the same point is that (e.g.) the SQL UNION operator applied to tables *t1* and *t2* can quite legitimately produce a result containing—even consisting entirely of!—rows that appear in neither *t1* nor *t2*.

Part II

CODD'S EARLY WRITINGS

I use the phrase "Codd's early writings" here to refer to the following papers:

- "Derivability, Redundancy, and Consistency of Relations Stored in Large Data Banks"

- "A Relational Model of Data for Large Shared Data Banks"

- "Relational Completeness of Data Base Sublanguages"

- "A Data Base Sublanguage Founded on the Relational Calculus"

- "Further Normalization of the Data Base Relational Model"

- "Interactive Support for Nonprogrammers: The Relational and Network Approaches"

These papers were staggering in their originality. Among other things, they changed, and changed permanently, the way database management was perceived in the IT world; more specifically, they transformed what had previously been nothing but a ragbag of tricks and ad hoc techniques into a solid scientific endeavor. They also, not incidentally, laid the foundation for an entire multibillion dollar industry. Together, they provided the basis for a technology that has had, and continues to have, a major impact on the very fabric of our society. Thus, it's no exaggeration to say that Codd is the intellectual father of the modern database field.

To the foregoing, I'd like to add this: Codd's relational model has been with us now for almost 50 years. And I for one think it very telling that, in all that time, no one has managed to invent any kind of new theory, one that might reasonably supplant or seriously be considered superior to the relational model in any way. In my opinion, in fact, no one has even come close to inventing such a theory (though there have been many attempts, as I'm sure you're aware, but attempts that in my opinion have universally failed).

And yet ... And yet, here we are—as I've said, almost 50 years later—and what do we find? Well:

- First, the teaching of relational theory, in universities in particular, seems everywhere to be in decline. What's more, what teaching there is seems not to have caught up—at least, not fully, and certainly not properly—with the numerous developments in relational theory that have occurred since publication of those early papers of Codd's.

- Second, no truly relational DBMS has ever been widely available in the commercial marketplace.

Let me offer some evidence in support of the first of the foregoing claims (evidence for the second is, I'm sorry to say, all around us and all too plain to see). At the beginning of my seminar "SQL and Relational Theory," I ask attendees the following series of questions in order to test their relational knowledge before we get properly started:

1. What exactly is first normal form?

2. What's the connection between relations and predicates?

3. What's semantic optimization?

4. What's an image relation?

5. Why is semidifference important?

6. Why doesn't deferred integrity checking make sense?

7. What's a relation variable?

8. What's prenex normal form?

9. Can a relation have an attribute whose values are relations?

10. Is SQL relationally complete?

11. Why is *The Information Principle* important?

12. How does XML fit with the relational model?

Now, attendees on that seminar are expected to be, and usually are, experienced database professionals (typically database administrators or database application developers). They often have a computer science degree. In my experience, however, they're almost universally incapable of answering even one of the foregoing questions satisfactorily.[1] Frankly, I very much doubt whether the average university class deals with these issues properly (perhaps not at all, in some cases). What's more, much the same can be said of the majority of the numerous database textbooks currently available—at least the ones I'm aware of.

Sadly, it seems to me that part of the blame for this depressing state of affairs has to be laid at Codd's own door. The fact is, those early writings of his, brilliantly innovative though they undoubtedly were, did suffer from a number of defects, some of which I'll be examining in this part of the book. And it's at least plausible to suggest that some of the sins to be observed in the present database landscape—sins of both omission and commission—can be regarded, with hindsight (always perfect, of course), as deriving from the defects in question.

The Extent of Codd's Contribution

Some 20 years ago or so I wrote a series of twelve articles for the Miller Freeman monthly magazine *Intelligent Enterprise*, beginning with the October 1998 issue.[2] The overall title for the series was "30 Years of Relational," because they were written in part to celebrate the relational model's forthcoming 30th birthday (August 19th, 1999). As I wrote at the time:

> [These articles are intended] to serve as a historical account and ... analysis of E. F. Codd's (huge!) contribution to the field of database technology. Codd's relational model, [described in] a startlingly novel series of research papers, was a revolution at the time, albeit one that was desperately needed. Now, however, it seems that—despite the fact that the entire multibillion dollar database industry is founded on Codd's original ideas—those ideas are in danger of being ignored or forgotten (or, at best, being paid mere lip service to). Certainly we can observe many examples today of those ideas being flouted in (among other things) database products, database designs, and database applications. It thus seems appropriate to take another look at Codd's original papers, with a view to assessing their true significance and restating, and reinforcing, their message for a new generation of database professionals.

And later I went on to say this:

> [The papers in question] are certainly unusual in one respect: They stand up very well to being read—and indeed repeatedly *re*read—over 30 years later! (How many papers can you say *that* of?) At the same time, it has to be said too that they're not particularly *easy* to read, nor to understand ... The writing is terse and a little dry, the style theoretical and academic, the notation and examples

---

[1] You might think I'm exaggerating people's lack of awareness here, but I'm not. I often encounter people on my seminars who've never even heard of Ted Codd, let alone read any of his papers. And in 1980, when I approached my manager in IBM— the Technical Planning manager for DB2, IBM's flagship relational (or at least would-be relational) product!—to ask permission to use some of my time in nominating Codd for the ACM Turing Award, I discovered that he, the manager in question, had never even heard of either the Turing Award or ACM. At least he'd heard of Codd, though.

[2] Those articles were later collected into a book, *The Database Relational Model: A Retrospective Review and Analysis* (Addison-Wesley, 2001). By the way, I believe that earlier book still provides a useful overview of Codd's achievement overall, and the present book is certainly not meant to replace or displace it.

mostly rather mathematical in tone. As a consequence, I'm sure I'm right in saying that, to this day, only a tiny percentage of database professionals have actually read them. So I thought it would be interesting, and (I also thought) useful, to devote a short series of articles to a careful, unbiased, retrospective review and assessment of [those] papers.

And then I went on to summarize Codd's major contributions, somewhat as follows:

- His biggest overall achievement was to make database management into a science; in other words, he put the field on to a solid scientific footing, by providing a theoretical framework—the relational model—within which a variety of important problems could be addressed in a scientific manner. Thus, the relational model really serves as the basis for a *theory* of data. (Indeed, the term "relational theory" is preferable in some ways to the term "relational model," and it might have been nice if Codd had used it. But he didn't.)

- As a consequence of the previous point, he introduced a welcome and sorely needed note of clarity and rigor into the database field.

- He introduced not only the relational model in particular, but the whole idea of a data model in general.

- He stressed the importance of the distinction, regrettably still widely misunderstood, between model and implementation.

- He saw the potential of using the ideas of predicate logic as a foundation for database management.

- He defined both a relational algebra and a relational calculus as a basis for dealing with data in relational form.

- He defined (albeit only informally) what was probably the first relational language, "Data Sublanguage ALPHA."

- He introduced the concept of functional dependence and defined the first three normal forms (1NF, 2NF, 3NF).

- He defined the key notion of essentiality.

Now, I stand by everything I've said above, as well as by all of the nice things I said about Codd's work in those twelve articles. But I think the time has come for a closer, more critical look at these matters. That's the primary purpose of this part of the present book. Before I do so, however, I'd like to repeat something I said on the dedication page: namely, that I'd like to make it as clear as possible that the analysis, comments, and criticisms in the chapters that follow are all offered in, and should be construed in, the spirit of the extracts cited on that page from William Dunham and David Hilbert. I admire and am hugely grateful for the work Codd did in the late 60s and early 70s and documented in his early writings. Indeed, I owe my very livelihood to him and that work! But I also feel it's important not to be blinded by such feelings into uncritical acceptance of everything Codd said or wrote, either at that time or subsequently. Nor do I feel it appropriate to accept Codd as the sole authority on relational matters. Indeed, it's to his credit that Codd himself is on record as agreeing with this position. In an interview in *Data Base Newsletter 10*, No. 2 (March 1982), he stated explicitly that "I see relational theory as simply a body of theory to which many people are contributing in different ways." And, of course, numerous people have indeed made contributions to relational theory since it was first introduced (contributions that in some cases I consider to be very significant indeed), though details of most of those contributions are unfortunately beyond the scope of the present book. To repeat, the book is about Codd's writings on the subject, not about other people's.

Chapter 2

The First Two Papers

It was fifty years ago today
Dr Edgar showed us all the way
—with apologies to Lennon & McCartney

The relational model originated in two papers by E. F. Codd:

- "Derivability, Redundancy, and Consistency of Relations Stored in Large Data Banks," IBM Research Report RJ599 (August 19th, 1969)—referred to throughout this chapter as the 1969 paper

- "A Relational Model of Data for Large Shared Data Banks," *Communications of the ACM 13*, No. 6 (June 1970)—referred to throughout this chapter as the 1970 paper

By the way, the 1970 paper is usually credited with being the seminal paper in the field, as indeed I'm sure you know. However, that characterization is a little unfair to its 1969 predecessor; in fact, the 1970 paper was essentially just a somewhat revised and extended version of the 1969 paper. For that reason, I think it's reasonable to treat the two papers together, and that's what I plan to do in the present chapter.

Now, I claimed in the introduction to this part of the book that Codd's early papers suffered from certain defects—and here I claim that, unfortunately, this criticism applies to the 1969 and 1970 papers in particular. The purpose of the present chapter is to provide evidence in support of this latter claim. I'll buttress my arguments with a variety of quotes from the papers in question (actually the quotes are all taken from the 1970 paper specifically, except where otherwise indicated).

WHAT'S THE RELATIONAL MODEL?

It's a curious fact that, despite its title, the 1970 paper nowhere says exactly what the relational model consists of. (Actually the 1969 paper doesn't do so either.) Indeed, what it does say in this connection suggests rather strongly that it consists of a structural component only. Here are several examples to illustrate the point:

■ A model based on *n*-ary relations ... and the concept of a universal data sublanguage are introduced.

That "and" suggests rather strongly that the model and the "universal data sublanguage" (i.e., the collection of operators, such as join) are separate and distinct things. Moreover, a later remark in the 1970 paper makes it quite clear in connection with that "sublanguage" that Codd isn't just talking about syntax here—he means an abstract language.

■ [The model] provides a means of describing data with its natural structure only ... Accordingly, it provides a basis for a high level data language ... .

These two sentences taken separately and together suggest rather strongly again that the model and the operators are different things.

■ The adoption of a relational model of data, as described above, permits the development of a universal data sublanguage based on an applied predicate calculus.

Once again there seems to be an implication that the model is concerned with structure only.

■ The relational view (or model) of data described in Section 1 ... .

"The relational view (or model)" is indeed described in Section 1 as claimed.[1] However, it isn't properly *defined* there. Indeed, not only is it not defined there, but all that section does in this connection is describe the model's structural aspects, or in other words relations as such—it has nothing to say about either operators or integrity constraints, except for a brief mention of keys and foreign keys. (As an aside, I note that the fact that keys and foreign keys *are* briefly discussed in this context might be one of the reasons why, in practice, key and foreign key constraints are typically bundled in with structural definitions—as in SQL, for example—instead of being treated in the same uniform manner as integrity constraints in general.)

To pursue the point a moment longer, what *is* defined in Section 1 is the term *relation*. However, given that (a) that definition actually occurs in subsection 1.3 of that section, (b) that subsection is titled "A Relational View of Data," (c) that term *view* (as used by Codd here) has already been equated with the term *model*, and (d) that subsection 1.3 makes no mention of the operators, the clear implication once again is that the operators aren't part of the model.

As an aside, I note that the first of Codd's papers to contain an actual definition of the relational model was "Extending the Database Relational Model to Capture More Meaning" (*ACM Transactions on Database Systems 4*, No. 4), which didn't appear until December 1979. What this latter paper said was as follows (paraphrasing somewhat):

---

[1] I note in passing that the text quoted actually *appears* in Section 1. An early example of self-reference?

The relational model consists of (1) a collection of time-varying tabular relations, (2) the entity and referential integrity rules, and (3) the relational algebra.

This definition might be criticized on a variety of grounds—*tabular* in particular is a little odd—but at least it does make it clear that the operators are included. As for that *time-varying*, see later in the present chapter.

To return for a moment to the mistaken idea that the relational model consists of a structural component only: Actually this misconception seems to be quite widespread and persists to this day, as the following quotes from a variety of well known database textbooks indicate:

- In this chapter, we first study the fundamentals of the relational model, which provides a very simple yet powerful way of representing data. We then describe three formal query languages [*viz., relational algebra, tuple calculus, and domain calculus*] ... (from Abraham Silberschatz, Henry F. Korth, and S. Sudarshan, *Database System Concepts*, 4th edition, McGraw-Hill, 2002).

- Chapter 5 The Relational Data Model and Relational Database Constraints ... Chapter 6 The Relational Algebra and Relational Calculus (from Ramez Elmasri and Shamkant B. Navathe, *Fundamentals of Database Systems*, 4th edition, Addison-Wesley, 2004).

- This chapter presents two formal query languages [*viz., relational algebra and relational calculus*] associated with the relational model (Raghu Ramakrishnan and Johannes Gehrke, *Database Management Systems*, 3rd edition, McGraw-Hill, 2003).

And I could cite numerous further examples—including, I'm sorry to say, somewhat similar text from the first two editions of my own book *An Introduction to Database Systems* (Addison-Wesley, 1975 and 1977).

"A" Relational Model?

The 1970 paper not only fails to give a proper definition of *the* relational model, it sometimes uses the term "*a relational model*" to refer to some user's perception of some specific database. (Hence, perhaps, the modern and continuing confusion over the two quite distinct meanings of the term *data model*—see Chapter 6 of the present book.) Here are a couple of examples:

- There are usually many alternative ways in which a relational model may be established for a data bank.

- To sum up, it is proposed that ... users should interact with a relational model of the data consisting of a collection of time-varying [relations].

Incidentally, that phrase "consisting of" suggests once again that the—or a?—relational model is concerned with structure only.

WHAT'S A RELATION?

Following on from the previous section, I now observe that the 1970 paper isn't even totally clear on what it means by the term *relation*. Subsection 1.3 ("A Relational View of Data") begins thus:

> The term *relation* here is used in its accepted mathematical sense. Given sets $S_1, S_2, ..., S_n$ (not necessarily distinct), R is a relation on these n sets if it is a collection of n-tuples each of which has its first element from S_1, its second element from S_2, and so on. We shall refer to S_j as the jth *domain* of R.

Note in particular that the "domains" of any given relation—more on that topic later in the present section, also in the next—are here quite explicitly considered to have an ordering ("left to right").[2] Now, the paper does subsequently go on to say that "users [should] deal, not with relations which are domain-ordered but with *relationships*, which are their domain-unordered counterparts." But almost all of the subsequent discussions in the paper (in several later writings also), as well as the title of the 1970 paper and indeed the very term *relational model* itself, emphasize relations as such, not those "relationships" or "domain-unordered counterparts to" relations. Accordingly, it's hard to escape the conclusion that one of the biggest flaws to be observed in SQL today—namely, that it relies on its tables having a left to right ordering to their columns—has its origin in Codd's 1970 paper.

Here are some further quotes from the 1970 paper that have to do with what exactly a relation is:

- [See the] remarks below on domain-ordered and domain-unordered relations.

  But the paper has already stated explicitly that relations are domain-ordered by definition. As far as that paper is concerned, therefore, *domain-unordered relation* is, or should be, simply a contradiction in terms.

- Consider an example [involving a relation] called *part* which is defined on the following domains ... (5) quantity on hand, (6) quantity on order.

  "Quantity on hand" and "quantity on order" would surely be distinct *attributes* defined on the *same* domain. Indeed, the 1970 paper very frequently uses *domain* when *attribute*

---

[2] Note too the implicit assumption here, made explicit later in other writings by Codd, that every relation has at least one "domain," and hence that the important relations TABLE_DEE and TABLE_DUM (see Chapter 3) are excluded.

would clearly be correct, or at least much more appropriate. In fact, however, it never mentions the term *attribute* at all—at least, not as a component of a relation.[3] (As a matter of fact, it never mentions the term *tuple* as an abbreviation for *n*-tuple, either. Taken together, these omissions are more than a little surprising, given that relations in the relational model are today universally understood to consist specifically of attributes and tuples.)

■   ... simple domains—domains whose elements are atomic (nondecomposable) values.

Unfortunately, the 1970 paper gives no adequate definition for the term *atomic value*.[4] This omission led to a massive misunderstanding in the database community at large as to what exactly it means to say a relation is in first normal form—a misunderstanding that persists, widely, to the present day. Indeed, it's not unreasonable to suggest that Codd himself might have been a little confused over this issue, to judge not only by the 1970 paper but also by certain of his later writings (see Part III of this book).

■   Nonatomic values can be discussed within the relational framework. Thus, some domains may have relations as elements.

Two questions here. First, what about other "nonatomic" values, such as lists or sets? Are they permitted? Second, are relations allowed to contain such "nonatomic" values or aren't they? The 1970 paper never really gives a clear, straightforward answer to this question.[5]

■   For expository reasons, we shall frequently make use of an array representation of relations, but it must be remembered that this particular representation is not an essential part of the relational view being expounded.

First of all, it's interesting to see that Codd suggests representing relations as arrays, not tables (in fact, it's a little surprising to find that the term *table* doesn't occur in the paper at all). Second, to suggest that relations might be thought of in terms of arrays is really rather strange—not to say actively misleading—given that it's a sine qua non of arrays that they have both an ordering to their rows and an ordering to their columns, and relations have

---

[3] Oddly enough, the 1969 paper does mention the domain vs. attribute distinction.

[4] The closest it gets to such a definition is in the following loose characterization of the distinction between what it calls "simple" and "nonsimple" domains: "The terms attribute and repeating group in present database terminology are roughly analogous to simple domain and nonsimple domain, respectively." That being said, however, it seems virtually certain that what Codd meant by "atomic values" was nothing more nor less than what in programming language circles are referred to as *scalar* values. But as I've had occasion to remark elsewhere—see, e.g., my book *SQL and Relational Theory: How to Write Accurate SQL Code* (3rd edition, O'Reilly, 2015)—"scalarness" isn't an absolute. It isn't even formally defined (indeed, the very same value might be regarded as scalar in some contexts and nonscalar in others). Now, it would surely be unwise to require the formal relational model to rely on such a fuzzy notion in any formal way; thus, if this understanding of what Codd meant by "atomic values" is in fact correct, then I think it must be rejected.

[5] By contrast, the 1969 paper explicitly does allow relations to contain such values.

nothing analogous to either. As a consequence, Codd's caveat, to the effect that the array representation "is not an essential part of the relational view being expounded," seems much too weak. What *is* an essential part of the "view being expounded" is that the row and column ordering inherent in the suggested array representation must be explicitly ignored.

Unfortunately, the 1970 paper then goes on to make matters worse by frequently and repeatedly talking in terms of arrays and columns when what it really means is relations and attributes. For example:

■   A binary relation has an array representation with two columns. Interchanging these columns yields the converse relation.

No, it doesn't—it yields *an array representation* of "the converse relation" (not to mention that the very term *converse relation* is meaningless in the context of the relational model anyway).[6] This is just one of several places where the paper itself falls into the very trap it explicitly warns us against, of confusing a relation with its array representation. No wonder so many people continue to make essentially the same mistake to this very day.

■   A relation whose domains are all simple can be represented in storage by a two-dimensional column-homogeneous array of the kind discussed above.

Represented in storage (specifically, in the form of an array) is unfortunate, suggesting as it does a "direct image" style of implementation (which is, sadly, the style found in all mainstream SQL products today, to a first approximation). *Two-dimensional* is unfortunate too—to this day, far too many people seem to think that "two-dimensional relations" are incapable of representing "*n*-dimensional data" (or indeed most other data that occurs in practice, come to that).

■   Some more complicated [storage representation] is necessary for a relation with one or more nonsimple domains.[7] For this reason ... the possibility of eliminating nonsimple domains appears worth investigating.

The stated reason is a very bad one!—suggesting as it does that representation in storage is the major concern. Also, does "appears worth investigating" mean that "eliminating nonsimple domains" *must* be done (assuming it's possible), or are we merely talking about something that might be desirable but isn't absolutely required?

---

[6] Note carefully too that Codd is quite definitely talking about "domain-ordered relations" here, not their "domain-unordered counterparts."

[7] The paper uses the term *data structure*, not *storage representation*, but it's clear from the context that storage representation is what's meant.

■ The simplicity of the array representation ... is not only an advantage for storage purposes ... but also for communication of bulk data between systems ... The communication form ... would have the following advantages ... :

Again the phrase *for storage purposes* is unfortunate. (So too is the phrase *communication of bulk data between systems*, come to that.) Anyway, the first of the advantages the paper goes on to mention is: "It would be devoid of pointers." Of course, this state of affairs clearly implies that the arrays seen by the user are devoid of pointers also, but this latter fact, strangely enough, is *not* cited as an advantage. In other words, the crucially important fact that database relations per se are supposed to "be devoid of pointers" is nowhere spelled out explicitly.[8]

■ A first-order predicate calculus suffices if [every relation in the] the collection of relations is in [first] normal form.

There seems to be a suggestion here that second-order logic is necessary otherwise. It's not clear to me whether such is in fact the case, but I do think this remark is the source of some further confusion. And while I'm on the subject of logic, let me also point out what seems to be a fairly major omission: namely, the omission, from both the 1970 paper and its 1969 predecessor, of any mention of the crucial connection between relations and predicates.[9]

WHAT'S A DOMAIN?

I've already mentioned the 1970 paper's lack of clarity over domains vs. attributes. In fact, however, there's a further point of confusion that arises from the notion of domains as described in Codd's writings. To elaborate: As far as I and many other writers are concerned, domains in the relational world are indistinguishable from *types* in the programming languages world.[10] But the 1970 paper doesn't discuss this equivalence at all; in fact, it doesn't even mention it. Au contraire, in fact: In later writings Codd went to great lengths to argue the opposite point of

---

[8] Indeed, this fact doesn't seem to have been spelled out explicitly in any of Codd's writings until 1979, when the following text appeared in his paper "Extending the Database Relational Model to Capture More Meaning" (*ACM Transactions on Database Systems 4*, No. 4, December 1979): "Between ... relations there are no structural links such as pointers. Associations between relations are represented solely by values." However, a couple of remarks that do at least strongly hint at such a state of affairs can be found in his 1971 paper "Normalized Data Base Structure: A Brief Tutorial," Proc. ACM SIGFIDET Workshop on Data Description, Access, and Control (San Diego, Calif., November 11th-12th, 1971).

[9] The first of Codd's writings to spell out this connection explicitly seems to have been the paper I've mentioned a couple of times already, "Extending the Database Relational Model to Capture More Meaning" (*ACM Transactions on Database Systems 4*, No. 4, December 1979).

[10] This observation does *not* apply to what SQL calls domains, which aren't domains in the relational sense at all. Rather, they're merely a kind of factored out "common column definition," with a number of rather strange properties that have nothing to do with the relational model as such and are therefore beyond the scope of this chapter.

view, viz., that domains and types are different things. For example, in his paper "Domains, Keys, and Referential Integrity in Relational Databases" (*InfoDB 3*, No. 1, Spring 1988), he draws a distinction between what he calls "basic data types" and "extended data types," and goes on to say that "extended data types" are domains but "basic data types" aren't. Here's a quote from that paper:

> Each domain is declared as an extended data type (not as a mere basic data type) ... The distinction between extended ... and basic data types is NOT that the first is user defined and the second is built into the system.

The following table from that same paper purports to summarize the differences between the two—the differences as seen by Codd, that is—though as far as I'm concerned all it manages to do is raise a whole host of further questions:

#	Basic Data Type	Extended Data Type
1	property-oriented name	object-oriented name
2	a property of an object	an object
3	not independently declarable	independently declarable
4	range of values NOT specifiable	range of values specifiable
5	applicability of >, < not specifiable	applicability of >, < specifiable
6	two database values with the same basic data type need not have the same extended data type	

A detailed discussion of all of these alleged differences would be out of place in the present chapter; suffice it to say that all that's happening here is that Codd is confusing types and representations (or so it seems to me, at any rate).[11] Further evidence in support of this claim is provided by several further remarks in that same *InfoDB* paper. I'll content myself with quoting just one such here:

> With special authorization ... a user may employ the DOMAIN CHECK OVERRIDE qualifier in his [*sic*] command, if a special need arises to "compare apples with oranges."[12]

The "apples and oranges comparisons" Codd is referring to here are comparisons involving domains that are (by definition) logically distinct but share the same physical representation—for

---

[11] More on this confusion in Chapter 4. By the way, the significance of the important logical difference between types and representations is nicely captured in the following quote from "On Understanding Types, Data Abstraction, and Polymorphism" (*ACM Computing Surveys 17*, No. 4, December 1985), by Luca Cardelli and Peter Wegner: "A major purpose of type systems is to avoid embarrassing questions about representations, and to forbid situations in which these questions might come up."

[12] In later writings, Codd (rather unfortunately, in my opinion) used the term "semantic override" in place of "domain check override." The term "command" is unfortunate too—"expression" would be much better.

example, a comparison to see whether the physical representation of a certain supplier number is the same as that of a certain part number.

WHAT'S A TIME-VARYING RELATION?

Ever since the early 1990s, Hugh Darwen and I have been doing our best to call attention to the fact that there's a logical difference between relations as such (meaning relation values), on the one hand, and relation variables (which we abbreviate to just *relvars*) on the other. Codd's 1970 paper uses the qualifier *time-varying* in an attempt to get at the same distinction. For example, he says at one point that "The totality of data in a data bank may be viewed as a collection of time-varying relations." However, it's my belief that the phrase *time-varying relation* has been the source of a very great deal of confusion. Since relations simply don't vary with time (as indeed the definition of the term *relation* in the first paragraph of subsection 1.3 of the 1970 paper makes quite clear), it follows that a "time-varying relation," whatever else it might be, certainly isn't a relation. In particular, therefore, given that the operators—join, projection, and so on—defined elsewhere in the paper all apply to relations as such, what does it mean to apply them to a "time-varying relation"? Note that Codd certainly does assume they apply, as is evidenced by several remarks in Section 2.2 ("Redundancy") of the 1970 paper and elsewhere.

Consider also the following quote:

> As time progresses, each *n*-ary relation may be subject to insertion of additional *n*-tuples, deletion of existing ones, and alteration of components of any of its existing *n*-tuples.

"Relation" here surely ought to be "time-varying relation" or (better) "relation variable" (variables can be updated, values can't). Also, the 1970 paper nowhere mentions the fundamental operation of relational assignment, an oversight that perhaps led to the omission of that operator from SQL, as well as from most other proposed relational or would-be relational languages. As noted in Chapter 1, INSERT, DELETE, and UPDATE are convenient shorthands, but they're all, in the final analysis, defined in terms of relational assignment. And a model as such—which after all is what the 1970 paper is supposed to be all about—ought surely to be concerned with fundamentals, not with mere shorthands that might happen to be convenient for the user.

While I'm on the subject of updates, I note that the 1970 paper also has this to say:

> Deletions which are effective for the community (as opposed to the individual user or subcommunities) take the form of removing elements from declared relations.

Well, it's frankly not clear what this remark is supposed to mean (especially given the qualification in parentheses)—it looks a little mysterious to me. As far as I know, however, it didn't lead to anything, so perhaps we can simply ignore it.

WHAT'S A KEY?

The 1970 paper is quite muddled over the concept of keys in general and primary keys in particular. Consider the following quote:

> Normally, one domain (or combination of domains) of a given relation has values which uniquely identify each element (*n*-tuple) of that relation. Such a domain (or combination) is called a *primary key* ... A primary key is *nonredundant* if it is either a simple domain (not a combination) or a combination such that none of the participating simple domains is superfluous in uniquely identifying each element. A relation may possess more than one nonredundant primary key ... Whenever a relation has two or more nonredundant primary keys, one of them is arbitrarily selected and called *the* primary key of that relation.

I have several comments on this extract.

1. First of all, keys of any kind represent certain integrity constraints, and integrity constraints apply to variables, not values (since they constrain the effects of updates, and updates apply to variables, not values). Thus, "relation" should be "time-varying relation" or (better) "relation variable" throughout.

2. "Domain" should be "attribute" throughout.

3. The term *simple domain* doesn't mean here what it means elsewhere in the paper (viz., a domain whose values are "atomic").

4. The "combination" consisting of no attributes at all should be allowed. *Note:* Of course, this possibility isn't explicitly excluded by the text quoted; but the term "combination" (used here and elsewhere in the paper), rather than the term "set," does tend to suggest that the intended interpretation is "one or more," not "zero or more."[13]

5. That opening "Normally" is quite puzzling—it suggests that what the paper calls a primary key is in fact optional.[14] Worse, it actually suggests that "a given relation" might not have a "domain (or combination of domains) which uniquely identify each [tuple]" at all, and hence that duplicate tuples might be legitimate! Of course, I'm quite certain this interpretation isn't what Codd intended, but it would surely have been better to have used

---

[13] Further evidence that this interpretation is the one intended can be found in various later writings by Codd. For example, in his book *The Relational Model for Database Management Version 2* (Addison-Wesley, 1990), we find this: "A primary key may consist of a simple column or a combination of columns. When it consists of a combination of columns, the key is said to be *composite*." It's hard to believe that Codd intended that a key of degree zero should be thought of as composite.

[14] But the paper does later say "Each [relation] declaration ... identifies the primary key for that relation," which suggests that primary keys are mandatory after all.

more careful wording. As it is, he lays himself open to attack by critics of the deconstructionist persuasion.[15]

6. Note that the extract allows a "relation" to have any number of primary keys, and moreover that such keys are allowed to be "redundant" (better: *reducible*). In other words, what the paper calls a primary key is what later (and better) became known as a *superkey*, and what the paper calls a nonredundant (better: *irreducible*) primary key is what later became known as a *candidate* key or (better) just a *key*.

7. Finally, "*the* primary key" as defined in the final sentence of the extract quoted is indeed what the term *primary key* later came to denote. But I reject that concept anyway. I don't believe the kind of arbitrariness involved—i.e., in selecting the primary key—has any place in a formal system such as the relational model is supposed to be.

Here's another quote on primary keys (though actually what it says is surely intended to apply to keys in general, not just to primary keys in particular):

No primary key has a component domain which is nonsimple.

And the paper goes on to say "The writer knows of no application" that would require this condition to be relaxed. Well, we could perhaps argue over the precise meaning of the term *require* here; however, there are certainly applications for which keys defined on "nonsimple domains" do seem to be the most natural design.[16]

So much for keys as such; now I turn to foreign keys. I have two quotes in this connection:

■ We shall call a domain (or domain combination) of relation *R* a *foreign key* if it is not the primary key of *R* but its elements are values of the primary key of some relation *S* ... .

Foreign keys were invented by Codd, but his definition of the concept changed several times over the years; the definition just quoted is the one he gave in the 1970 paper, but he gave different definitions in 1969, 1979, 1988, and 1990.[17] In particular, observe that the foregoing (1970) definition includes the strange and clearly unnecessary restriction that a foreign key not be the primary key of its containing relation (or relvar, rather). Codd later

---

[15] Deconstruction in general is a useful and effective technique of literary criticism. This isn't the place for a detailed explanation, but what it boils down to is this: You can judge a writer's intent only by what he or she has actually said, not by what you might possibly think he or she might possibly have wanted to have possibly said, but didn't.

[16] Examples of such applications can be found in the paper "What First Normal Form Really Means" in my book *Date on Database: Writings 2000-2006* (Apress, 2006).

[17] An annotated history of these various definitions can be found in my paper "Inclusion Dependencies and Foreign Keys" in the book *Database Explorations: Essays on The Third Manifesto and Related Topics* (Trafford, 2010), by Hugh Darwen and myself.

and silently dropped that restriction, but he never dropped the restriction that the target of a foreign key had to be a primary key specifically.[18]

■ It is a remarkable fact that several existing information systems ... fail to provide data representations for relations which have two or more identical domains.

This remark is clearly incorrect on its face; a relation with, e.g., two attributes both defined on the domain of integers surely can't give rise to any special difficulties of implementation. From the context, however, it seems that what Codd was really getting at here is that systems often provide direct support for many to one relationships but fail to provide direct support for many to many relationships, especially if the relationship in question is between entities of the same type, as occurs in (e.g.) the well known "bill of materials" application. That is, such a system might not allow (its analog of) a "time-varying relation" to have (its analog of) n foreign keys for $n > 1$, especially if two or more of those "foreign keys" need to reference the same target. This criticism applies to XML, for example, though of course XML didn't exist in 1970. However, it's interesting to note that it doesn't apply to IMS (which did exist at the time), despite the fact that IMS is usually perceived as being a hierarchic system.[19]

WHAT ABOUT THE OPERATORS?

Although (as I've tried to show) the 1970 paper is at best unclear as to whether the relational operators are part of the model—not to mention whether they apply to "time-varying relations"—it does have a lot to say about such operators. With hindsight, however, it seems to me that some of the things it does say are a little strange. For example:

■ Since relations are sets, all of the usual set operations are applicable to them. Nevertheless, the result may not be a relation; for example, the union of a binary relation and a ternary relation is not a relation.

These remarks are undoubtedly true, but they constitute the sole mention of "the usual set operations" (union in particular) in the entire paper. The clear implication is that (a) union and the rest are included in the proposed set of operators, and (b) there's no requirement for what Codd referred to in later papers as *union compatibility*.[20] A further implication is that there's no requirement for what later came to be called *closure* (relational closure, that is,

---

[18] To its credit, SQL never abided by either of these restrictions.

[19] And despite the fact also that the very next sentence in Codd's 1970 paper, immediately following the sentence already quoted, is: "The present version of [IMS] is an example of such a system"!

[20] But I reject "union compatibility" as such anyway. In our work on *The Third Manifesto* Hugh Darwen and I have replaced, and subsumed, that notion by a carefully thought out notion of *relation type*.

meaning that the result of every relational operation is itself a relation). Indeed, this latter notion—which later came to be regarded as crucial—isn't mentioned in the paper at all. (It might be germane to mention here that SQL as originally defined in fact failed to abide by the closure requirement, a shortcoming that wasn't corrected, at least in the standard version of that language, until 1992.)

■ *Join.* Suppose we are given two binary relations, which have some domain in common. Under what circumstances can we combine these relations to form a ternary relation which preserves all of the information in the given relations?

The join concept is in many ways one of Codd's most important contributions. It's unfortunate, therefore, that—in my opinion, at any rate—the discussion of that topic in the 1970 paper is quite confusing:[21] so much so, in fact, that it can be hard in places to see the forest for the trees. For example, it might not be immediately obvious to a modern reader—though the foregoing quote, which opens the discussion, does suggest as much— that the paper is primarily, albeit not exclusively, concerned with what we would now call *nonloss* joins.[22] Nonloss joins are crucially important in what subsequently became known as normalization theory, but that theory isn't part of the relational model; rather, it's a separate theory that's built on top of the relational model.[23] To put the point another way: Join as such is just an operator. Whether or not some particular join is nonloss is a separate question, one that's significant in certain important contexts but is, or should be, irrelevant as far as the relational model itself is concerned.

■ A binary relation R is *joinable* with a binary relation S if there exists a ternary relation U such that [the projection of U on its first and second attributes is equal to R and the projection of U on its second and third attributes is equal to S].[24] Any such ternary relation is called a join of R with S.

Observe that—quite apart from the fact that it assumes that relations have a left to right ordering to their attributes[25]—this definition implies the following: If X is the second attribute of relation R and Y is the first attribute of relation S (and if those two attributes are

---

[21] The discussion in the 1969 paper is essentially identical.

[22] Actually the term *nonloss join* has at least two different meanings. In this chapter I use it in the following sense (and that sense only): The join j of relations $r1$ and $r2$ is nonloss if and only if the projection of j on the attributes of $r1$ is equal to $r1$ and the projection of j on the attributes of $r2$ is equal to $r2$.

[23] It is, however, only fair to mention that it was Codd himself who established the foundations of normalization theory (now more usually referred to as dependency theory). His paper on the topic, "Further Normalization of the Data Base Relational Model," is discussed in Chapter 5 of the present book.

[24] Our modern understanding of the term is rather different; today we would say that two relations are joinable if and only if attributes with the same name are of the same type.

[25] And quite apart also from the fact that it implies that R might be joinable with S while S isn't joinable with R—and that, even if joinability applies in both directions (as it were), the join of R with S and the join of S with R will in general be distinct (as indeed the 1970 paper subsequently and explicitly admits).

defined on the same domain, of course), then *R* can be joined with *S only if the set of X values in R is the same as the set of Y values in S* (or, loosely, only if the projections of *R* on *X* and *S* on *Y* are equal).[26] Oddly, however, the paper then goes on to give a definition of the natural join of *R* with *S* that doesn't require *R* and *S* to be "joinable" in the foregoing sense!—indeed, that definition is close to the one we use today.

The paper then gets into a fairly extensive discussion of what it calls *cyclic* joins. But that discussion is back to front, in a sense. What it really has to do with is not so much join as such but what we now know as *join dependencies*, and in particular with the possibility that a given relation might be nonloss decomposable into three or more projections but not into two. Indeed, the very fact that no one at the time seemed to realize that such matters were the real topic lends weight to my claim that the discussion overall wasn't as clear as it might have been. Be that as it may, the paper gives an example, in its Figs. 8 and 9, to illustrate the foregoing possibility (the possibility, that is, that a relation might be nonloss decomposable into three projections but not into two). Unfortunately, however, Fig. 8 in the paper contains at least one mistake, which makes it difficult to understand exactly what's going on. At the very least, the fourth row of T in that figure should be either changed (but how?) or deleted.[27]

■   [It] appears that an adequate collection [of operators is] projection, natural join, tie, and restriction.[28]

Here Codd is touching on what he would later come to call *relational completeness*. However, that "adequate" list of operators should certainly include (relational) union and difference. By contrast, it's hard to see why tie is included, or even what purpose that operator serves at all.

■   Arithmetic functions may be needed in the qualification or other parts of retrieval statements. Such functions can be defined in [the host language] *H* and invoked in [the data sublanguage] *R*.

It's good to see Codd tacitly endorsing the idea of supporting relational operators such as EXTEND. Unfortunately, he fails to give further guidance as to how those "arithmetic functions" might actually be "invoked in *R*" (the relational operators defined in the paper don't seem to have any room for such invocations).

---

[26] Note that (in accordance with footnote 22) this condition is both necessary and sufficient to guarantee that the join of *R* with *S* is nonloss.

[27] Oddly enough, the counterpart to Fig. 8 in the 1969 paper does appear to be correct (to be specific, it omits that fourth row of T). On the other hand, at least one republished version of the 1970 paper—viz., the one in Phillip LaPlante, *Great Papers in Computer Science* (West Publishing, 1996)—manages to introduce at least one additional mistake of its own. *Caveat lector.*

[28] Codd's restriction operator here isn't quite the same as the operator of that name as now understood, but the differences aren't important for present purposes. As for the tie operator, it can be defined as follows: Given a relation *r* with attributes *A1*, *A2*, ..., *An*, the *tie* of *r* returns the relation containing just those tuples of *r* for which the *A1* and *An* values are equal. (Incidentally, note the reliance on left to right attribute ordering in this definition.)

By the way, the terms *arithmetic*, *retrieval*, and *statements* in the foregoing quote are all somewhat misleading, in my view. For my part, I would greatly prefer to replace the first sentence by something along the following lines: "Relational expressions might need to contain invocations of computational functions" (and that qualifier *computational* might not be necessary, either).

■ It is well known that ... it is unnecessary to [be able to] express every formula of the selected predicate calculus [in the data sublanguage]. For example, just those in prenex normal form are adequate.

Actually prenex normal form is *not* adequate, as I've shown elsewhere.[29]

■ The network model ... has spawned a number of confusions, not the least of which is mistaking the derivation of connections for the derivation of relations ... A lack of understanding of relational composition[30] has led several system designers into what may be called the *connection trap*. This trap may be described in terms of the following example. Suppose each supplier description is linked by pointers to the descriptions of each part supplied by that supplier, and each part description is similarly linked to the descriptions of each project which uses that part. A conclusion is now drawn which is, in general, erroneous: namely that, if all possible paths are followed from a given supplier via the parts he [*sic*] supplies to the projects using those parts, one will obtain a valid set of all projects supplied by that supplier.

Far be it from me to defend "the network model," but this criticism really has nothing to do with the network model as such—it applies equally to the relational model, mutatis mutandis.[31] "Derivation of connections" *is* "derivation of relations"! The mistake consists in misinterpreting the relations so derived. It's the quoted text that's confused.

And What about Relational Comparisons?

The algebra of sets is usually thought of as including a partial ordering operator called set inclusion, denoted by the symbol "⊆". Here's the definition: The expression $s1 \subseteq s2$, where $s1$ and $s2$ are sets, evaluates to TRUE if and only if every element of $s1$ is also an element of $s2$ (i.e., if and only if $s1$ is a subset of $s2$). So if, as seems likely, Codd meant to pattern his algebra of relations after the algebra of sets, it would have been reasonable to define an analogous

---

[29] E.g., in my paper "A Remark on Prenex Normal Form" in the book *Database Explorations: Essays on The Third Manifesto and Related Topics* (Trafford, 2010), by Hugh Darwen and myself.

[30] Relational composition is a generalization of conventional functional composition. In its simplest form it can be defined as follows: Let relation $r1$ have attributes A and B and let relation $r2$ have attributes B and C, and let attributes B of $r1$ and B of $r2$ be of the same type (i.e., let $r1$ and $r2$ be joinable, either in Codd's sense or as that term is now understood). Then the composition of $r1$ and $r2$ is the projection on A and C of the join of $r1$ and $r2$.

[31] By the way, Codd really shouldn't have used the phrase "the network model" here if, as he later argued, no abstract network model even existed at the time. See his remarks on such matters in his paper "Data Models in Database Management" (*ACM SIGMOD Record 11*, No. 2, February 1981).

relational inclusion operator. More generally, it would have been reasonable, and indeed useful, to define a full array of relational comparison operators: equality ("="), inclusion ("⊆"), proper inclusion "⊂"), and so on. Sadly, however, neither the 1970 paper nor its 1969 predecessor mentioned any such operators (at least, not explicitly).[32]

Note: Actually the foregoing omission is a trifle odd, inasmuch as the discussion of redundancy in both papers certainly assumed (at least implicitly) the ability to compare two relations for equality if nothing else. What's more, the definitions Codd himself gave for his relational division operator in various later publications all explicitly invoked the operation of relational inclusion! Be that as it may, the fact that relational comparisons are still to this day omitted from nearly all database textbooks (and from the SQL language as well, come to that) can, I think, fairly be traced back to the lack of any mention of such operators in Codd's first two papers.

WHAT ABOUT DATA INDEPENDENCE?

Here's the opening sentence from the abstract to the 1970 paper:

> Future users of large data banks must be protected from having to know how the data is organized in the machine (the internal representation).

I agree strongly with this position, of course, implying as it does that there must be a rigid distinction between model and implementation. But several later remarks in the paper blur that distinction considerably. For example, subsection 1.6 is titled "Expressible, Named, and Stored Relations." Clearly, any notion of some given relation being stored—i.e., *physically* stored, in some kind of "direct image" form, with each stored record corresponding to a single tuple from the relation in question[33]—is counter to the objective of users being "protected from having to know how the data is organized in the machine." In fact, subsection 1.6 nowhere discusses "stored relations" anyway! The title is presumably a hangover from the 1969 paper, where such a notion *was* discussed. (Here's a quote from that earlier paper: "The large, integrated data banks of the future will contain many relations of various degrees *in stored form*"—emphasis

---

[32] Codd did subsequently require such operators to be supported in what he called Version 2 of the model—see his book *The Relational Model for Database Management Version 2* (Addison-Wesley, 1990)—but he didn't discuss them in detail or even define them. (The pertinent text, on page 365 of that book, reads in its entirety thus: "[The relational language] also includes set comparators such as SET INCLUSION.")

[33] One reviewer objected here that Codd's talk of stored relations didn't necessarily imply a "direct image" style of implementation (especially since the very next quote in the present chapter, also taken from the 1970 paper, explicitly refers to "declarations which indicate ... how relations are represented in storage," perhaps suggesting some degree of choice and variability in physical representation). But other remarks of Codd's quoted elsewhere in the present chapter do strongly suggest a direct image style. And in any case (and more to the point), that very phrase *stored relation* implies—at least to me—that there's some kind of one to one mapping between relations and storage structures, and in my view the assumption of such a mapping has already prejudiced the debate. In my book *Go Faster! The TransRelational™ Approach to DBMS Implementation* (2002, 2011, http://bookboon.com), I argue strongly that it's a good idea that there not necessarily be any such one to one mapping.

added.) Indeed, the whole idea of some relations being "stored" ones was a mistake in that earlier paper, a mistake partially but not totally excised from the 1970 paper. For example, here are some more quotes from this latter:

- [The host language] permits declarations which indicate ... how these relations are represented in storage.

- Once a user is aware that a certain relation is stored ...

- ... [then that user will] expect to be able to exploit it using any combination of its arguments as "knowns" and the remaining arguments as "unknowns" ... This is a system feature ... which we shall call ... *symmetric exploitation* of relations. Naturally, symmetry of performance is not to be expected.

Actually there's no a priori reason why symmetry of performance shouldn't be expected, unless—as the extract quoted here does tacitly seem to assume—we're dealing with a "direct image" style of implementation (which is indeed, as noted earlier, what we do find in most if not all mainstream SQL products today). Thus, once again we find the 1970 paper tacitly endorsing the notion that certain relations will be physically stored as such (or, rather, the notion that their array representation will be physically stored as such). *Note:* By the way, "arguments" in the foregoing quote ought really to be *parameters* or (perhaps better) *attributes*.

 As an aside, I note that the 1970 paper goes on to say "To support symmetric exploitation ... [for] a relation of degree n, the number of [access] paths to be named and controlled is n factorial." It's a little hard to argue with this claim since the term *access path* isn't defined, but shouldn't the number of paths be 2^n, not n factorial? After all, there are 2^n combinations of attributes that might be used as "knowns."

WHAT ABOUT INTEGRITY?

The 1970 paper has quite a lot to say about integrity. However, it mostly doesn't use that term, it uses the term *consistency* instead—not unreasonably, because the only integrity constraints it considers in any detail[34] are ones having to do with data redundancy specifically, as the following quote (from subsection 2.3 of the paper, "Consistency") makes clear:

---

[34] Apart from key and foreign key constraints, discussed earlier both in this chapter and in the 1970 paper.

Whenever the named set of relations is redundant ... we shall associate with that set a collection of [constraint] statements which define all of the redundancies which hold independent of time between the member relations[35] ... Given a collection of C of time-varying relations, an associated set Z of constraint statements, and an instantaneous value V for C, we shall call the state (C, Z, V) *consistent* or *inconsistent* according as V does or does not satisfy Z.

There's just one issue—a very important one!—arising in connection with this topic that I'd like to comment on here. Here first is the relevant extract from the paper:

> There are, of course, several possible ways in which a system can detect inconsistencies and respond to them. In one approach the system checks for possible inconsistency whenever an insertion, deletion, or key update occurs.[36] Naturally, such checking will slow these operations down. If an inconsistency has been generated ... and if it is not remedied within some reasonable time interval, either the user or someone responsible for the ... integrity of the data is notified. Another approach is to conduct consistency checking as a batch operation once a day or less frequently.

I regard these remarks as unfortunate in the extreme. Indeed, I regard them as the source of a serious mistake to be observed in SQL and elsewhere: namely, the decision to allow the checking of certain integrity constraints to be "deferred," typically to the end of the transaction (i.e., "COMMIT time"). In strong contrast, it's my very firm position that all integrity checking needs to be "immediate" (i.e., done whenever an update is requested that might cause the constraint in question to be violated, at the time the request in question is made). Let me elaborate:

■ First of all, to say the database is consistent merely means, formally speaking, that it conforms to all declared integrity constraints. But it's crucially important that databases *always* be consistent in this sense; indeed, a database that's not consistent in this sense, at some particular time, is like a logical system that contains a contradiction. And in a logical system with a contradiction, you can prove anything; for example, you can prove that $1 = 0$. What this means in database terms is that if the database is inconsistent in the foregoing sense, you can never trust the answers you get from queries (they may be false, they may be true, and you have no way in general of knowing which they are); all bets are off. As far as declared constraints are concerned, in other words, the system simply *must* do the checking whenever a pertinent update occurs; there's no alternative, because (to say it

---

[35] It's a sad comment on the state (or agility, or lack thereof) of the database industry that, to this day, no mainstream product actually provides this functionality.

[36] I don't know why Codd singles out key updates specifically here; surely integrity checking should be performed on *all* updates (all pertinent updates, at any rate)? Even if (as he says) he wants to limit his attention to violations of consistency as such, surely he should at least be worrying about foreign key updates as well. Or is the phrase "key updates" supposed to cover foreign key updates as well?

again) not to do that checking is to risk having a database for which all bets are off. In other words, immediate integrity checking is logically required.

■ What's more, I don't agree that immediate checking will necessarily slow the system down. If the user has bothered to declare the constraint, presumably he or she wants it enforced—for otherwise there's no point in declaring it in the first place. And if the user wants the constraint enforced, and if the system isn't going to do it (by which I mean do it properly, by which I mean doing immediate checking on all pertinent updates), then the user is going to have to do it instead. Either way, the checking does have to be done. And I would hope the system could do that checking more efficiently than the user! Thus, I think that, far from updates being slowed down, they should be speeded up, just so long as the system does the right thing and shoulders its responsibility properly.

Now, to be charitable, what I think Codd might have been getting at by his suggestion that integrity checking could be deferred was what has since come to be known as "eventual consistency." But if so, then I think he was confusing consistency in the formal sense and consistency as conventionally (and informally) understood, meaning consistency as understood in conventional real world terms, outside the world of databases. Suppose there are two items A and B in the database that, in the real world, we believe should have the same value. They might, for example, both be the selling price for some given commodity, stored twice because stored data replication is being used to improve availability. If A and B in fact have different values at some given time, we might certainly say, informally, that there's an inconsistency in the data as stored at that time. But that "inconsistency" is an inconsistency as far as the system is concerned only if the system has been told that A and B are supposed to be equal—i.e., only if "$A = B$" has been stated as a formal integrity constraint. If it hasn't, then (a) the fact that $A \neq B$ at some time doesn't in and of itself constitute a consistency violation as far as the system is concerned, and (b) importantly, the system will nowhere rely on an assumption that A and B are equal. In other words, if all we want is for A and B to be equal "eventually"—i.e., if we're content for that requirement to be handled in the application layer—all we have to do as far as the database system is concerned is omit any declaration of "$A = B$" as a formal constraint. No problem, and in particular no violation of the relational model.

AND WHAT ABOUT NULLS?

I've deliberately saved until last one of the biggest mistakes of all: *nulls*. One of my reasons for doing so is that the 1969 and 1970 papers actually have nothing at all to say about the issue—quite correctly, in my view, since nulls (at least in the sense in which they're usually understood, involving a foundation in n-valued logic for some $n > 2$) have no part to play in a formal system like the relational model, which is firmly based on conventional two-valued logic. Indeed, Codd never discussed nulls in any detail until the 1979 paper I've mentioned several times already:

viz., "Extending the Database Relational Model to Capture More Meaning" (*ACM Transactions on Database Systems 4*, No. 4). In other words, Codd's relational model did perfectly well without nulls for some ten years. I would prefer to keep it that way.

APPENDIX: RELATIONS REVISITED

Here again, repeated from the body of the chapter, is the 1970 paper's definition of a relation:

> Given sets S_1, S_2, ..., S_n (not necessarily distinct), R is a relation on these n sets if it is a collection of *n*-tuples each of which has its first element from S_1, its second element from S_2, and so on. We shall refer to S_j as the *j*th *domain* of R.

Now, I've already shown that this definition leaves quite a lot to be desired:

■ First of all, it quite clearly defines something that's a *value*, whereas the term *relation* often has to be understood in the literature to mean not a value but a *variable*.[37] (Later in the paper, Codd introduces the term *time-varying relation* to mean something like what I'd prefer to call a relation variable, but the term "time-varying relation" has problems of its own.)

■ Second, it fails to mention the term *tuple* (though it does at least mention the term from which *tuple* derives, *n-tuple*).

■ Third, it also fails to mention the term *attribute*.

■ Fourth, it clearly says there's a left to right ordering to the components of a tuple, and hence to the attributes of a relation.

■ Fifth, it fails to acknowledge that the unfamiliar term *domain* denotes exactly the same thing as the much more familiar term *type* does.

And so on (the foregoing list of flaws isn't exhaustive). What's more, most of the mainstream textbooks unfortunately give definitions that are little more than a regurgitation of Codd's 1970 definition, or something very like it. Here by contrast is the way I'd prefer to deal with the issue ... Recognizing that (a) relations have headings and bodies, and (b) headings are made out of attributes and bodies are made out of tuples, I'd approach the issue one step at a time, like this:[38]

---

[37] Analogous remarks apply to the term *table* as used in SQL contexts.

[38] These definitions assume that some brief explanation (not deep) has already been given as to what a type is.

Definition (heading): A *heading H* is a set, the elements of which are *attributes*. Let *H* have cardinality *n* ($n \geq 0$); then the value *n* is the *degree* of *H*. A heading of degree zero is *nullary*, a heading of degree one is *unary*, a heading of degree two is *binary*, ..., and more generally a heading of degree *n* is *n-ary*. Each attribute in *H* is of the form *<Aj,Tj>*, where *Aj* is the *attribute name* and *Tj* is the corresponding *type name* ($0 < j \leq n$), and the attribute names *Aj* are all distinct.

Definition (tuple): Let heading *H* be of degree *n*. For each attribute *<Aj,Tj>* in *H*, define a *component* of the form *<Aj,Tj,vj>*, where the *attribute value vj* is a value of type *Tj*.[39] The set—call it *t*—of all *n* components so defined is a *tuple value* (or just a *tuple* for short) over the attributes of *H*. *H* is the *tuple heading* (or just the heading for short) for *t*, and the degree and attributes of *H* are, respectively, the degree and attributes of *t*.

Definition (body): Given a heading *H*, a *body B* conforming to *H* is a set of *m* tuples ($m \geq 0$), each with heading *H*. The value *m* is the *cardinality* of *B*.

Definition (relation): Let *H* be a heading, and let *B* be a body conforming to *H*. The pair *<H,B>*—call it *r*—is a *relation value* (or just a *relation* for short) over the attributes of *H*. *H* is the *relation heading* (or just the heading for short) for *r*, and the degree and attributes of *H* and the cardinality of *B* are, respectively, the degree, attributes, and cardinality of *r*.

These definitions pin down the notion of a relation precisely, and they form the basis of a sound, thorough, modern, and detailed understanding of what the relational model is all about.

---

[39] Actually *Tj* is uniquely determined by *Aj*, and so it would be possible to define a component as an *<Aj,vj>* pair instead of an *<Aj,Tj,vj>* triple. I prefer to define it as a triple simply in order that the clause "where the *attribute value vj* is a value of type *Tj*" might make sense as it stands, instead of having to be expanded to "where the *attribute value vj* is a value of the type *Tj* of attribute *Aj*."

As an aside, I note that since every value is of exactly one type, absent type inheritance, *Tj* is uniquely determined by *vj* as well. If we wanted to take inheritance into account, we would have to define a component as an *<Aj,Tj,vj>* triple where *vj* is a value of *some subtype of* type *Tj*—or, equivalently, as an *<Aj,vj>* pair where *vj* is a value of some subtype of the type *Tj* of attribute *Aj*, of course. See my book *Type Inheritance and Relational Theory: Subtypes, Supertypes, and Substitutability* (O'Reilly, 2016) for further explanation.

Chapter 3

The Completeness Paper

A condition of complete simplicity ...
And all shall be well and
All manner of thing shall be well

—T. S. Eliot:
Four Quartets: Little Gidding (1942)

The paper I'll be referring to in this chapter as "the completeness paper" for short is just one in that series of papers by E. F. Codd that I characterized in the preface to this book as "staggering in their originality." Here's a full citation:

■ "Relational Completeness of Data Base Sublanguages," IBM Research Report RJ987 (March 6th, 1972); republished in Randall J. Rustin (ed.), *Data Base Systems: Courant Computer Science Symposia Series 6* (Prentice-Hall, 1972)

Of all of Codd's early papers this one is surely the most formal, and for that reason it's probably also the one that's the most difficult to understand. Let me therefore state for the record just what the paper did:[1]

1. It defined a *relational algebra*—i.e., a set of operators, such as join and projection, for deriving a relation from some given set of relations.

2. It defined a *relational calculus*—i.e., a notation, based on predicate calculus, for defining a relation in terms of some given set of relations.

3. It defined a notion of *relational completeness* ("a basic yardstick of selective power"). Basically, a language L is said to be relationally complete if and only if it's as powerful as

---

[1] Or what it tried to do, rather, since I'll be arguing later that at least in some respects the paper didn't quite achieve what it attempted. *Note:* Codd's 1969 and 1979 papers also touched on most of the points identified in the list of achievements I cite here. To be specific, they defined a set of algebraic operators (point 1); they suggested that predicate calculus would be a possible basis on which to define a "data sublanguage" (point 2); they suggested that such a language "would provide a yardstick of linguistic power for all other proposed data languages" (point 3); and they suggested rather strongly that predicate calculus would be, not just a possible, but in fact the *best*, basis on which to define a data sublanguage (point 5).

the calculus (see point 2)—i.e., if and only if for every possible expression of that calculus, there's a logically equivalent expression in that language *L*.

4. It presented an algorithm ("Codd's reduction algorithm") for reducing an arbitrary expression of the calculus as defined under point 2 to a logically equivalent expression of the algebra as defined under point 1, thereby:

    a. Showing that the algebra was relationally complete, and

    b. Providing a possible basis for implementing the calculus.

5. Finally, it offered some opinions in favor of the calculus as opposed to the algebra as a basis on which to define a general purpose relational language—what the paper referred to as "a query language (or other data sublanguage)."

Overall, the paper was dramatically different in just about every possible way from other database publications at the time. In particular, as I've indicated, it had a heavily formal (i.e., logical and/or mathematical) flavor. Now, I'm all for formalism in its place; in particular, I'm all for the precision that formalism can lead to. As I've said, however, the formalism in the case at hand had the unfortunate effect of making the paper quite difficult to understand.[2] Moreover, as a consequence of this latter fact, I believe it also had the effect of obscuring certain errors in the presentation. At least it's true that the errors in question weren't noticed, so far as I'm aware, for quite a long time. The purpose of the present chapter, then, is to clarify the contributions of the completeness paper, and also to raise a few pertinent questions.

STRUCTURE OF THE PAPER

The completeness paper consists of five main sections, as follows:

1. Introduction
2. A Relational Algebra
3. Relational Calculus
4. Reduction
5. Algebra versus Calculus

A couple of cosmetic points arise right away. First, note the indefinite article in the title of Section 2 and the lack of any article at all in the title of Section 3. To people unfamiliar with

---

[2] I first read the paper myself when it was published in 1972 and I was working for IBM, and I certainly had difficulty with it—though not perhaps as much as my manager, who came into my office one day with a huge grin on his face, brandishing the paper and saying "I've found it! I've found it! I've found the piece of Codd that passeth all understanding."

concepts such as algebra and calculus in general, this state of affairs might tend to suggest that there could be several different relational algebras, but only one relational calculus. Well, it's true that several different relational algebras have been defined (Codd himself described quite a few over the years). But at least two different versions of relational calculus have been defined as well, viz., the tuple relational calculus and the domain relational calculus,[3] and Section 3 might thus have better been titled "A Relational Calculus," with the indefinite article. The specific calculus defined in that section is a tuple calculus.

The second point is: Why are these things called an algebra and a calculus, anyway? As a matter of fact, I wrote a paper some years ago addressing precisely these questions,[4] and I don't propose to repeat the discussions of that paper here. I will, however, give definitions of the terms *algebra* and *calculus*, taken from my book *The New Relational Database Dictionary* (O'Reilly, 2016) but lightly edited here:

> **Definition (algebra):** A formal system consisting of (a) a set of elements and (b) a set of read-only operators that apply to those elements, such that those elements and operators together satisfy certain laws and properties (almost certainly closure, probably commutativity and associativity, and so on); also known as an *algebraic structure* or an *abstract algebra*. The word algebra itself derives from Arabic *al-jebr*, meaning a resetting (of something broken) or a combination. *Note:* The foregoing definition is admittedly not very precise, but the term just doesn't seem to have a very precise definition, not even in mathematics.

> **Definition (calculus):** A system of formal computation (the Latin word *calculus* means a pebble, perhaps used in counting or some other form of reckoning). *Note:* Relational calculus in particular is an applied form of predicate calculus, tailored to operating on relations. Predicate calculus in turn has to do with predicates and connectives and the inferences that can be made using such predicates and connectives.

PRELIMINARY DEFINITIONS

Before discussing its major topics as such (i.e., relational calculus and relational algebra), the completeness paper presents a number of preliminary definitions, definitions that in my view raise a number of issues right away. In fact, they (i.e., the definitions in question) suffer from two major flaws that unfortunately permeate the entire paper. By way of illustration, consider the following quote from Section 2.1 ("Objective"):

---

[3] The names are slightly illogical—tuple calculus is so called because its range variables represent tuples, domain calculus is so called because its range variables represent, not domains as the name might suggest, but *elements of* domains. (In any case, I greatly prefer the term *type* to the term *domain*, and the term *value* (of some type) to the term *element* (of some domain).)

[4] "Why Is It Called Relational Algebra?"—a chapter in my book *Logic and Databases: The Roots of Relational Theory* (Trafford, 2007). *Note:* Despite its title, that chapter does have something to say about relational calculus also.

For notational and expository convenience, we deal with domain-ordered relations; that is, the individual domains of a given relation can be identified as the first, second, third, and so on ... [In] many practical data bases the relations are of such high degree that names rather than position numbers would be used to identify domains when actually storing or retrieving information.

This quote touches on both of the claimed "major flaws." To be specific:

■ First, the term *domain* would much better be replaced by the term *attribute* throughout. Indeed, there are many definitions in the paper as a whole where the term *domain* is used when *attribute* would clearly be better, and I'll offer more detailed commentary to that effect on some but not all of those definitions in what follows. Here let me just note that the term *attribute*, rather unfortunately, doesn't appear in the paper at all! This state of affairs might be one source of the confusion over domains vs. attributes that persisted in the database world for many years (and continues in some circles to the present day).

■ Second, what the quote is saying is that throughout the paper relations are to be regarded as having a left to right ordering to their attributes. Now, it's true that Codd says he adopts this position only for "notational and expository convenience,"[5] but the fact remains that:

   a. Most if not all of the individual operator definitions in the paper rely heavily on that left to right ordering assumption, and converting them into definitions having no such reliance is a fairly nontrivial task. As a result, the definitions in question are, to say the least, far from ideal. (In fact, despite Codd's claim of "convenience," I know from direct experience that the definitions are actually much easier to formulate if that left to right ordering assumption is dropped.)

   b. To put the point another way, what the paper *doesn't* do is define an algebra of relations as such—relations as they're supposed to be in the context of the relational model, that is, meaning that (by definition) they have no left to right ordering to their attributes. As a consequence, the paper doesn't even touch on the crucial importance—the importance, that is, in the definition of a truly useful and usable relational algebra—of proper attribute naming. Nor does it discuss the related (and also crucially important) issue of relation type inference.

   c. Moreover, it's a sad truth that, in SQL in particular, "relations" (or tables, rather) do have a left to right ordering to their "attributes" (or columns, rather), and it seems

---

[5] He also says in Section 1 ("Introduction") that he "would propose that domain names be used instead of domain numbers" (in a language based on relational algebra, that is). But this remark is little more than an aside, and it's easily overlooked (especially since it appears in the paper well before either relations as such or the algebra have even been discussed).

quite likely that the completeness paper is the source, or one of the sources, of this particular SQL error.[6]

In addition, note that the text cited says only that (paraphrasing slightly) "names rather than position numbers would be used to identify domains *in many practical data bases*" (my italics). This wording suggests rather strongly that "position numbers"—with all that such numbers entail—will sometimes be acceptable after all.

The next section, Section 2.2 ("Introductory Definitions"), then goes on to give the preliminary definitions mentioned above, all of them based where applicable on that left to right ordering assumption. I'd like to repeat and comment on certain of those definitions here. For typographic and comprehensibility reasons, however, I'll frequently make use of wording and notation in my versions of those definitions (and indeed throughout the present chapter) that differs from the wording and notation used in the completeness paper as such.

Definition (expanded cartesian product): The expanded cartesian product XCP (*D1, D2, ..., Dn*) of *n* sets *D1, D2, ..., Dn* is defined by:[7]

```
XCP ( D1 , D2 , ... , Dn )  ≝
              { ( d1 , d2 , ... , dn ) : dj ∈ Dj for j = 1, 2, ..., n }
```

Several points arise in connection with this definition. First of all, the paper doesn't actually say as much, but the expression (*d1, d2, ..., dn*) here is meant to denote the ordered *n*-tuple consisting of *d1* as its first component, *d2* as its second component, and so on. However, the paper does at least say that the elements of an expanded cartesian product "are called *n-tuples*, or just *tuples* for short."

Second, the paper goes on to say the following:

When *n* = 1, XCP (*D1*) = *D1*, since no distinction is made between a 1-tuple and its only component.

But this is clearly wrong! There certainly *is* a distinction—a logical difference, in fact—to be observed between a 1-tuple and its only component. To put the point another way, the elements of XCP (*D1, D2, ..., Dn*) are always tuples, while the elements of *D1, D2, ..., Dn* are typically not

---

[6] Some of the many unfortunate consequences of this serious SQL error are described in detail in *The Naming of Columns*, by Hugh Darwen (writing as Andrew Warden), originally published in March 1988 in Issue 3 of *The Relational Journal* and later republished in our joint book *Relational Database Writings 1985-1989* (Addison-Wesley, 1990). See also (a) the paper "A Sweet Disorder" in my book *Date on Database: Writings 2000-2006* (Apress, 2006) and (b) my book *SQL and Relational Theory: How to Write Accurate SQL Code* (3rd edition, O'Reilly, 2015). *Note:* For the remainder of this chapter I'll refer to this latter book as just *SQL and Relational Theory*, for brevity.

[7] The symbol "≝" in this definition means "is defined as." The completeness paper frequently uses a plain "=" symbol where "≝" would be more appropriate, but I'm sure that was done purely for typographical reasons.

tuples, and indeed usually aren't. In particular, therefore, if the elements of *D1* are *d11, d12, ...*, *d1m* (say), then the elements of XCP (*D1*) are the *tuples* (*d11*), (*d12*), ..., (*d1m*).

Third, the paper should also, but doesn't, consider the important case of $n = 0$. For the record, XCP ( ) is a set containing exactly one tuple: namely, the unique tuple with no components, also known as the empty tuple.

To continue with the preliminary definitions:

> **Definition (relation):** *R* is a relation on the sets *D1, D2, ..., Dn* if and only if it is a subset of XCP (*D1, D2, ..., Dn*). The value *n* is the *degree* of *R*. The sets on which a relation is defined are called its underlying *domains*.

Having given this definition, the paper goes on to say:

> For data base purposes, we are concerned with [domains] consisting of integers and character strings (other types of primitive elements may be included in this definition if desired, with only minor changes in some of the definitions [to come]).

Frankly, I don't know why these remarks are included in the paper at all.[8] As far as I can see, there are just two points in the paper that rely (but shouldn't!) on what I'll call "the integers and character strings" assumption:

- The first is the definition of a *simple domain* (see below).

- The second is a further assumption (e.g., in the definition of the θ-restriction operator, q.v.) that all of the operators "<", ">", "≤", and "≥" are defined for the values contained in a "simple domain." Of course, these operators *are* defined in the case of integers and character strings, but they're not—at least, not necessarily—in the case of other "primitive elements" (consider, for example, a "simple domain" of complex numbers[9]).

Now, it's an unfortunate fact that for many years there was a widespread perception in the database world at large to the effect that relational databases were good only for simple things like integers and character strings. And I venture to suggest that it was text such as that quoted above that might well have been one of the sources of that misconception. (Note in particular in this connection Codd's use of the qualifier "primitive" in the text cited above.)

---

[8] Perhaps what Codd had in mind here was something to do with his long-standing but mistaken belief that there's a difference in kind between "basic data types" and "domains as extended data types" (to use his own terminology). But if so, then I've already dealt with that belief on his part in Chapter 2 of this book

[9] I thought of using the "simple domain" of truth values as another example here. Unfortunately, however, SQL in particular does allow "<" (etc.) to be used with truth values! To be specific, it defines the comparison "FALSE < TRUE" to evaluate to TRUE. PS: Actually, the definition of "<" (etc.) for the "simple domain" of character strings can be somewhat nontrivial too, as the case of SQL sadly also demonstrates.

Anyway, let me get back to the definitions as such. The next is:[10]

Definition (simple domain): A simple domain is a set all of whose elements are integers, or a set all of whose elements are character strings.

I've already discussed that business of integers or character strings (see above). But note one logical consequence of this definition as stated: As far as the completeness paper is concerned, there are apparently just two "simple domains"! After all, having two distinct domains of, say, integers doesn't seem to make very much sense.[11]

Anyway, what's really going on here? It seems to me that a "simple domain" is just a domain as usually understood; the qualifier "simple" is introduced purely in order to distinguish domains as such from what the paper calls "compound" domains—see the next definition below—which aren't really domains at all within the meaning of the act, though Codd is trying to pretend they are.

So what *is* "a domain as usually understood"? In my opinion, it's nothing more nor less than a *type*, as this latter notion is generally understood. As far as the foregoing definition is concerned, therefore, I think it would be sufficient, and preferable, to appeal to the familiar notion of a type, and then just to say that a domain is a type *tout court*.

Definition (compound domain): A compound domain is the expanded cartesian product of a finite number k ($k \geq 1$) of simple domains;[12] k is the *degree* of the compound domain.

Well, I've already said I don't think a "compound domain" is a domain. To spell the point out, I believe the concept is introduced purely so that later in the paper an expression such as

```
A = B
```

—where *A* and *B* are "compound domains" (or "compound attributes," rather) with component simple domains (or attributes, rather) *A1, A2, ..., An* and *B1, B2, ..., Bn*, respectively—can be used as an abbreviation for

```
A1 = B1 AND A2 = B2 AND ... AND An = Bn
```

---

[10] Actually I think there's a definition missing here—I think Codd must have meant to define a domain to be either a simple domain or a compound domain. (On the other hand, the situation is complicated by the fact that, as I'll be explaining in just a moment, I don't really think "compound domains" should be regarded as domains at all.)

[11] Perhaps he was thinking that, e.g., two distinct domains might be defined, each containing some integers and not others (odd integers vs. even integers, perhaps). But he never discussed such a possibility in any detail, neither in the completeness paper nor in any subsequent publication, and of course it opens up a whole host of further questions. See my book *Type Inheritance and Relational Theory: Subtypes, Supertypes, and Substitutability* (O'Reilly, 2016) for a detailed discussion of such questions.

[12] Note, therefore, that the elements of a compound domain are tuples, while the elements of a simple domain (at least as defined in the completeness paper) are scalars.

And I don't think the rather trivial ability to abbreviate in this fashion—which is solely a matter of syntax, please observe—is sufficient to justify the introduction of a whole new concept ("compound domains"). Note in particular that a compound domain can't have a compound domain as a component, a state of affairs that should surely give us some pause.[13]

> **Definition (union compatibility):** Two simple domains are union compatible if and only if both are domains of integers or both are domains of character strings. Two compound domains D, E are union compatible if and only if they are of the same degree m and for every j ($j = 1, 2, ..., m$) the jth simple domain of D is union compatible with the jth simple domain of E. Two relations R, S are union compatible if and only if the compound domains of which R and S are subsets are union compatible.

There seems to be some confusion here ... To repeat a point already touched on above, why would there ever be more than one domain of integers, or more than one domain of character strings? Here, surely, is one place where we *really* need to be clear on the logical difference between domains and attributes. Personally, I would replace the first sentence of the foregoing definition by something like the following:

Two attributes are union compatible if and only if they're defined on the same domain.[14]

And then, of course, there would be knock-on effects for the rest of the definition. But I don't want to get into those knock-on effects here, because I don't really believe in the notion of union compatibility, as such, anyway. Indeed, I regard that notion as ad hoc at best. Now, in our work on *The Third Manifesto*, Hugh Darwen and I replace and subsume the union compatibility notion by a carefully thought out notion of *relation type*. But I don't want to get into details of that replacement notion here, either, because it would be very much out of place in the present chapter. In what follows, therefore, I'll stick with the notion of union compatibility as defined above, even though it's not at all to my taste.

RELATIONAL ALGEBRA

I turn now to the completeness paper's Section 2. The algebra defined in that section consists of the following operators:

---

[13] As Jim Gray once said to me: "Anything in computer science that's not recursive is no good."

[14] I don't actually believe in this definition either, for reasons to be touched on in just a moment. The trouble is, I can't give you my preferred replacement for the definition without going over a lot of preliminary material first, and that preliminary material would really be out of place in the present context.

product
union
intersection
difference
projection
join
division
restriction

The subsections that follow offer specific comments on each of these operators in turn.

Product

Codd first defines an auxiliary operator he calls tuple concatenation:

Definition (tuple concatenation): Let $d = (d1,d2,...,dm)$ and $e = (e1,e2,...,en)$ be tuples. Then the concatenation $d \,||\, e$ is the $(m+n)$-tuple defined by:

$$d \,||\, e \;\stackrel{\text{def}}{=}\; (\; d1 \,,\; d2 \,,\; ... \,,\; dm \,,\; e1 \,,\; e2 \,,\; ... \,,\; en\;)$$

Note that, owing to the left to right ordering assumption, tuple concatenation isn't commutative—that is,

$$d \,||\, e \;\neq\; e \,||\, d$$

(in general). It is, however, associative—that is,

$$(\,d \,||\, e\,) \,||\, f \;=\; d \,||\, (\,e \,||\, f\,)$$

Codd then goes on to define his product operator thus:

Definition (product): Let relations R and S be of degrees m and n, respectively. Then the product TIMES (R,S) is a relation of degree $m+n$, defined by:

$$\text{TIMES}\;(\;R\,,\;S\;) \;\stackrel{\text{def}}{=}\; \{\; r \,||\, s \,:\, r \in R \text{ AND } s \in S\;\}$$

Note that this operator, though also "expanded" in a sense, is not the same as the expanded cartesian product operator XCP previously defined. To spell the point out, the input for XCP is a set of sets, while for TIMES it's a pair of relations. (The output in both cases is a relation, though.) Note too that this operator, like the tuple concatenation operator on which it's based, is associative but not commutative.

Personally, however, I would greatly prefer to replace the operator as just defined by one that (a) is commutative as well as associative and (b) doesn't rely on the left to right ordering assumption. Here's my preferred definition:

> **Definition (product, preferred):** Let relations *r1* and *r2* have no attribute names in common. Then the product of *r1* and *r2* is the relation with heading the set theory union of the headings of *r1* and *r2* and body the set of all tuples *t* such that *t* is the set theory union of a tuple from *r1* and a tuple from *r2*.

And then I would generalize the definition to deal with any number *k* of relations ($k \geq 0$) as input. Note, however, that the definition does rely on the concepts of *heading* and *body*, concepts that aren't defined, or indeed even mentioned, in the completeness paper. However, they're discussed informally in Chapter 1 of the present book and defined formally in the appendix to Chapter 2.

Note: Actually my preferred version of TIMES is strictly unnecessary anyway, because it turns out to be just a degenerate case of my preferred version of join (see later in this chapter). In other words, there might be ergonomic reasons to support a TIMES operator, but there aren't really any logical ones.

Union, Intersection, Difference

The completeness paper doesn't actually define these operators but merely says they're "defined in the usual way, except that they are applicable only to pairs of union compatible relations." But those definitions, if they'd been included, would surely have looked something like this:

> **Definition (union, intersection, difference):** Let relations *R* and *S* be union compatible. Then the union UNION (*R,S*), the intersection INTERSECT (*R,S*), and the difference DIFFERENCE (*R,S*) are defined by:

```
UNION ( R , S )          def   { t : t ∈ R OR t ∈ S }
INTERSECT ( R , S )      def   { t : t ∈ R AND t ∈ S }
DIFFERENCE ( R , S )     def   { t : t ∈ R AND NOT ( t ∈ S ) }
```

Note: I would like to see UNION and INTERSECT generalized to return the union and intersection, respectively, of any number *k* of union compatible relations ($k \geq 0$).[15]

---

[15] These generalizations might not be necessary as far as the formal theory is concerned, but they're highly desirable from a human factors point of view. *Note:* The same goes for the analogous generalization of TIMES, of course—assuming TIMES is supported at all, that is—and similarly for JOIN (see later).

Projection

The completeness paper builds up to a definition of projection via a sequence of steps, which I'll state in somewhat paraphrased form and comment on as we go:

1. Let t be a tuple of the m-ary relation R. For $j = 1, 2, ..., m$, the notation $t[j]$ designates the jth component of t.

    Comment: I see no need to drag in relations as such yet. I would prefer to talk simply in terms of "a tuple t of degree m" (though in fact the completeness paper never defines the term *degree* in connection with tuples).

2. We extend the notation to a list $A = (j1, j2, ..., jk)$ of integers from the set $\{1, 2, ..., m\}$ thus:

    ```
    t [ A ]  ≝  ( t [ j1 ] , t [ j2 ] , ... , t [ jk ] )
    ```

    Points arising:

    a. Previously the expression $(j1, j2, ..., jk)$ would have been taken to mean a tuple, not a list. However, since tuples have a left to right ordering to their components as far as the completeness paper is concerned, I guess a tuple *is* a list.

    b. Although the completeness paper doesn't say as much, we've now effectively defined a tuple projection operator. It's not part of the relational algebra as such, of course, but tuple projection is in fact a useful operator to have.[16]

    c. Note the logical difference between, e.g., $t[1]$ and $t[(1)]$—the first returns a component (of tuple t) and the second a tuple (a "subtuple" of tuple t).

    d. The completeness paper says the integers $j1, j2, ..., jk$ are "not necessarily distinct," but I don't see anything to be gained from allowing them not to be (?).

3. The paper says "When the list A is empty, $t[A] = t$"—but this is clearly wrong. There's a logical difference between $t[]$ and t! In fact, $t[]$ is the empty tuple (i.e., the unique tuple with no components).[17]

---

[16] Tuple analogs of other relational operators such as union are useful too.

[17] The empty tuple (*aka* the 0-tuple) is discussed in the paper *Table_Dee and Table_Dum*, by Hugh Darwen (writing as Andrew Warden), first published in November 1988 in Issue 8 of *The Relational Journal* and later republished in our joint book *Relational Database Writings 1985-1989* (Addison-Wesley, 1990). *Note:* As its title might suggest, this paper was the one that introduced the names TABLE_DEE and TABLE_DUM. TABLE_DEE and TABLE_DUM are the only relations of degree zero—TABLE_DEE contains just one tuple (the 0-tuple, of course) and TABLE_DUM contains no tuples at all. See *SQL and Relational Theory* for further discussion.

4. Let R and A be as above. Then the projection $R[A]$ of R on A is defined by:

$$R\ [\ A\ ]\ \overset{\text{def}}{=}\ \{\ t\ [\ A\ ]\ :\ t \in R\ \}$$

The paper then goes on to observe that "When A is a permutation of the list $(1, 2, ..., m)$, $R[A]$ is a relation whose domains are the same of those of R except for a change in order of appearance." As far as the paper is concerned, this observation is both correct and significant— if "relations" do have a left to right ordering to their "domains," then some kind of "permute" operator is clearly necessary. For example, suppose R has attributes X and Y (in that order) and S has attributes Y and X (in that order), and suppose further that the two X's are defined on domain DX and the two Y's are defined on domain DY ($DX \neq DY$). Then R and S aren't "union compatible," but, e.g., $R[(1,2)]$ and $S[(2,1)]$ are. (Of course, $R[(1,2)]$ is just R.)

The paper then gives several examples of projection (in all of which, however, it omits the parentheses enclosing the list of domain numbers over which the projection is to be taken, a state of affairs that lends weight to the argument that the paper's choice of notation often leaves something to be desired).[18]

I'd like to close this subsection by giving my own preferred definition of projection (one that doesn't rely on left to right attribute ordering, of course):

Definition (projection, preferred):[19] Let relation r have attributes called $A1, A2, ..., An$ (and possibly others). Then the projection of r on $\{A1, A2, ..., An\}$ is the relation with heading $\{A1,A2,...,An\}$ and body consisting of all tuples t such that there exists a tuple in r that has the same value for each of attributes $A1, A2, ..., An$ as t does.

Join

The completeness paper—rather unfortunately, in my opinion—uses the term "join" to mean not the *natural* join operator, which is what it usually means today, but rather the much less useful θ-*join* operator (where "θ" denotes any of the usual scalar comparison operators[20] "=", "$\neq$", "<", ">", "$\leq$", and "$\geq$"):

---

[18] Oddly enough it makes the exact opposite mistake in connection with the product operator, inserting parentheses that aren't just unnecessary but are in fact logically incorrect.

[19] This definition makes use of a simplified notation for headings. See Chapter 2, footnote 38.

[20] Which the paper confusingly calls *relations*. Of course, they *are* relations, but I don't think it helps the poor reader who's struggling to understand the completeness paper overall to call them such, when "comparison operators" does the job at least as well. After all, we could with equal justification refer to union, projection, etc., as relations too (and in fact they are).

PS: Given that (e.g.) "<" is a relation, an interesting question is: What exactly are the domains of that relation? (Yes, I do mean domains, not attributes.) *Your answer here.*

Definition (θ-join):[21] The θ-join of relation R on domain A with relation S on domain B is defined by:

```
R [ A θ B ] S  ≝  { r || s : r ∈ R AND s ∈ S AND r [ A ] θ s [ B ] }
```

Every element of $R[A]$ must be *θ-comparable* with every element of $S[B]$,[22] where "x is θ-comparable with y" means that $x \, θ \, y$ is either true or false (not undefined).

Note: I take the θ-comparability requirement as here defined to imply among other things that:

a. If "domains" A and B are compound, then θ must be either "=" or "≠".[23]

b. This version of the algebra—note that phrase "true or false (not undefined)"—apparently has no provision for "nulls" (and a good thing too).

The paper then goes on to say:

The most commonly needed join is the join on "=", which we call the equi-join. In the case of the equi-join, two of the domains of the resulting relation are identical in content. If one of the redundant domains is removed by projection, the result is the natural join of the given relations ...

So in the algebra as defined in the completeness paper, natural join isn't regarded as a primitive operator (it's a projection of an equi-join, and this latter in turn is a restriction of a product). I regard this downplaying of the significance of natural join as quite unfortunate; I would greatly prefer (a) to take the unqualified term *join* to mean the natural join specifically (unless the context demands otherwise), and then (b) to regard that operator as one of the primitives. Note in particular that (as mentioned earlier) product can be regarded as a degenerate case of natural join.

I'd like to close this subsection by giving for the record my own preferred definition of join (meaning natural join specifically):

Definition (join, preferred): Let relations *r1* and *r2* be such that attributes with the same name are of the same type. Then the join of *r1* and *r2* is the relation with heading the set

---

[21] Here's another place where "domain" *really* needs to be replaced by "attribute" (twice).

[22] In later writings Codd would say rather that (a) *attributes* A and B must be defined on the *same* domain, and (b) θ must apply to values from that domain. (Unless, he would probably add, "domain check override" is in effect—but "domain check override," *aka* "semantic override," is another ad hoc notion that I really don't want to get into here.)

[23] Although in his 1990 book on RM/V2, Codd tried (but failed) to give some meaning to operators such as "<" for "compound domains." See Chapter 8 for further discussion.

theory union of the headings of *r1* and *r2* and body the set of all tuples *t* such that *t* is the set theory union of a tuple from *r1* and a tuple from *r2*.

I would also generalize this definition to deal with any number *k* of relations ($k \geq 0$).

Division

Of the operators defined in the completeness paper, division is far and away the most complicated—so much so, in fact, that I don't think it's worth trying to comment on it in detail here. Let me just say that:

a. It suffers from numerous problems, problems I've discussed in detail elsewhere;[24]

b. I think it's fair to say that Codd introduced it purely in order to be able to make use of it in the reduction algorithm he discusses later in his paper; and in any case

c. It isn't primitive—it can be expressed in terms of product, difference, and projection, as Codd himself notes later in his paper.

Restriction

Here's the completeness paper's definition of restriction (or "θ-restriction," rather):

Definition (θ-restriction):[25] Let *R* be a relation and let *A*, *B* be domain-identifying lists for *R*. The θ-restriction of *R* on domains *A*, *B* is defined by:

$$R [A \theta B] \stackrel{\text{def}}{=} \{ r : r \in R \text{ AND } r [A] \theta r [B] \}$$

Every element of *R[A]* must be θ-comparable with every element of *R[B]*.[26]

Note that the operator is defined here is considerably less general than restriction as usually understood (though it's adequate for the purposes of the reduction algorithm to be discussed later in the paper).[27] For the record, I'll give my own preferred definition of restriction here:

---

[24] See my paper "A Brief History of the Relational Divide Operator" in the book *Database Explorations: Essays on The Third Manifesto and Related Topics*, by Hugh Darwen and myself (Trafford, 2010).

[25] Here's yet another place where the term *domain* really needs to be replaced by the term *attribute*. And why does the definition call *A* and *B* "domain-identifying lists"? Surely "domains, possibly compound," or just "domains," would be better?

[26] Footnote 22 applies here also.

[27] Or is it? Codd's θ-restriction appears to have nothing analogous to a relational calculus "join term" that compares an attribute value and a literal. The paper does give an example in Table 1 (page 13) of an algebraic expression involving such a comparison, but the syntax used in that example doesn't conform to that defined elsewhere in the paper (for θ-restriction in particular).

Definition (restriction, preferred): Let *r* be a relation and let *bx* be a restriction condition on *r* (implying in particular that every attribute reference in *bx* identifies some attribute of *r*). Then the restriction of *r* according to *bx* is the relation with heading the same as that of *r* and body consisting of all and only those tuples of *r* for which *bx* evaluates to true.

Note: A restriction condition on *r* is, loosely speaking, a boolean expression that can be evaluated (yielding either true or false) for any given tuple of *r* by examining just that tuple in isolation—i.e., without having to examine any other tuple in *r* or any other relation in the given set of relations.

RELATIONAL CALCULUS

I think it's fair to say that, at least for a reader with no training in formal logic, Section 3 of the completeness paper is the hardest to understand. Therefore, instead of going through that section point by point as I did above in connection with Section 2 and the relational algebra, what I'll try to do is explain the calculus as such—the tuple relational calculus, that is—in terms of a series of simple examples. And I won't use the syntax from the completeness paper in those examples, either, since I (and many others also, I feel quite sure) find it a trifle intimidating; instead, I'll use the syntax I introduced in my book *An Introduction to Database Systems* (8th edition, Addison-Wesley, 2004). Moreover, I'll feel free to skip details here and there if I feel they would interfere unduly with the main flow of the presentation. However, I will at least relate concepts introduced by the examples to terms defined in the completeness paper, where it makes sense to do so.

As usual, my examples will all be based on the familiar suppliers-and-parts database, with sample values as shown in Fig. 1.1 in Chapter 1. (For convenience, I've repeated that figure as Fig. 3.1 overleaf.) The first example is a query: "Get supplier number and status for suppliers who either are located in London or supply part P1 or both." Here's a calculus formulation of this query:

```
RANGEVAR SX  RANGES OVER S ;
RANGEVAR SPX RANGES OVER SP ;

( SX.SNO , SX.STATUS ) WHERE SX.CITY = 'London'
                           OR EXISTS SPX ( SPX.SNO = SX.SNO
                                           AND SPX.PNO = 'P1' )
```

S

SNO	SNAME	STATUS	CITY
S1	Smith	20	London
S2	Jones	10	Paris
S3	Blake	30	Paris
S4	Clark	20	London
S5	Adams	30	Athens

P

PNO	PNAME	COLOR	WEIGHT	CITY
P1	Nut	Red	12.0	London
P2	Bolt	Green	17.0	Paris
P3	Screw	Blue	17.0	Oslo
P4	Screw	Red	14.0	London
P5	Cam	Blue	12.0	Paris
P6	Cog	Red	19.0	London

SP

SNO	PNO	QTY
S1	P1	300
S1	P2	200
S1	P3	400
S1	P4	200
S1	P5	100
S1	P6	100
S2	P1	300
S2	P2	400
S3	P2	200
S4	P2	200
S4	P4	300
S4	P5	400

Fig. 3.1: The suppliers-and-parts database—sample values (same as Fig. 1.1)

Explanation: The two RANGEVAR statements define SX and SPX to be *range variables* that range over suppliers (S) and shipments (SP), respectively. What this means is that, at any given time, SX denotes some tuple in S and SPX denotes some tuple in SP.[28] The rest of the text of the example, which I take to be more or less self-explanatory, denotes the query as such. Some remarks on terminology:

■ Range variables are actually called *tuple* variables in the completeness paper, but they're not variables in the usual programming language sense, they're variables in the sense of logic. Since (a) *tuple variable* is the obvious term for a variable in the usual programming language sense whose values are tuples, and (b) we're almost certain to need such variables in a real programming language that deals with relational databases, I prefer to use the term *range variable* for the construct currently under discussion.

■ The RANGEVAR statements correspond to what the completeness paper calls *range terms*, and the rest of the text corresponds to what the completeness paper calls, for reasons not explained, an *alpha expression*. In the interest of accuracy, however, I note that range terms in the completeness paper aren't separated out into definitional statements of their own as in the foregoing example, but are actually incorporated directly into the pertinent alpha expression itself. (SQL does the same thing, incidentally. An SQL analog of the

---

[28] By "some tuple in S" here, I really mean "some tuple in the relation that's the current value of relvar S" (and similarly for "some tuple in SP," of course). But the completeness paper doesn't discuss the issue of relation values vs. relation variables at all (it doesn't even mention "time-varying relations," except in a throwaway remark in the introduction). As far as the present chapter is concerned, therefore, I choose to avoid overt discussion of such matters myself as much as possible.

foregoing query might begin SELECT SX.SNO, SX.STATUS FROM S AS SX ... , and that "S AS SX" is effectively a range term.)

The general form of an alpha expression (using my own syntax) is:

```
proto tuple [ WHERE bool exp ]
```

Intuitively speaking, this expression yields a relation with body consisting of all possible values of the prototype tuple ("proto tuple") for which the boolean expression ("bool exp") evaluates to true. For example, in the case of the alpha expression in the example above, the result, given the sample data values shown in Fig. 3.1, looks like this:[29]

SNO	STATUS
S1	20
S2	10
S4	20

I note, however, that Section 3 of the completeness paper doesn't actually say anything about the evaluation of alpha expressions, nor does it define the result of such an evaluation. On the contrary, it's concerned merely with syntax, i.e., with the rules according to which an alpha expression can be said to be well formed. The semantics of such an expression are given, in effect, by the reduction algorithm in Section 4 of the paper. *More terminology:* What I'm calling the prototype tuple and the boolean expression (within an alpha expression) are called the *target list* and the *qualification*, respectively, in the completeness paper. Also, the paper uses a colon (":") instead of the keyword WHERE to separate them.

In its simplest form, then (which is all I propose to discuss here), the prototype tuple in an alpha expression consists of a parenthesized sequence of *range attribute references* separated by commas, where a range attribute reference in turn takes the form:

```
range variable name . attribute name
```

Examples are SX.SNO and SX.STATUS.[30]

---

[29] At this point, a good question to ask is: How do we know the result relation has the heading shown? Actually the completeness paper doesn't address this (rather important!) question at all. However, the fact is that rules can be defined that will ensure that all of the result relations shown in this chapter, and in fact throughout this book, do indeed have the headings I show for them. Further details would be out of place here but can be found in many places—e.g., in my book *SQL and Relational Theory*.

[30] In these and subsequent examples I'll assume range variables SX and SPX are as previously defined. *Note:* Since the completeness paper assumes left to right ordering (and doesn't deal with attributes anyway), it uses what it rather inappropriately calls *indexed tuples* in place of my range attribute references. For example, in place of SX.SNO and SX.STATUS it might use the "indexed tuples" SX[1] and SX[3], respectively.

As for the boolean expression, it can take all of the usual forms, plus either of the following *quantified* forms:

```
EXISTS range variable name ( bool exp )
FORALL range variable name ( bool exp )
```

Consider the alpha expression *pt* WHERE *bx*. Any range variable mentioned in *bx* must either be *bound* (by EXISTS or FORALL) or be mentioned in *pt* (and it can't be both). Thus, the following are all valid alpha expressions:

```
( SX.SNO ) WHERE SX.STATUS > 10
( SX.SNO , SX.CITY , SPX.PNO ) WHERE SX.SNO = SPX.SNO
( SX.SNO ) WHERE EXISTS SPX ( SPX.SNO = SX.SNO AND SPX.PNO = 'P2' )
( SPX.PNO )
```

(Omitting the WHERE and the boolean expression, as in the last of the foregoing examples, is equivalent to specifying WHERE TRUE.) By contrast, the following are *not* valid alpha expressions (in each case, why not?):

```
( SX.SNO ) WHERE SPX.PNO = 'P2'
( SPX.SNO , SPX.PNO ) WHERE SX.CITY = 'London'
( SPX.SNO ) WHERE EXISTS SPX ( SPX.QTY < 300 )
```

More terminology: Let *r*, *r1*, and *r2* be range variables (not necessarily distinct) and let *A* and *B* be attributes. In the context of an alpha expression, then, comparisons of the form

```
r1.A θ r2.B
```

or

```
r.A θ literal
```

are referred to in the completeness paper as *join terms*.

To wind up this section, let me get back to range variables. The examples I gave earlier—

```
RANGEVAR SX  RANGES OVER S ;
RANGEVAR SPX RANGES OVER SP ;
```

—suggest rather strongly that range variables must be defined in terms of just one of the given relations. In fact, however, the completeness paper also allows a range variable to range over any relation that can be formed by taking unions and/or intersections and/or differences of relations from the given set. What it doesn't allow, however, is for the expression defining the range of a given range variable to involve any projections. As a consequence, there are certain unions that can be formulated in the completeness paper's relational algebra but not in its relational calculus—for example, the union of supplier cities and part cities, in the case of the suppliers-and-parts database.[31]   In other words, the completeness paper's relational algebra is in fact strictly more powerful than its relational calculus (i.e., it's actually "more than" relationally complete).   Of course, this state of affairs was unintended, and Codd himself quickly recognized the deficiency (I have a personal note from him dated April 7th, 1972, correcting his original oversight).   But it does mean that the definition of relational completeness in the paper as such is slightly defective, relying as it does on the paper's definition, which is defective in turn, of range variables—or range terms, rather.[32]

CODD'S REDUCTION ALGORITHM

Section 4 ("Reduction") of the completeness paper begins thus:

> The objective of this section is to show that the relational algebra defined in Section 2 is relationally complete. We proceed by exhibiting an algorithm for translating any simple alpha expression ... into a semantically equivalent algebraic expression T.[33]

I don't propose to discuss that algorithm—which these days is usually referred to more explicitly as *Codd's reduction algorithm*—in any detail here. If you're interested, you can find a detailed example of the algorithm in action in my book *An Introduction to Database Systems* (8th edition, Addison-Wesley, 2004). However, I do want to repeat Codd's own brief overview of the algorithm from Section 4 of the paper:

> The reduction algorithm ... may be best understood by supposing for the moment that, instead of merely producing several algebraic expressions (which are finally combined into one composite expression T), these expressions are evaluated as they are produced. The effect of this evaluation would be roughly as follows. First, the ranges of the cited tuple variables are generated by retrieving certain data base relations and by taking unions, intersections, and differences as necessary. Second, a cartesian product of these ranges is formed. From this product the final relation is eventually extracted. Third, tuples that do not satisfy the combination of join terms are removed from the product. Fourth, the remaining product is whittled down by projection and division to satisfy the quantification in the alpha expression. Finally, a projection as specified by the target list is performed, and we have the required relation.

---

[31] Note that this problem occurs only with union, not with intersection or difference. For example, given range variables SX and PX ranging over S and P, respectively, the intersection of supplier cities and part cities is given by (SX.CITY) WHERE EXISTS PX (PX.CITY = SX.CITY), and the difference between supplier cities and part cities, in that order, is given by (SX.CITY) WHERE NOT EXISTS PX (PX.CITY = SX.CITY).

[32] Not too many people seem to have noticed the defect, though (in almost 50 years!), and I can't help wondering whether it's the arguably excessive formalism of Section 3 that's the reason why not. Certainly that formalism makes it quite hard to see the forest for the trees in general.

[33] The paper distinguishes between simple and other ("nonsimple") alpha expressions, but that distinction can safely be ignored for present purposes.

I'd like to examine this overview a piece at a time, starting with the sentence beginning "First, the ranges." I'll use the query from the previous section—"Get supplier number and status for suppliers who either are located in London or supply part P1 or both"—to illustrate various points as we proceed. Just to remind you, here again is a calculus formulation of that query:

```
RANGEVAR SX  RANGES OVER S ;
RANGEVAR SPX RANGES OVER SP ;

( SX.SNO , SX.STATUS ) WHERE SX.CITY = 'London'
                    OR EXISTS SPX ( SPX.SNO = SX.SNO
                                AND SPX.PNO = 'P1' )
```

First, the ranges of the cited tuple variables are generated by retrieving certain data base relations and by taking unions, intersections, and differences as necessary: In the example, "the cited tuple variables" are the *range* variables SX and SPX, and the corresponding ranges are the suppliers relation S and the shipments relation SP, respectively. So these two relations are retrieved. I'll use the symbols s and sp to denote the retrieved copies of S and SP, respectively. *Note:* No unions, intersections, or differences are needed in this example since no such operators are involved in the definitions of the range variables.

Second, a cartesian product of these ranges is formed: We form TIMES (s,sp). Given the sample data shown in Fig. 3.1, that product—let's call it x—contains $5 \times 12 = 60$ tuples.[34]

From this product the final relation is eventually extracted: But surely there's something wrong here! Suppose we modify the sample data in Fig. 3.1 so that SP is empty (but nothing else is changed—meaning, intuitively, that we still have five suppliers and six parts, but none of those suppliers supplies any of those parts). Our sample query thus effectively reduces to just "Get supplier number and status for suppliers who are located in London," and the correct result is clearly as follows:

SNO	STATUS
S1	20
S4	20

---

[34] By the way, it's a little improper to talk about "the" cartesian product of the pertinent ranges, since the completeness paper's product operator isn't commutative. E.g., if there are three ranges, then there are actually six different products, in general. Of course, this problem goes away if (as suggested earlier in the chapter) we adopt a revised version of cartesian product for which commutativity does apply.

But if SP is empty, the cartesian product *x* is clearly empty too—so how can the foregoing correct result possibly be "eventually extracted" from that product?[35]

Be that as it may, let's continue with our original sample data (with SP not empty, and 60 tuples in the product *x*). The next step is:

Third, tuples that do not satisfy the combination of join terms are removed from the product: "The combination of join terms" in the case at hand is:

```
SX.CITY = 'London' OR ( SPX.SNO = SX.SNO AND SPX.PNO = 'P1' )
```

Applying this restriction condition—for that's what it is—to the 60 tuples of *x* gives a result *y* consisting of 25 tuples (twelve for supplier S1, twelve for supplier S4, and one for supplier S2).

Fourth, the remaining product[36] is whittled down by projection and division to satisfy the quantification in the alpha expression: Projection corresponds to existential quantification (EXISTS) and division to universal quantification (FORALL). In the example, therefore (which involves an EXISTS but no FORALL), we project away the attributes corresponding to shipments, thanks to the quantification EXISTS SPX. We're left with a relation *z*, effectively just the following restriction of relation *s*:

SNO	SNAME	STATUS	CITY
S1	Smith	20	London
S2	Jones	10	Paris
S4	Clark	20	London

Finally, a projection as specified by the target list is performed, and we have the required relation: In the example, we project the relation *z* just shown over SNO and STATUS to obtain the desired final result:

---

[35] Here's a possibly simpler example to illustrate the same point. Let relations A, B, and C each have just one attribute, H; let A and B each contain just one tuple (with H value *h* in both cases) and let C be empty; let AX, BX, and CX be range variables ranging over A, B, and C, respectively; and consider the expression (AX.H) WHERE EXISTS BX (BX.H = AX.H) OR EXISTS CX (CX.H = AX.H). In other words, and now spelling the point out explicitly, it seems to me that Codd is making a tacit assumption that if the boolean expression contains two or more join terms, then those join terms are connected by AND and not by OR.

[36] "The remaining product" here has to be interpreted as meaning what's left of the product *x* (namely, *y*) after the restriction specified in the previous step has been applied. But strictly speaking *y* isn't a product, as such, at all, and it shouldn't be referred to as one.

SNO	STATUS
S1	20
S2	10
S4	20

———— ♦ ♦ ♦ ♦ ♦ ————

Well, I've demonstrated at least one puzzle, or problem, with Codd's reduction algorithm. Here's another example of a query for which the algorithm also appears to fail:

```
RANGEVAR SX   RANGES OVER S ;
RANGEVAR SPX RANGES OVER SP ;
RANGEVAR PX   RANGES OVER P ;

( SX.SNO , SX.STATUS ) WHERE FORALL PX
                    ( EXISTS SPX ( SPX.SNO = SX.SNO AND
                                   SPX.PNO = PX.PNO ) )
```

("Get supplier number and status for suppliers who supply all parts"). Suppose there are no parts (i.e., P is empty). Then this expression should logically give supplier number and status for every supplier represented in S—but again the algorithm will yield an empty result, for essentially the same reason as before (viz., an empty intermediate relation produced as the result of the second step). Note that this example doesn't involve any ORs.

———— ♦ ♦ ♦ ♦ ♦ ————

There's another puzzle, too. The very first step in the completeness paper's detailed description of the reduction algorithm reads as follows:

Convert *V* to prenex normal form (if it is not already in this form) ...

V here denotes the boolean expression in the WHERE clause of the original alpha expression. Now, there's clearly an assumption here that every boolean expression is equivalent to one that's in prenex normal form (PNF). But is that assumption reasonable? Well, here's a slightly simplified definition of PNF:

Definition (prenex normal form): A boolean expression is in prenex normal form, PNF, if and only if (a) it's quantifier free or (b) it's of the form Qx (p), where Qx is a quantifier and p in turn is a boolean expression in PNF. Thus, a PNF expression takes the form

```
Q1 x1 ( Q2 x2 ( ... ( Qn xn ( q ) ) ... ) )
```

where (a) $n \geq 0$, (b) each of $Q1$, $Q2$, ..., Qn is either EXISTS or FORALL, and (c) the boolean expression q—the *matrix*—is quantifier free.

In other words (loosely), a boolean expression is in PNF if and only if the quantifiers, if any, all appear at the beginning.

Now, it's true that many boolean expressions do have a PNF equivalent. But it's not true that they all do! Indeed, the boolean expression in our original sample query—

```
SX.CITY = 'London' OR EXISTS SPX ( SPX.SNO = SX.SNO AND SPX.PNO = 'P1' )
```

—is one that doesn't.[37] So what are the implications of this state of affairs for the reduction algorithm?

CALCULUS vs. ALGEBRA

Despite the various flaws identified in the present chapter, the algebra and the calculus and the reduction algorithm can certainly all be "cleaned up" in such a way as to meet all of Codd's original objectives in this connection—in particular, the objective that the algebra and the calculus have exactly equivalent functionality.[38] Given that equivalence, then, what are the relative merits of the two formalisms? Section 5 of the completeness paper offers some opinions in this connection. Before discussing those opinions, however, I'd like to make a few observations of a more general nature:

- *Implementation:* As noted earlier, the algebra can serve as a vehicle for implementing the calculus. That is, given a calculus based language such as QUEL or Query-By-Example, one approach to implementing that language would be to take the user's original request (which is basically just a calculus expression) and apply the reduction algorithm to it, thereby obtaining an equivalent algebraic expression. That algebraic expression will consist of a set of algebraic operations, which are by definition inherently implementable.[39]

- *Purpose:* There seems to a widespread misconception concerning the purpose of the algebra (and the calculus too, come to that, but for simplicity I'll limit my attention here to

---

[37] See my paper "A Remark on Prenex Normal Form" in the book *Database Explorations: Essays on The Third Manifesto and Related Topics*, by Hugh Darwen and myself (Trafford, 2010), for further discussion..

[38] See, e.g., the paper "Equivalence of Relational Algebra and Relational Calculus Query Languages Having Aggregate Functions," by Anthony Klug (*Journal of the ACM 29*, No. 3, July 1982).

[39] In fact, a pioneering paper on optimization—"A Data Base Search Problem," by Frank P. Palermo (IBM Research Report RJ1072, July 27th, 1972, republished in Julius T. Tou (ed.), *Information Systems: COINS IV*, Plenum Press, 1974)—is based on exactly this approach; it implements a given calculus expression by executing an appropriate sequence of algebraic operations, applying a variety of optimizations to those operations as it does so.

the algebra specifically). To spell the point out, many people seem to think the algebra is meant purely for formulating queries[40]—but it's not; rather, it's meant for writing *relational expressions*. Those expressions in turn serve many purposes, including query but certainly not limited to query alone. Here are some other important ones:

a.   Defining views and snapshots

b.   Defining a set of tuples to be inserted, deleted, or updated (or, more generally, defining a set of tuples to serve as the source for some relational assignment)

c.   Defining constraints (though here the relational expression or expressions in question will be just subexpressions of some boolean expression)

d.   Serving as a basis for research into other areas, such as optimization and database design[41]

e.   Serving as a yardstick against which the power of database languages in general can be measured (see the next bullet item below)

And so on (the foregoing list isn't meant to be exhaustive).

■ *Relational completeness:* Codd suggests in his completeness paper that a general purpose relational language "should be at least relationally complete in the sense defined in this paper," and defines a language to be complete in this sense if and only if it has "at least the selective power of the relational calculus."[42] Given some proposed relational language *L*, then, it becomes desirable to be able to prove that *L* is relationally complete. And if the calculus and the algebra are logically equivalent, then it's sufficient (and usually easier) to show that it's as powerful as the algebra, rather than the calculus. For example, to show that SQL is relationally complete, we would need to demonstrate

a.   That there exist SQL counterparts to each of the primitive operators restriction, projection, product, union, and difference, and then

---

[40] This particular misconception is supported rather strongly by the very term *query*, of course, also by the associated term *query language*. Indeed, both of these terms occur several times in the completeness paper itself.

[41] Various "nice" properties of the algebra are important in this connection: commutativity, associativity, distributivity, and so on (thanks to Hugh Darwen for this observation).

[42] "Selective power" is Codd's term. Personally I much prefer the term *expressive* power.

b. That the operands to those SQL counterparts can be denoted by arbitrary SQL expressions, meaning that the SQL operators can be nested and combined in arbitrary ways.[43]

By the way, Codd stresses in his completeness paper the fact that relational completeness is only a *basic* measure of "selective power."[44] To quote:

> In a practical environment [that power] would need to be augmented by a counting and summing capability, together with the capability of invoking ... library functions tailored to that environment.

And elsewhere:

> Relational completeness represents a very basic selective power, which in most practical environments would need to be enhanced.[45]

Despite these caveats, however, Codd notes that relational completeness means, in effect, that queries can be formulated "without resorting to programming loops or any other form of branched execution—an important consideration when interrogating a data base from a terminal."

So which is preferable?—the algebra or the calculus? In one sense, this question is unimportant; given the complete interchangeability of the two formalisms, the difference is essentially one of style, not substance. In my own experience, it seems that people familiar with programming tend to prefer the algebra (because it's basically operators—restriction, etc.—and programmers understand operators), while end users tend to prefer the calculus (because it's a little "closer to natural language"[46]). To repeat, however, I don't really think the difference is all that important.

Note: The difference in question is sometimes characterized as being analogous to that between procedural and nonprocedural languages, in the sense that the algebra is *prescriptive* (i.e., procedural) while the calculus is *descriptive* (i.e., nonprocedural). Indeed, this characterization might even be helpful from an intuitive point of view. However, it's not really

---

[43] As a matter of fact fact SQL is *not* relationally complete, because it lacks the ability to take projections over the empty set of attributes and hence fails to support the crucially important relations TABLE_DEE and TABLE_DUM (see footnote 17). PS: That business of "nesting and combining the operators in arbitrary ways" has to do with the all important property of *closure*, of course. It's interesting to note, therefore, that the completeness paper in fact never mentions that property at all!

[44] Indeed, the point is worth stressing that relational completeness doesn't necessarily imply other kinds of completeness. In particular, it certainly doesn't imply computational completeness.

[45] I can think of several other features that would need to be added too—for example, relation literals.

[46] If your knowledge of the calculus derives only from the completeness paper and nothing else, you might find this claim a little surprising! In fact, however, the calculus can easily be wrapped up in "syntactic sugar" and made much more palatable to the average user than the completeness paper might lead one to expect.

valid, of course (nor is it accurate), given the logical equivalence between the two. To repeat, the difference is really just a difference in style.

Anyway, Codd concludes his paper with some brief arguments in support of his own opinion that the calculus is to be preferred. His arguments are as follows (paraphrasing considerably):

■ *Extendability:* As noted above, a real language will surely need to be able to invoke various "library functions," and extending the calculus to support such invocations seems to be straightforward:

    a.   Such invocations could appear as part of the "prototype tuple," where they would have the effect of transforming the result of evaluating the alpha expression.

    b.   They could also appear in place of one of the comparands in a "join term," where they would have the effect of generating the actual comparand.

    c.   If they return a truth value, they could be used in place of a "join term."

    Codd claims that "such enhancements readily fit into the calculus framework," whereas extending the algebra seems to be much less straightforward and would "give rise to circumlocutions." I'm not at all sure I agree with these claims, however—grafting the operators EXTEND and SUMMARIZE[47] on to the original relational algebra (which is more or less what's needed to do the job) seems fairly straightforward to me.

■ *Ease of capturing the user's intent* (important for optimization, authorization, and so forth): Codd claims that because it permits the user "to request data by its properties" instead of by means of "a sequence of algebraic operations," the calculus is a better basis than the algebra for this purpose. Again I'm not at all sure I agree, however, given that any request that can be stated as a single calculus expression can equally well be stated as a single algebraic expression. *Note:* The concept of *lazy evaluation*, pioneered by the PRTV prototype, is relevant here.[48]

■ *Closeness to natural language:* Codd makes the point that most users shouldn't have to deal directly with either the algebra or the calculus as such. And he continues:

---

[47] Actually support for EXTEND would suffice, especially if image relations are supported as well (which I think they should be). Once again, see *SQL and Relational Theory* for further discussion.

[48] See S. J. P. Todd: "The Peterlee Relational Test Vehicle—A System Overview," *IBM Systems Journal 15*, No. 4 (1976). See too the discussion of WITH clauses in *SQL and Relational Theory* (also mentioned in Chapter 4 of the present book).

However, requesting data by its properties is far more natural than [having to devise] a particular algorithm or sequence of operations for its retrieval. Thus, a calculus-oriented language provides a good target language for a more user oriented source language.

Once again, however, I don't really agree, for essentially the same reason as under the previous bullet item. But I do want to point out that because they're more systematically defined, the calculus and the algebra are both much more suitable than SQL as such a target! (By the way, it's worth noting in passing that for implementation purposes, many SQL systems effectively convert SQL internally into something rather close to the algebra anyway.[49])

MISCELLANEOUS COMMENTS

This final section consists of a few further general comments on the completeness paper that don't belong neatly in any of the foregoing sections and yet I don't want to lose. The first two are, I suppose, pretty minor:

- Fig. 2 on page 8 of the paper is quite confusing, because the various appearances of the domain labels "D1", "D2", and "D3" don't always mean the same thing. In fact, the examples in that figure demonstrate rather clearly why it's necessary to distinguish between domains and attributes! (I've made the point repeatedly earlier in this chapter— and complained about it, too—that the completeness paper doesn't make that distinction, but should.) What's more, the picture is muddied by the fact that Fig. 3 on page 9 of the paper suddenly changes style and does use domain labels ("A", "B", etc.) that do mean the same thing on each appearance.

- There are a few places—not many—where the writing is a trifle sloppy. Now, I know it's hard to avoid sloppiness entirely (sometimes such sloppiness can even be a good thing), but I think it's a little unfortunate in a paper that's generally meant to be very precise and formal indeed. Here are a couple of examples:

  a. On page 10, the paper says: "In the case of the equi-join, two of the domains are identical in content." Of course, *domains* here should be *attributes*, but even with that correction the statement is still not very precise. What it should say is something like this: "In the case of the equi-join, each tuple of the result contains the same value in each of the pertinent attributes."

---

[49] I say "rather close to" because the algebra in question can't be a true *relational* algebra, on account of the fact that SQL tables aren't true relations.

b.   On page 16, the paper says: "[The purpose of the indexed tuple $r[N]$] is to identify the Nth component of ... tuple r." But r here isn't a tuple! What the paper should say is something like this: "The purpose of the indexed tuple $r[N]$ is to identify the Nth component of the tuple that's the current value of the tuple variable r."

My third and final comment is perhaps a little more substantial. The fact is, the paper refers repeatedly to the fact that the relations in the database must all be *normalized*, meaning they must be in what Codd elsewhere calls *first normal form* (1NF). Now, I've argued elsewhere[50] that Codd's definition of first normal form might always have been a little confused—in fact, it's my opinion that relations are *always* in 1NF, by definition—but in the present context it's clear that Codd just means that the relations in question are such that their underlying domains contain scalar values (e.g., integers or character strings) only. OK, fine; for present purposes, let's accept that definition. *But it's not at all clear why that requirement is imposed.* That is, it's not at all clear what if anything goes wrong with the algebra, or the calculus, or the reduction algorithm, or indeed any other part of the completeness paper, if relations aren't normalized in the foregoing sense.

---

[50] See, e.g., Chapter 2 of the present book.

Chapter 4

The ALPHA Paper

The letter alpha (α) represents various concepts in physics and chemistry, including alpha radiation, angular acceleration, alpha particles, alpha carbon, and strength of electromagnetic interaction ... [It] also stands for thermal expansion coefficient of a compound in physical chemistry. It is also commonly used in mathematics in algebraic [formulas] representing quantities such as angles. Furthermore, in mathematics, the letter alpha is used to denote the area underneath a normal curve in statistics ... In zoology, it is used to name the dominant individual in a wolf or dog pack ... Alpha was derived from aleph, which in Phoenician means "ox."

—Wikipedia

The paper I'll be referring to in this chapter as "the ALPHA paper" for short is, of course, another of E. F. Codd's early papers on relational matters. Here's a full citation:

■ "A Data Base Sublanguage Founded on the Relational Calculus," IBM Research Report RJ893 (July 26th, 1971); republished in Proc. 1971 ACM SIGFIDET Workshop on Data Description, Access and Control, San Diego, Calif. (November 1971)

This paper made a huge impression on me when I first read it, in draft form, in early 1971. I was employed by IBM Hursley at the time (in the U.K.) and was working in the Advanced Technology Department where, along with a colleague, Paul Hopewell, I had the job of trying to define extensions to the "high level language" PL/I in order to provide database functionality. And I think it's fair to say that both Paul and I found the paper extremely influential—I might almost say inspiring—and it helped considerably in shaping our thoughts as to what our PL/I language extensions might look like.[1]

---

[1] I don't want to give a false impression here—Paul and I did work for some considerable time on defining those extensions (and Paul even implemented a prototype to demonstrate and test them), but they were never accepted by the IBM powers that be (viz., the PL/I "Language Control Board") as a formal part of the PL/I language as such. I do still have a copy of our final report, though ("Revised Functional Specifications for PL/I Data Base Support"), dated April 1971. Incidentally, it's interesting to note that (a) the earlier version of the document of which this was a revision actually (and independently) proposed something very much like SQL's "IN *subquery*" construct, but (b) the revised version jettisoned that approach and replaced it by something much more akin to relational calculus. A pity SQL didn't do the same! (The reason we made the change was that the "IN *subquery*" construct—or our analog of that construct, rather—simply wasn't helpful for an important class of queries that relational calculus dealt with rather elegantly: viz., queries involving universal quantification.)

Be that as it may, what the paper does is describe what Codd called Data Sublanguage ALPHA, a language "founded on the relational model ... and also on the relational calculus."[2] Regarding this latter, Codd gives the following as a reference:

■ E. F. Codd: "Relational Completeness of Data Base Sublanguages," [presented at] *Courant Computer Science Symposia Series 6: Data Base Systems* (May 24th-25th, 1971)

Note, however, that (a) this reference is to a *presentation*, and (b) that presentation was given in May 1971, several weeks prior to first publication of the ALPHA paper. The paper on which that presentation was based wasn't published—not even as an IBM Research Report— until March 1972, or in other words nearly nine months later:

■ E. F. Codd: "Relational Completeness of Data Base Sublanguages," IBM Research Report RJ987 (March 6th, 1972); republished in Randall J. Rustin (ed.), *Data Base Systems: Courant Computer Science Symposia Series 6* (Prentice-Hall, 1972)

Moreover, there a few technical discrepancies (some of them to be discussed in the present chapter) between the ALPHA paper and this latter paper, and it really isn't clear in such cases which of the two publications represented the more recent thinking on Codd's part. However, I should at least note that the latter paper (which is much the more formal of the two) uses the term *alpha expression* to refer to what would more conventionally be called just a *relational* expression—i.e., an expression that evaluates to a relation—and that presumably is the reason for the name ALPHA.

Anyway, what I plan to do in the present chapter is give a very brief overview of the ALPHA language in the section immediately following, and then follow up that overview with some more detailed commentary and criticisms in subsequent sections.

OVERVIEW

ALPHA was always meant to be merely a "sublanguage," suitable for incorporation, with appropriate syntactic modification, into either (a) languages used by users at a terminal interacting with "a shared, formatted data base" or (b) "host programming languages [such] as PL/I, COBOL, or Fortran" (or both, of course).[3] As such, it provides facilities for:

---

[2] Actually Codd's text here is a little odd. Nowadays it's generally understood that the relational model *includes* a set of relational operators, and those operators can be exposed to the user in either algebraic or calculus form (or possibly in some other form that's logically equivalent to the algebra and the calculus). Thus, to suggest, as the quoted text apparently does, that the relational calculus is somehow separate from the model is a little strange. Perhaps Codd just wanted to stress the point that ALPHA is based on the calculus and not the algebra.

[3] So the ALPHA paper pioneered, at least in concept, the idea that later came to be called the *dual mode principle*—i.e., the principle that any relational operation that can be invoked interactively can also be invoked from an application program and vice versa.

■ Creating and dropping what we would now call base relations[4]

■ Retrieving some relation derived from the given base relations

■ Inserting a set of tuples into some given base relation

■ Deleting a set of tuples from some given base relation

■ Modifying a set of tuples in some given base relation

Computational and other conventional programming language facilities are deliberately omitted.

Note: The ALPHA paper overall is quite informal; in particular, one thing it doesn't do is give a full BNF grammar for the language. Nor does it give detailed semantics for those aspects it does describe. As a consequence, please understand that the present chapter is necessarily somewhat informal too. In a few places, in fact, I'm afraid it's going to involve a certain amount of guesswork on my part, though I'll try to make it clear whenever such is the case.

DATA DEFINITION

Early papers on SQL (or SEQUEL, as it then was) made much of the fact that the language was much more than just a query language, as this latter term was generally understood at the time (i.e., it provided many features over and above just the ability to retrieve data from the database). Indeed, the title of one of those papers explicitly described the language as "a unified language for data definition, manipulation, and control." All of which is fair enough; it *is* a strong feature of SQL that there are no artificial boundaries between such things as data definition and data manipulation, and hence that, e.g., new relations—or tables, rather, in the SQL context—can be added to the database at any time without having to shut the system down.

What's perhaps not generally known, however, is that it was ALPHA that showed the way; I mean, it was the ALPHA paper that was the first to suggest that such things might be possible. These days, of course, we're so used to the idea that languages should be "unified" in the foregoing sense that it might be hard to appreciate what a breakthrough it was at the time. But a breakthrough is what it was; it was a major departure from the way things had been done in older, prerelational systems such as IMS, and it was a major contribution.

---

[4] Or base relvars, rather. Unfortunately, however, the ALPHA paper—like all of Codd's writings, and indeed like the vast bulk of the relational literature both then and ever since—refers to both relation *values* (relations for short) and relation *variables* (relvars for short) simply as relations, unqualified. In the present chapter, therefore, I'm going to be more or less forced to do the same thing (much against my own better judgment!). PS: The ALPHA paper not only fails to mention relvars, it doesn't even mention the term *time-varying relation*—a term that was used in Codd's 1969 and 1970 papers in an attempt to get at the relation vs. relvar distinction, but in my opinion one that suffers from problems of its own (see Chapter 2).

That said, it must be said too that the ALPHA paper is rather short on details in this connection. In fact, most of what it does have to say, in the case of data definition operations in particular, has to do with the creation and dropping of base relations and nothing more. Here's the essence of what it has to say on these specific topics:

(*Creating a New Base Relation*:) The relation must be declared; this involves giving it a name, specifying its domains and naming its attributes, and identifying its primary key ... All of this information must be entered in those relations that catalog the data base relations. The authorization constraints for the new relation must be set up in the relations that describe such constraints. These preparatory "gold plating" steps will be dealt with in a later paper.[5]

(*Dropping an Existing Base Relation*:) If *R* is the name of a data base relation, execution of the statement

```
DROP R
```

has the effect of removing all information about *R* from the data base catalog. Further, if any tuples of *R* still exist, they are deleted.

Points arising:

■ Note the phrase "specifying its domains and naming its attributes." As that phrase indicates, the ALPHA paper, unlike the relational completeness paper, does distinguish between domains and attributes,[6] and I'm very glad it does (though it still doesn't do so as clearly as I would like).

■ The reference to primary keys is a little unfortunate. Frankly, the idea that a relation always has to have exactly one "primary" key—meaning in particular that if it has two or more "candidate" keys, we're supposed to choose one and make it somehow more equal than the others—was a notion that was always a little hard to swallow.[7]

■ As far as I'm aware, the ALPHA paper was the first of Codd's papers to mention the catalog, and in particular the first to mention the fact that the catalog itself should consist of relations. Once again the point seems obvious now, but it wasn't at all obvious back then.

---

[5] But no such paper ever materialized.

[6] This state of affairs tends to suggest that (despite their respective publication dates) the completeness paper was probably written first and the ALPHA paper second.

[7] Because, unlike other aspects of the relational model, it seems to be founded not so much on logic but more on some kind of vague notion of "good design." See Appendix A, "Primary Keys Are Nice but Not Essential," of my book *Database Design and Relational Theory: Normal Forms and All That Jazz* (O'Reilly, 2012). In the present chapter I won't distinguish between primary and other keys, referring to them all as just keys, unless I'm in the context of the ALPHA language as such and am forced by that context to make such a distinction.

For example, what passes for the catalog in IMS is certainly not structured as an IMS database![8]

■   Note (a) the reference to authorization constraints, and (b) the absence of any similar reference to integrity constraints.[9] Both are important in practice, I suppose, but if I had to choose just one I think I'd have to say the latter are *more* important, or at least more fundamental, and I therefore regard the omission as something else about the ALPHA paper that I find a little unfortunate.

■   As for DROP—doubtless the inspiration for that rather unorthodox choice of name for analogous operators in SQL—I note merely that the ALPHA paper does briefly discuss the dropping of domains as well as relations, but has nothing to say about the complementary operation of creating one. (Though it does give some examples, as we'll see below.)

■   I note for completeness also, for what it's worth, that the ALPHA paper has nothing at all to say about either views or snapshots.

The paper also gives some sample domain and base relation definitions, which I adapt below to serve as a definition for the suppliers-and-parts database (see Fig. 1.1 in Chapter 1 or Fig. 3.1 in Chapter 3):[10]

```
DOMAIN SNO     CHAR(5)
       SNAME   CHAR(15)
       STATUS  NUM(5,0)
       CITY    CHAR(20)
       PNO     CHAR(20)
       PNAME   CHAR(30)
       COLOR   CHAR(8)
       WEIGHT  NUM(3,1)
       QTY     NUM(5,0)

RELATION S  ( SNO , SNAME , STATUS , CITY )            KEY SNO
RELATION P  ( PNO , PNAME , COLOR , WEIGHT , CITY )    KEY PNO
RELATION SP ( SNO , PNO , QTY )                        KEY ( SNO , PNO )
```

Well, a few obvious points arise here too! The first has to do with the distinction between domains and attributes once again. Sadly, the example misses an obvious trick: Instead of

---

[8] I remember writing a paper myself in the early 1970s about what seemed to me to be a novel and constructive idea: viz., the idea that the catalog itself should be a relational database, with all that that entails. But I never published that paper—I wasn't familiar with the "publish or perish" mantra in those days—and now it's disappeared down the memory hole.

[9] There are subsequent brief references to key and foreign key constraints, but none to integrity constraints in general.

[10] As the example indicates, the ALPHA paper underlines keywords such as DOMAIN and RELATION. For consistency, therefore, I'll do the same in the present chapter.

specifying attributes as attribute-name / domain-name pairs (which would make the distinction very clear), it simply gives each attribute the same name as its underlying domain.

The second point has to with the distinction Codd draws—mistakenly, I firmly believe—between domains and types. Consider, e.g., the following definition from the example:

```
DOMAIN ... PNO CHAR(20)
```

Presumably this definition is to be interpreted as saying that (a) PNO is the name of a domain, and (b) that domain is of a certain character string type;[11] so here, apparently, we have character strings as a type and not a domain. Yet in his paper on relational completeness (see Chapter 3), Codd makes it abundantly clear that character strings can be regarded as a domain. So what exactly is the difference between a domain and a type? I don't believe there is one; I believe rather that Codd is simply confused here over types (or domains, if you must), on the one hand, vs. representations on the other. That is, it seems to me in the example that CHAR(20) is meant to be the type (or domain) for the underlying internal or physical *representation* of values of type (or domain) PNO—and indeed the type (or domain) for the underlying physical representation of values of type (or domain) CITY as well, come to that. To put the matter another way, I think Codd thought there was a difference between domains and types, domains being visible to users and types being under the covers and hidden. But the difference he should have been getting at wasn't a difference between domains and types at all (there isn't one), but rather a difference between types and representations.[12]

My next point has to do with integrity constraints. Consider domains STATUS and QTY, both of which are defined to be of type NUM(5,0). Suppose that (as the sample values shown In Fig. 1.1 or Fig. 3.1 might suggest) status values must always be multiples of 10 and quantities must always be multiples of 100. Then it would make sense to be able to specify that the corresponding NUM(5,0) values are constrained accordingly. But the ALPHA paper never addresses such issues.

A couple of final points:

---

[11] I don't know if Codd would regard, e.g., CHAR(20) and CHAR(5) as two different types or just one; as far as the present discussion is concerned, it's really a secondary issue. For the record, however, I would say that (a) CHAR is really a *type generator*; (b) CHAR(20) and CHAR(5) are different invocations of that type generator (the "20" in CHAR(20) and the "5" in CHAR(5) denoting arguments to those invocations); and hence (c) those different invocations do indeed represent different types. (I do know the term *type generator* was never used by Codd himself, though.) Similar remarks apply to NUM, of course, mutatis mutandis. See my book *SQL and Relational Theory: How to Write Accurate SQL Code* (3rd edition, O'Reilly, 2015) for further discussion of such matters.

[12] If I'm right here, it would go some way toward explaining some of the very strange claims Codd makes elsewhere regarding the alleged difference between types and domains, or— to use terms introduced by Codd in some of his later writings—the alleged difference between "basic data types" and "extended data types" (the former being regarded by Codd as types per se and the latter as domains). See Chapter 1 for further discussion of such matters.

PS: There's yet another logical difference that's relevant to the present discussion: namely, that between physical and possible representations. I don't want to go into more detail on that difference here, though, because it would take us much too far afield. See *The Third Manifesto* for further discussion.

■ It's a very minor matter, of course, but I don't know why Codd chose to "factor out" the keyword <u>DOMAIN</u> in the domain definitions but not the keyword <u>RELATION</u> in the base relation definitions.

■ The <u>KEY</u> specification on a base relation definition identifies the primary key, specifically, of the pertinent base relation. What happens if a given relation has two or more keys isn't discussed. Note too that the example includes no "<u>FOREIGN KEY</u>" specifications.

RETRIEVAL OPERATIONS

Of course, the most strikingly novel aspect of ALPHA—the aspect that made it drastically and dramatically different from any other computer language that I at any rate had seen before—was its support, in its retrieval operations, for arbitrarily complex boolean expressions, including support for quantified expressions in particular. (As with various other matters already discussed in this chapter, such support seems obvious now, but it wasn't at all obvious back then.) Let's consider an example. In Chapter 3 I gave the following as an example of a query against the suppliers-and-parts database ("Get supplier number and status for suppliers who either are located in London or supply part P1 or both"):

```
RANGEVAR SX  RANGES OVER S ;
RANGEVAR SPX RANGES OVER SP ;

( SX.SNO , SX.STATUS ) WHERE SX.CITY = 'London' OR
                             EXISTS SPX ( SPX.SNO = SX.SNO AND
                                          SPX.PNO = 'P1' )
```

I refer you to that previous chapter for a detailed explanation of this example, including an explanation of the *range variables* SX and SPX in particular. (*Note:* The ALPHA paper refers to them not as range variables but as *tuple* variables, but I gave my reasons in that previous chapter for preferring the former term.) As I also explained in that same chapter, however, the example in question uses my own syntax—specifically, syntax from my book *An Introduction to Database Systems* (8th edition, Addison-Wesley, 2004). Here's what the same example would look like using the syntax of the ALPHA paper:

```
RANGE S  SX
RANGE SP SPX

GET W1 ( SX.SNO , SX.STATUS ) : ( SX.CITY = 'London' ) ∨
                                ( ∃ SPX ( ( SPX.SNO = SX.SNO ) ∧
                                          ( SPX.PNO = 'P1' ) ) )
```

Points arising:

■ Codd states explicitly in his paper that he "does not attach any importance to the syntax of ALPHA." However, he has to use *some* syntax to illustrate his ideas, and the syntax he does use is unfortunately a little daunting, involving as it does the use of mathematical symbols instead of keywords. To be specific, he uses:

:	*instead of*	WHERE
∧	*instead of*	AND
∨	*instead of*	OR
¬	*instead of*	NOT
∃	*instead of*	EXISTS
∀	*instead of*	FORALL

He also uses lots of parentheses in order not to have to rely on any specific operator precedence rules, and for consistency I'll do the same in the present chapter, for the most part.

■ The symbol W1 in the example denotes a *workspace*. Workspaces are used in ALPHA as a kind of buffer or staging area between the database and the data structures available in the host language. The assumption is that the host language probably doesn't support relations as such and so can't access data in its (relational) database form directly, but *can* access such data when it's converted to array form in a workspace. To quote from the paper:

> Data transmitted from the data base to a workspace W is placed in W [in the form of] a rectangular array[13] with the following properties:
>
> 1. Data items are homogeneous within each column.
>
> 2. Different columns may have dissimilar types of data items.
>
> 3. All rows consist of distinct tuples.
>
> In addition, each column is headed by a workspace attribute name.

Note in particular, therefore, that while a relation as such has no left to right ordering to its attributes and no top to bottom ordering to its tuples, its workspace representation has both.

---

[13] Not as a table, observe! The ALPHA paper rather surprisingly never mentions the possibility that relations might conveniently be perceived by the user as tables.

- The parenthesized expression following the workspace reference and preceding the colon—(SX.SNO, SX.STATUS), in the example—is called the *target list*. The boolean expression following the colon is called the *qualification*.

- ALPHA includes a feature by which quantifiers can be moved out of the qualification portion of a <u>GET</u> statement and into the range variable definitions.[14] Consider the following example ("Get supplier number and status for suppliers who supply all parts"):

```
RANGE S   SX
RANGE P   PX
RANGE SP  SPX

GET W2 ( SX.SNO , SX.STATUS ) :
      ∀ PX ( ∃ SPX ( ( SPX.SNO = SX.SNO ) ∧ ( SPX.PNO = PX.PNO ) ) )
```

Moving the quantifiers into the range variable definitions, this becomes:

```
RANGE S   SX
RANGE P   PX   ALL    /* universal quantification   */
RANGE SP  SPX  SOME   /* existential quantification */

GET W2 ( SX.SNO , SX.STATUS ) :
              ( SPX.SNO = SX.SNO ) ∧ ( SPX.PNO = PX.PNO )
```

Note in particular that now we've been able to drop two pairs of matching parentheses, since they're no longer necessary.

Personally, though, I'm not convinced that moving quantifiers into the range variable definitions in this way is a good idea. Consider the following revised form of the example:

```
RANGE S   SX
RANGE SP  SPX  SOME   /* existential quantification */
RANGE P   PX   ALL    /* universal quantification   */

GET W2 ( SX.SNO , SX.STATUS ) :
              ( SPX.SNO = SX.SNO ) ∧ ( SPX.PNO = PX.PNO )
```

Note the reordering of the <u>RANGE</u> statements in particular! In general, the order in which the <u>RANGE</u> statements appear defines the order in which the quantifiers would appear if they were moved back into the boolean expression, and of course it's crucially important to get that order right, because changing the order changes the meaning of the expression.[15] Here's what the <u>GET</u> statement would look like in this latter example if the quantifiers were moved back:

---

[14] But only if the boolean expression in question is in prenex normal form.

[15] Unless the quantifiers are all of the same kind (i.e., all existential or all universal), in which case the order doesn't matter.

```
GET W2 ( SX.SNO , SX.STATUS ) :
     ∃ SPX ( ∀ PX ( ( SPX.SNO = SX.SNO ) ∧ ( SPX.PNO = PX.PNO ) ) )
```

(I'll leave interpretation of this revised formulation as an exercise for you.) For such reasons, I feel that specifying the quantification via the RANGE statements is likely to be somewhat error prone, and I won't do it myself in the remainder of this chapter.

■ Regarding workspaces, the ALPHA paper goes on to say the following:

> A relation [that] has been deposited in a workspace ... may be used for retrieval purposes as an extension of the collection of relations in the data base ... This feature ... is particularly helpful in breaking down very complicated queries into a sequence of much simpler ones.

Here's an example to illustrate the point (it's based on one in the ALPHA paper, but I've altered it somewhat to make it apply to the suppliers-and-parts database). The query is "Get supplier number and city for suppliers who supply at least those parts supplied by supplier Jones"). ALPHA formulation:

```
RANGE S  SX
RANGE SP SPX

GET W1 ( SPX.PNO ) :
              ∃ SX ( ( SX.SNAME = 'Jones' ) ∧ ( SX.SNO = SPX.SNO ) )

/* W1 now contains (the array representation of) a unary relation */
/* giving part numbers for all parts supplied by any supplier    */
/* called Jones                                                  */

RANGE S  SZ
RANGE SP SPZ
RANGE W1 WZ

GET W2 ( SZ.SNO , SZ.CITY ) :
     ∀ WZ ( ∃ SPZ ( ( SPZ.SNO = SZ.SNO ) ∧ ( SPZ.PNO = WZ.PNO ) ) )
```

Now, I've argued elsewhere myself that breaking a complicated query down into smaller subqueries is often desirable from a human factors point of view. However, I don't think it's desirable to break something that's logically just one query down into a series of separate *statements*, as ALPHA does—I think there's a better way. In outline, that "better way" would involve:

a. Making ALPHA expression- instead of statement-oriented (a minor change, syntactically speaking, but a major one semantically)

b. Replacing the keyword GET by assignment syntax (this is just a cosmetic change)

c. Introducing a <u>WITH</u> clause for assigning a name to the result of an intermediate expression

Given these changes, a better formulation for the given query might look something like this:

```
RANGE S  SX
RANGE S  SZ
RANGE SP SPX
RANGE SP SPZ
RANGE T1 TZ

W2 := WITH ( T1 := ( SPX.PNO ) :
                        ∃ SX ( ( SX.SNAME = 'Jones' ) ∧
                               ( SX.SNO = SPX.SNO ) ) ) :
        ( TZ.SNO , TZ.CITY ) :
                  ∀ TZ ( ∃ SPZ ( ( SPZ.SNO = SZ.SNO ) ∧
                                 ( SPZ.PNO = TZ.PNO ) ) )
```

The <u>WITH</u> clause introduces a temporary name T1 for the relation defined by the specified subexpression (i.e., part numbers for parts supplied by Jones). However, it doesn't require any retrieval, as such, to be done (i.e., it doesn't require the result of that subexpression to be materialized). The assignment to W2 then yields the desired final result.

Why is this approach better? Because it still allows for the breaking down of a complicated query into smaller subqueries, but it does so without giving up on the goal—important for reasons of optimizability and the like that rely on the system being able to capture the user's overall intent—of formulating the entire query as a single expression or single statement.[16]

There are quite a lot more things I want to say about the retrieval aspects of the ALPHA language (some of them comparatively minor, though), but I'll leave those to the section "More on Retrieval," later. Before then, I want to say something about ALPHA's update features.

UPDATE OPERATIONS

ALPHA supports three statements of an updating nature, viz., <u>PUT</u>, <u>DELETE</u>, and <u>UPDATE</u>.[17] Note right away, therefore, that one thing it doesn't do is support a relational assignment

---

[16] The approach sketched here was pioneered in the PRTV system and is supported by **Tutorial D** and even (albeit to a very limited extent) by SQL.

[17] Thereby doing nothing to alleviate the perennial confusion between lowercase update, meaning updates in general, and uppercase UPDATE, meaning the UPDATE operator specifically (or <u>UPDATE</u>, rather, in the case of ALPHA). I'll attempt to avoid that confusion in the present chapter by using the term *modify* to refer to uppercase UPDATE (or <u>UPDATE</u>).

statement as such. Nor does it mention the fact that <u>PUT</u>, <u>DELETE</u>, and <u>UPDATE</u> are all in essence just shorthand for such an assignment. Of course, prerelational systems typically supported the same three operations (or analogs of them, rather) and didn't support en bloc assignment, so ALPHA can be regarded as simply following tradition here—but it's a pity it did, because most subsequent relational languages, including SQL in particular, then followed suit and did the same thing. As a consequence, to this day there's still little understanding in the industry at large that:

a.   Relational assignment is the only update operator that's logically necessary,

and moreover that

b.   Logically, the tuples to be inserted or deleted or updated constitute a *relation*, the body of which of course consists of a *set* of tuples, of (in general) arbitrary cardinality. Now, it's true that thinking in terms of inserting or deleting or modifying an individual tuple can often be intuitively useful. However, it's logically incorrect, and in fact it can lead to serious misunderstandings in this often problematic area.

Anyway, let's take a closer look at the three operators.

PUT

Suppose workspace WSP1 contains (the array representation of) a set of shipment tuples.[18]   Then the statement

```
PUT WSP1 SP
```

causes those tuples to be inserted into base relation SP. Moreover, according to the paper, "the system checks that no duplicate values of the primary key are introduced" by such an operation.[19] But that's more or less the totality of what it has to say about integrity constraint checking ... In the case at hand in particular, it has nothing to say about checking the foreign key constraints connecting SP to S and P.[20] (Note in this connection that <u>PUT</u> always operates on a single target relation—there's nothing analogous to *The Third Manifesto*'s multiple assignment

---

[18] However, recall that each column in the workspace is supposed to be headed by an attribute name. In the case of <u>PUT</u> in particular, it's not clear where these names might come from, since arrays as usually understood—I mean, arrays as supported in typical programming languages—don't have named columns, and so just writing an array from somewhere else in memory into the workspace isn't going to be sufficient.

[19] It doesn't say whether the operation is all or nothing, however. That is, what happens if some of the tuples to be inserted have primary key values that already exist and others don't?

[20] Elsewhere the paper does recognize the existence of those constraints (it even uses the term *foreign key* in connection with them), but it doesn't say anything about how such constraints might be either defined or enforced.

feature,[21] according to which, e.g., tuples might be inserted into all three of S, P, and SP "simultaneously.")

The ALPHA paper also gives another example of PUT, one that I find a little troubling. The following is a slightly revised form of the example in question. Suppose workspace WSP2 contains the array representation, not of a set of shipment tuples as such, but rather of just a set of supplier-number / part-number pairs. Then the statement

```
PUT WSP2 SP
```

will convert each of those pairs into a triple by "appending the absent value" [*sic*] as the value of the QTY attribute, and will then insert the resulting triples into base relation SP. I'll have more to say about the concept of "absent values" in the subsection "Missing Information," later (part of the section "More on Retrieval").

DELETE

DELETE neither needs nor takes any workspace operand. Here's a simple example:

```
RANGE PX P

DELETE PX : ( PX.PNO = 'P6' )
```

The target list needs no enclosing parentheses, since it always consists of a single range variable name.[22] Now, that range variable must presumably range over a base relation and not a workspace, though the paper doesn't actually say as much; however, it does say "A single DELETE statement removes tuples from precisely one data base relation (no more, no less)." Now, I might be reading too much into that "no more, no less," but it could be interpreted—perhaps rather charitably—as saying that, in the example, the DELETE will fail if there are currently any tuples for part P6 in relation SP (because it won't cascade to delete those tuples as well).

The paper also fails to state what happens if there are no tuples in the target satisfying the qualification.

Here's another example ("Delete all shipments from Paris suppliers"):

---

[21] In fact, ALPHA's update operations always take just one base relation operand. Codd justifies this state of affairs by merely asserting rather airily that it "avoids unwarranted complexity." Hmmm ...

[22] Unqualified range variable names can be used in the target list in GET, too. For example, if SX is a range variable ranging over the suppliers relation S, then an appearance of SX, unqualified, in a GET target list is shorthand for SX.SNO, SX.SNAME, SX.STATUS, SX.CITY (though what sequence these implicit attribute references appear in doesn't seem to be specified). And if the GET target list contains just one entry—in particular, if it consists of just a range variable name—then the enclosing parentheses can be omitted, too, but for simplicity I'll ignore this latter possibility in my examples.

```
RANGE SX  S
RANGE SPX SP

DELETE SPX : ∃ SX ( SX.CITY = 'Paris' AND SX.SNO = SPX.SNO )
```

UPDATE

ALPHA requires data that's to be modified to be retrieved into a workspace first. However, the retrieval is done not via GET but via a new statement, HOLD, which is like GET but additionally "warns the system to be prepared to return modified data to the elements supplying the retrieved data" (?). Here's an example ("Subtract 100 from the shipment quantity for all shipments of part P3"):

```
RANGE SPX SP

HOLD WQ ( SPX.QTY ) : ( SPX.PNO = 'P3' )

WQ.QTY := WQ.QTY - 100   /* host language */

UPDATE WQ
```

Well, there are several rather odd things going on here ... Note first of all that the HOLD statement is retrieving just the pertinent quantities; that is, after the retrieval, workspace WQ contains the array representation of a unary relation that's derived from SP by restricting it to just the tuples for part P3 and then projecting away the SNO and PNO values (and thereby also eliminating redundant duplicates, in general). Then the assignment—a host language operation—subtracts 100 from each of the quantities in WQ (so here we have to assume here that the host language supports array assignment). And then the UPDATE statement tells the system to apply the desired modification to the database somehow. To quote:

> Upon receipt of a HOLD the system retains enough primary key information ... so that it can perform the UPDATE properly ... The system may also suspend other ... accesses until this UPDATE is complete ...

I've already registered my objection to the primary key notion in general, and I certainly don't much care for the specific role assigned to it in the present context. What's more, the paper also says:

> If the value of the primary key in [the workspace] has changed when the UPDATE is received, the system balks and signals an error.

This text is hardly very clear (*what* primary key?), but what I *think* it means is that UPDATE can't be used to modify values of the primary key of a base relation—and this interpretation is supported by the fact that the paper's next example is titled, precisely, "Primary Key Update." To quote:

A sharp distinction is made between updates of primary keys ... and updates of other domains [*sic!*], because of the crucial role of primary keys in identification and search, and the high impact on the user community of changes in these keys.

Here's an example ("Change the primary key value for part P3 to P4"):

```
RANGE PX P

GET WP ( PX ) : ( PX.PNO = 'P3' )

DELETE PX : ( PX.PNO = 'P3' )

WP.PNO := 'P4' /* host language */

PUT WP P
```

In my opinion there are a whole host of further problems here. I'll leave it as an exercise for you to identify as many of those problems as you can, but on the whole I think I'd have to say that updating in general isn't exactly ALPHA's strongest feature.

MORE ON RETRIEVAL

Aggregate Operators

The ALPHA paper proposes support for "an expandable library of functions [that] can be invoked in queries," including the "rather important" ones COUNT, TOTAL, MAX, MIN, and AVERAGE [*sic no underlining*]. Here's an example of COUNT ("Get a count of the number of parts supplied by at least one supplier in a quantity greater than 100"):

```
RANGE SPX SP

GET W ( COUNT ( SPX.PNO ) ) : ( SPX.QTY > 100 )
```

Points arising:

■ The example is deliberately chosen to illustrate the point that the argument to COUNT is a *set*, meaning redundant duplicates are eliminated before the counting is done. Given the sample data in Figs. 1.1 and 3.1, for example, there are ten shipments with quantity greater than 100—but those shipments involve only five distinct part numbers, and so the final result (i.e., the count) is five, not ten.
   Note: In fact the ALPHA paper requires all of the aggregate operators to eliminate redundant duplicates from their argument before the corresponding aggregate is computed. However, it's obvious that duplicate elimination in this sense isn't always what's wanted.

For that reason Codd subsequently issued a corrigendum to his paper in which he proposed that duplicates be eliminated for COUNT and MAX and MIN but not for TOTAL and AVERAGE.

■ The syntax is unfortunate—the argument to the COUNT invocation is in fact the relation denoted by the expression

```
SPX.PNO : SPX.QTY > 100
```

(unnecessary parentheses omitted for clarity), and a more logical syntax for the example overall would therefore be:

```
GET W ( COUNT ( SPX.PNO : SPX.QTY > 100 ) )
```

Note: Of course, the foregoing language design error (which is what I would claim it is) is replicated in SQL, which would express the example thus[23]—

```
SELECT COUNT ( DISTINCT SPX.PNO ) FROM SP AS SPX WHERE SPX.QTY > 100
```

—instead of the following, which would be more logical:[24]

```
SELECT COUNT ( DISTINCT SPX.PNO FROM SP AS SPX WHERE SPX.QTY > 100 )
```

Here now is another example, to illustrate another point. The query is "For each part supplied, get the part number and the total quantity of that part, taken over all pertinent suppliers." (And let's assume for the sake of the example that the corrigendum mentioned above is in effect, so that duplicates in a TOTAL argument are retained, not eliminated.) Now, if we could use the more logical syntax sketched above, we could formulate this query straightforwardly like this (*warning! incorrect syntax coming up!*):

```
RANGE SPX SP
RANGE SPY SP

GET W ( SPX.PNO , TOTAL ( SPY.QTY : SPY.PNO = SPX.PNO ) )
```

Given ALPHA's syntax rules, however, the foregoing GET statement isn't valid, because the text within the inner parentheses isn't valid as a representation of the argument to a TOTAL invocation. By contrast, I *think*—though the ALPHA paper nowhere confirms the point—that the following GET statement would be valid (though I still find the syntax illogical):

---

[23] That intrusive DISTINCT is needed because SQL in effect does exactly the opposite of what ALPHA does (or originally did, at any rate)—namely, it retains duplicates in aggregate arguments (unless it's explicitly told not to).

[24] This design error is the direct cause of a well known defect in SQL: viz., that aggregate operator invocations can't be nested. For example, an expression of the form SELECT SUM (COUNT(...)) is illegal, in SQL.

```
GET W ( SPX.PNO , TOTAL ( SPY.QTY ) ) : SPY.PNO = SPX.PNO
```

However, for reasons that I have to say aren't exactly clear, the paper proposes formulating such queries in terms of something it calls *image functions*. Here's what the foregoing query would look like using an image function:

```
RANGE SPX SP

GET W ( SPX.PNO , ITOTAL ( SPX , PNO , QTY ) )
```

The expression ITOTAL (SPX,PNO,QTY) represents an invocation of the image function ITOTAL [*sic no underlining*]. Observe that SPX is a range variable ranging over the shipments relation, and PNO and QTY are attributes of that relation. Let the tuple currently represented by SPX be *sp*, and let the PNO value in *sp* be *pno*. Then the target list in the <u>GET</u> statement denotes that value *pno*, together with the total of all QTY values from shipment tuples *sp'* that have that same PNO value *pno* (i.e., the total of all QTY values from tuples *sp'* such that *sp'*.PNO = *sp*.PNO).

Well, I don't know about you, but I frankly don't find the foregoing idea—at least given the proposed syntax—very intuitive or easy to understand. I also think it would be completely unnecessary anyway, if only (as I've said) ALPHA took a more logical approach to the syntax of aggregate operator invocations in general. However, I will at least give one further image function example, in order to illustrate another point. The query is "Get part numbers for parts supplied by at least two different suppliers":

```
RANGE SPX SP

GET W ( SPX.PNO ) : ICOUNT ( SPX , PNO , SNO ) > 1
```

The point about this example is as follows: Given ALPHA's unorthodox syntax for regular aggregate operator invocations, such invocations can't appear in the boolean expression following the colon in a <u>GET</u> statement, and so an image function has to be used instead. With a more logical syntax, however, we could have written something like this—

```
RANGE SPX SP
RANGE SPY SP

GET W ( SPX.PNO ) : COUNT ( SPY.SNO : SPY.PNO = SPX.PNO ) ) > 1
```

—which I for one would find a great deal clearer.

"ORDER BY"

I believe ALPHA was the first language, or one of the first, to include support for what we would now usually call an ORDER BY clause, providing the ability to specify that the tuples of a result relation be returned in some user defined order. Here's a simple example:

```
RANGE SX S
GET W ( SX.SNO , SX.STATUS , SX.CITY ) : UP SX.CITY DOWN SX.SNO
```

("return result tuples in descending SNO sequence within ascending CITY sequence").

Quota Queries

The ALPHA paper also proposed support for "quota queries," something that as far as I know still hasn't been widely implemented (though various workarounds are possible). Here's an example ("Get supplier numbers for any two suppliers in Athens"):[25]

```
RANGE SX S
GET W ( 2 ) ( SX.SNO ) : SX.CITY = 'Athens'
```

This GET will return a relation of cardinality at most two (it'll be less than two if and only if there are fewer than two suppliers in Athens).

TOP and BOTTOM

TOP and BOTTOM [*sic no underlining*] are truth valued operators that, again, haven't been widely implemented, so far as I know. The expression TOP $(N,t.A)$ returns TRUE for tuple t of relation r if and only if the value of attribute A of that tuple is the Nth largest in r (and similarly for BOTTOM, mutatis mutandis). Here's an example ("Get part numbers for parts supplied in the largest of all current shipment quantities"):

```
RANGE SPX SP
GET W ( SPX.PNO ) : TOP ( 1 , SPX.QTY )
```

More on Range Variables

In Chapter 3 I said the following (more or less):

---

[25] I.e., any two will do, and we don't care which ones they are. Note, therefore, that quota queries can and often will be indeterminate.

Codd's completeness paper allows a range variable to range over any relation that can be formed by taking unions and/or intersections and/or differences of the given base relations. What it doesn't allow, however, is for the expression defining the range of a given range variable to involve any projections. As a consequence, there are certain unions that can be formulated in the completeness paper's relational algebra but not in its relational calculus—for example, the union of supplier cities and part cities, in the case of the suppliers-and-parts database. In other words, the completeness paper's relational algebra is in fact strictly more powerful than its relational calculus (i.e., it's actually "more than" relationally complete). Of course, this state of affairs was unintended, and Codd himself quickly recognized the deficiency (I have a personal note from him dated April 7th, 1972, correcting his original oversight).

In contrast to all of the above, in the ALPHA paper a range variable is limited to ranging over a single base relation.[26] Well ... Actually there are numerous issues here. First of all, the ALPHA paper never explicitly states that a range variable is limited to ranging over a single base relation, but it's clear from that personal note of April 7th, 1972, that Codd thought it did. In any case (and second), that same note removes that limitation from ALPHA, as well as removing the projection limitation from both ALPHA and from the relational calculus as such. Third, ALPHA always did allow a range variable to range over a workspace, a state of affairs that might go part way toward remedying the deficiency anyway. But this latter state of affairs raises a number of further questions! For example, what does it mean to say range variable WX ranges over workspace W if W contains (say) a projection of relation P at one time and the join of relations S and SP at another? Is such a situation even possible? (It is, in the ALPHA paper.) What's the lifetime of a range variable? What's the lifetime of a workspace name? How are workspaces declared? Ought they perhaps to be limited to a specific type of relation? And so on.

In addition to all of the above, there are a few minor syntactic issues having to do with range variables in general that I'd like to mention:

■ Let *BR* be a base relation. Then—in some circumstances but not all—ALPHA allows the name *BR* to be used in <u>GET</u> statements and the like to denote an implicitly defined range variable that ranges over the base relation with the same name. I deliberately haven't made use of this option in any of my examples—indeed, partly and precisely because of that "in some circumstances but not all"!— but I do at least want to point out that SQL does the same thing. For example, the SQL expression

```
SELECT SX.CITY FROM S AS SX WHERE SX.STATUS < 20
```

can legitimately be simplified to just:

```
SELECT S.CITY FROM S WHERE S.STATUS < 20
```

---

[26] This state of affairs tends to suggest that the ALPHA paper was written before the completeness paper (but see footnote 6).

Of course, it can be simplified still further to just:

```
SELECT CITY FROM S WHERE STATUS < 20
```

But this further simplification has no analog in ALPHA.

Attribute Names in Derived Relations

Consider the following example once again:

```
RANGE SPX SP

GET W ( COUNT ( SPX.PNO ) ) : ( SPX.QTY > 100 )
```

The question arises: What's the name of the single attribute of the result relation in this example? It must have a name, because that name is required to appear at the head of the corresponding column in the workspace. More generally, of course, the result of any relational expression *rx* must have a set of proper attribute names, in order that those names might be available for reference elsewhere in the expression of which *rx* might be just a part.

Sadly, this question is one that ALPHA does a really bad job on—so bad, in fact, that I'm not even going to try to explain exactly what its attribute naming rules are (actually I can't, because they're never spelled out in the paper in complete detail anyway). Let me just state for the record that the name of the sole result attribute in the example, according to the paper, would be something like this: COUNT_SPX_SNO.[27]

Piped Mode

"Piped mode" is another aspect of the ALPHA paper that I find a trifle unfortunate. It has to do with tuple at a time access to a relation. Consider the following query once again ("Get supplier number and status for suppliers who either are located in London or supply part P1 or both"):

```
RANGE S  SX
RANGE SP SPX

GET W1 ( SX.SNO , SX.STATUS ) : ( SX.CITY = 'London' ) ∨
                                ( ∃ SPX ( ( SPX.SNO = SX.SNO ) ∧
                                          ( SPX.PNO = 'P1' ) ) )
```

Here's the same query using "piped mode" (note that the original GET has been replaced by OPEN GET):

---

[27] There's an attempt on pages 15-16 of the paper to justify the ALPHA attribute naming rules in general (for base as well as derived relations), but that attempt seems to me to be completely off base. I mean, I find its argument completely specious.

```
RANGE S  SX
RANGE SP SPX

OPEN GET W1 ( SX.SNO , SX.STATUS ) : ( SX.CITY = 'London' ) ∨
                                      ( ∃ SPX ( ( SPX.SNO = SX.SNO ) ∧
                                                ( SPX.PNO = 'P1' ) ) )
```

OPEN <u>GET</u> is like opening a cursor in SQL; in particular, it doesn't retrieve anything. Now, however, each successive execution of

```
GET W1
```

will retrieve "the next" tuple of the result (in system defined order, unless the <u>OPEN</u> <u>GET</u> contains an appropriate ordering specification). This process will repeat until there are no more tuples to be retrieved or the user executes an appropriate <u>CLOSE</u> statement:

```
CLOSE W1
```

Now, tuple at a time access, or "piped mode," might be a comparatively harmless notion so long as we limit our attention to retrieval operations only (though even here I have reservations). Unfortunately, however, the paper proposes that it be used to support tuple at a time updating as well ... Thus, although the title of the present section is "More on Retrieval," I need to digress for a moment and talk about "piped mode <u>UPDATE</u>." Here's an example:

```
RANGE SPX SP

OPEN UPDATE WQ ( SPX.QTY ) : ( SPX.PNO = 'P3' )

HOLD W

WQ.QTY := WQ.QTY - 100  /* host language */

UPDATE WQ
```

Examples like the foregoing are probably the origin of SQL's "updating via cursor" feature (UPDATE *table* ... WHERE CURRENT OF *cursor*). And, of course, all such operations are strongly deprecated, because they represent a fundamental violation of the set level nature of the relational model.[28]

Note: To get back to the example for a moment, if it's discovered that some retrieved tuple doesn't need to be modified after all, then the following statement—

```
RELEASE WQ
```

---

[28] In particular they're likely to cause difficulties with integrity constraint checking. As we've seen, however, the ALPHA paper unfortunately doesn't have much to say in connection with integrity constraint checking anyway.

—can be used for that tuple instead of <u>UPDATE</u> WQ.

Missing Information

In his 1979 paper "Extending the Database Relational Model to Capture More Meaning" (*ACM Transactions on Database Systems 4*, No. 4, December 1979), Codd proposed an attack on the missing information problem based on the use of "nulls" and a corresponding three-valued logic (3VL). Indeed, that paper is usually cited as the primary source for Codd's nulls scheme and 3VL. In fact, however, the ALPHA paper shows that Codd was already thinking about the missing information problem as early as 1971. The following is more or less the entire content of a subsection of the ALPHA paper titled "Absent and Irrelevant Values":[29]

> In any practical data base there is a strong likelihood that some value or values are not presently available, while others never will be available because they are (for some reason) irrelevant ... The ramifications [of this state of affairs] ... are substantial.
>   First of all, a three-valued logic is needed, one which involves the truth values
>
>   <u>TRUE</u>, <u>FALSE</u>, <u>MAYBE</u>
>
> An explanation can be found in [*and here there's a reference to an IBM publication by Cantor, Dimsdale, and Hurwitz*[30]]. Secondly, when the final evaluation of a condition for eliciting a data item is completed and the result is <u>MAYBE</u>, the question arises: Should this item be included in the retrieved set or not? In ... ALPHA (in contrast to [*the IBM publication just cited*]), inclusion or exclusion of such items is under the control of the user through ... attachment or nonattachment of the keyword MAYBE_TOO [*sic no underlining*] on the pertinent retrieval request.

I regard these remarks as unfortunate in the extreme. Nulls and 3VL are widely regarded, by those who understand these things, as the single biggest mistake Codd made in connection with the relational model. Well, of course we should all be eternally grateful to him for his huge gift to society—his wonderful relational model—so I suppose we can allow him one mistake, and even forgive him for it ... For my own part, however, I do have to say I wish the mistake in question hadn't been quite such a major one.

---

[29] Note, however, that the subsection in question never actually explains what it means by an "absent value" (or an "irrelevant value," come to that). See the second example in the subsection discussing <u>PUT</u> operations, earlier in this chapter.

[30] D. Cantor, B. Dimsdale, and A. Hurwitz: "Query Language One (QL/1) Users Manual," IBM Scientific Center Report 320-2627, Los Angeles, Calif. (June 1969). I haven't been able to track down a copy of this publication, but—given the fact of its citation in the present context—I do wonder whether it could be the source for Codd's ideas and proposals regarding nulls and many-valued logics.

MISCELLANEOUS COMMENTS

Subsequent Work

Page 2 of the ALPHA paper identifies the following as one of Codd's principal reasons for publishing the paper in the first place:

> [This paper] is intended to provide a framework for subsequent papers on authorization principles, search tactics, and data representation techniques.

Well, I'm guessing here, but for the record:

- With respect to authorization principles, Codd did produce an IBM internal memo titled "Access Control Principles for Security and Privacy in Integrated Data Banks"—but he did that in July 1970, before the ALPHA paper was published. Perhaps he intended to beef that memo up and publish it outside IBM, but no such beefed up version ever materialized.

- With regard to search tactics, no paper by Codd on that topic ever materialized either. However, an important early paper on optimization—quite possibly the very first on the subject—was published in 1972 by a colleague of Codd's called Frank Palermo (see Chapter 3). Thus, it's possible that Codd, being aware of Palermo's research, had this paper in mind when he talked about a paper on search tactics. (On the other hand, Palermo's paper makes no use of the ALPHA language as such.)

- With respect to data representation techniques—which I take to mean representation techniques for data as physically stored under the covers—the only publication I'm aware of that (a) has anything to do with the subject and (b) has Codd as (co)author is a paper by D. Bjørner et al. titled "The GAMMA-0 *N*-ary Relational Data Base Interface: Specifications of Objects and Operations" (IBM Research Report RJ1200, April 11th, 1973). But like Palermo's paper, this paper—which incidentally was influential in the design of the storage and access component of the subsequent prototype System R, also from IBM Research—makes no use of the ALPHA language as such.

- In a similar vein, page 41 of the ALPHA paper says the following:

> Several additional features are desirable (in some cases necessary) to handle interlocking (for example, a means whereby certain operations may be temporarily excluded from specified portions of the data base), integrity preservation, virtual attributes, literal insertions, etc. ... These topics will be discussed in a later paper.

Unfortunately, however, no such paper or papers ever materialized.

"Data of Type RELATION"[31]

Page 9 of the ALPHA paper contains the following:

> For example, it might be desirable to introduce RELATION as a data type in Fortran.

In my opinion, however, RELATION is much better thought of not as a data type as such but rather as a *type generator* (like <u>CHAR</u> and <u>NUM</u> as discussed earlier).

Join Terms

Page 23 of the ALPHA paper contains the following text (edited very slightly here):

> Expressions of the form
>
> ```
>     T.D < U.E,   T.D = U.E,   T.D > U.E
> ```
>
> (where T, U are [range] variable names and D, E are attribute names) are called *join terms*, since they are the relational calculus counterparts of the relational algebraic operations *lo-join*, *equi-join*, and *hi-join*, respectively[32] ... Such expressions are permitted in ALPHA only in those cases where the units of the attribute T.D are system convertible into the units of U.E—for example, T.D could be in grams and U.E in pounds, if the system had a conversion algorithm it could invoke. A common special case ... occurs when T.D and U.E have the same units. For example, both attributes might refer to part numbers or both to ages in years.

Here Codd is confusing units and types (more evidence, to my mind, that he's also confused over types vs. representations). To be specific:

- If T.D and U.E both represent weights—i.e., if both are defined to be of type WEIGHT—it should be possible to compare them, regardless of what units they happen to be represented in under the covers. In fact, it should be possible for the user to be able to control whether a given WEIGHT value is presented to the user in question in grams, or pounds, or any other units that makes sense—again, regardless of what units such values happen to be represented in under the covers.

---

[31] I take my title for this subsection from Joachim W. Schmidt's paper "Some High Level Language Constructs for Data of Type Relation" (*ACM Transactions on Database Systems 2*, No. 3, September 1977). As my text immediately goes on to explain, however, I don't really think RELATION is a type, which is why I set my title in quotation marks.

[32] Here Codd gives a reference to his relational completeness paper—which is a little odd, because two of the three terms he mentions (*lo-join* and *hi-join*) don't appear anywhere in that paper. As a matter of fact I don't think they appear in any other of his writings, either.

■ Actually I think that what Codd was trying to get at in the foregoing quote has nothing to do with units at all; I think rather that what he was trying to deal with was the well known issue of *type conversion*. If T.D and U.E are of different types—say some <u>CHAR</u> type and some <u>NUM</u> type, respectively—then it should certainly be possible to convert the value of U.E to a character string and then compare that string with the value of T.D (which is a character string already, of course). The real question here is, I think, whether (a) the user should have to request that conversion explicitly or (b) the system should do the conversion implicitly on the user's behalf. Implicit conversion, also known as *coercion*, is supported by some languages (including SQL, incidentally) but is widely regarded as bad practice.[33]

Prenex Normal Form

Page 23 of the ALPHA paper also contains the following text:

> [All] qualifications can be converted to a logically equivalent formula with the quantifiers at the extreme left (prenex normal form) ... .

As I've demonstrated elsewhere,[34] this claim is incorrect.

Language Levels

Pages 41-44 of the ALPHA paper contain a series of good arguments—arguments that I basically agree with—in favor of supporting a truly high level database language such as ALPHA. I don't want to repeat those arguments here; however; I do want to take exception to one perhaps unimportant point. In the course of presenting those arguments, Codd repeatedly claims that the relational calculus is at a higher level of abstraction than the relational algebra (which he describes as merely "intermediate level"). I disagree with this claim; I think rather that they're both at the same level of abstraction, and that the difference between them is more one of style than of substance. However, I've presented detailed arguments in support of my position elsewhere—see the section "Calculus vs. Algebra" in Chapter 3 of this book—and I won't repeat them here.

---

[33] I remark in passing that the phrase "type conversion" isn't really very appropriate. When we talk of converting, say, some integer value to some character string type, we aren't really doing *anything* to that integer as such. Rather, we're simply applying a certain mapping to that integer value and thereby picking out and returning a certain character string value that corresponds to (or "is equivalent to") that given integer, under the mapping in question. In other words, the result isn't "the converted form" of the given integer, it's a whole different value (a character string, in fact).

[34] In my paper "A Remark on Prenex Normal Form" in the book *Database Explorations: Essays on The Third Manifesto and Related Topics*, by Hugh Darwen and myself (Trafford, 2010).

CONCLUDING REMARKS

When I first read the ALPHA paper, back in 1971, I'm sure you realize I did so with a much less critical eye ... At that time I was simply struggling to understand something that was radically new—radically new to me, at any rate—and I had neither the experience nor the judgment to see the blemishes in the paper that I observe now on rereading it, all these years later. (Hindsight is always perfect, of course.) But I certainly don't want my criticisms—and as you know by now, there are quite a lot of them—to be seen as detracting unnecessarily from what, after all, I still regard as a hugely important and original contribution. In closing, therefore, I'd like to repeat a few of the things I said in the introduction to this chapter—namely:

  a.   That the ALPHA paper made a huge and positive impression on me when I first read it;

  b.   That it had a major influence on the thinking of both my colleague Paul Hopewell and myself at the time; and

  c.   That it helped considerably in shaping our thoughts as to what our PL/I database language extensions might look like.

So, my thanks and sincere congratulations to Codd for writing it in the first place.

Chapter 5

The Further Normalization Paper

normalcy (an ill-formed word), normality
—Chambers Twentieth Century Dictionary (1972)

The paper I'm calling "the further normalization paper," or just "the normalization paper" for short, is of course yet another of the hugely important series of papers produced by E. F. Codd in the early 1970s. Here's a full citation:

■ "Further Normalization of the Data Base Relational Model," IBM Research Report RJ909 (August 31st, 1971); republished in Randall J. Rustin (ed.), *Data Base Systems: Courant Computer Science Symposia Series 6* (Prentice-Hall, 1972)

What this paper did was lay a foundation for the entire field of what subsequently became known as the theory of database dependencies, or just *dependency theory* for short. But what it didn't do—despite its title—was either change or add anything to the relational model itself! I'll elaborate on this point later; for now, let me just say that dependency theory is best thought of as a separate field in its own right, a field that's part of relational theory in general but not part of the relational model as such. Of course, the field of dependency theory is certainly built on top of the relational model—in particular, it's crucially reliant on the projection and join operators, which are certainly part of the model—but, to repeat, it's not part of that model as such. Rather, it's part (I'm tempted to say it's the academically respectable part) of the more general field of database design theory. So let me state for the record exactly what the normalization paper did do:

1. It introduced the crucially important notion of *functional dependence*,[1] a concept with major practical and theoretical implications.

2. It defined two "higher" normal forms, called second and third normal form, respectively. Those normal forms as such are perhaps of less interest now than they were back then, but

---

[1] Also known as functional dependency. The terms *dependence* and *dependency* are used more or less interchangeably in the literature. However, *dependence* seems slightly better for the concept in general and *dependency* seems slightly better for a specific instance of the concept (and when a plural is needed—as it is in connection with instances of the concept but not with the concept as such—*dependencies* seems to trip off the tongue a little better than *dependences* does).

the general concept they illustrated—viz., that of *levels of normalization*—remains significant, for both practical and theoretical reasons, to this day.

3. It helped lay the groundwork for what subsequently became known as *logical data independence*.

Sadly, one thing the paper didn't do was make a clear distinction between relation *values* (relations for short) and relation *variables* (relvars for short), and "further normalization" is one area—actually one of many—where making that distinction is really important. Quite apart from anything else, it (making the distinction, that is) is a huge aid to clarity of thinking, in an area where it's all too easy to get confused. Now, the normalization paper does *try* sometimes, but unfortunately not always, to make the distinction: For one thing, it sometimes describes the relations it talks about as *time-varying* (meaning they're not really relations at all but relvars), and for another it sometimes uses the term *state* to mean a particular value of some variable.[2] It also uses the qualifier *time-independent* to describe some condition that holds for all legitimate values of a "relation" (meaning all relations that can legitimately be assigned to some relvar), and the term *instantaneous tabulation* to refer to such a legitimate value.

So what I'll do in the present chapter is this: I'll begin by explaining the concept of functional dependence and various related matters in purely intuitive terms, using language derived from—where possible, actually taken from—the normalization paper as such. Then I'll get into a discussion of what's really going on in connection with these issues, using the more precise notions of relation value and relation variable to underpin that more formal discussion.

INFORMAL OVERVIEW

Here's how the normalization paper introduces the topic of functional dependence (the following text is very lightly edited here, mainly for typographical reasons[3]):

> When setting up a relational data base, the data base designer is confronted with many possibilities in designing the relations themselves, let alone deciding their representation in storage.[4] An important, in fact fundamental, consideration is that of identifying which attributes are functionally dependent on others. Attribute B of relation R is *functionally dependent* on attribute A of R if, at every instant of time, each value in A has no more than one value in B associated with it under R.

---

[2] The variables it applies this term to are actually database variables, not relation variables, but there's a clear and necessary implication that the term has to apply to relation variables as well.

[3] An analogous remark applies to quotes throughout this chapter.

[4] "Representation in storage" might seem a slightly odd thing to mention here, given that normalization has to do with the *logical* design of the database (i.e., the database as perceived by the user). Later in the paper, however, Codd—rather unfortunately, in my opinion—suggests that the concept of third normal form in particular might be relevant to physical design (i.e., physical storage considerations) as well. See footnote 39.

In other words, the projection of R on A and B is at every instant of time a function from the projection of R on A to the projection of R on B (this function can be, and usually will be, time-varying). We write R.A → R.B if B is functionally dependent on A in R, and R.A ↛ R.B if B is *not* functionally dependent on A in R. If both R.A → R.B and R.B → R.A hold, then at all times R.A and R.B are in one to one correspondence, and we write R.A ↔ R.B.

Pronunciation: For the purposes of the present chapter, an expression of the form R.A → R.B can be read as "R.B is functionally dependent on R.A," or as "R.A functionally determines R.B," or, more simply, just as "R.A arrow R.B."

By way of illustration, let the relation R referred to in the foregoing quote be as shown in Fig. 5.1:

ENO	ENAME	SALARY	DNO	BUDGET
E1	Adams	50K	D3	800K
E2	Boyd	60K	D2	900K
E3	Cope	45K	D1	800K
E4	Davis	75K	D2	900K
E5	Eliot	75K	D3	800K

Fig. 5.1: A relation concerning employees

As you can see, this relation concerns employees, and it has attributes ENO (employee number), ENAME (employee name), SALARY (employee salary), DNO (employee's department number), and BUDGET (budget for that department). Given the intuitively obvious semantics, then, here's one of the many functional dependencies that apply to this relation:

```
DNO → BUDGET
```

That is, whenever two tuples of R have the same value for DNO, they also have the same value for BUDGET (i.e., "each value in DNO has one value in BUDGET associated with it under R," to paraphrase Codd's definition).

Note: According to the text cited above, the foregoing functional dependency should more correctly be written thus:

```
R.DNO → R.BUDGET
```

But those "R." qualifications can be omitted if the context is clear, and I have my own reasons for preferring to omit them whenever I can (which, as it turns out, will be always).

Here are some more functional dependencies—hereinafter abbreviated FDs—that apply to that relation R of Fig. 5.1:

```
ENO → ENAME
ENO → SALARY
ENO → DNO
ENO → BUDGET
```

After all, it's certainly true that whenever two tuples of R have the same value for ENO, they also have the same value for, e.g., SALARY—because, of course, if two tuples have the same value for ENO, they must be the very same tuple (because employee numbers are unique, and ENO is a key for R). In other words, loosely: If K is a key, there'll always be "arrows out of K."

Relation R of Fig. 5.1 also illustrates a couple of further concepts that I'll be appealing to in later discussions:

■ First, consider the FD:

```
ENO → BUDGET
```

This FD certainly applies to R, but it does so precisely because the following two FDs also apply:

```
ENO → DNO
DNO → BUDGET
```

In general, in fact, if the FDs A → B and B → C both apply, then the *transitive* FD A → C applies as well, necessarily.

■ Second, consider the FD:

```
SALARY → SALARY
```

Again this is certainly an FD that applies to R (if two tuples have the same value for SALARY, then of course they have the same value for SALARY!), but it does so only in a rather trivial sense. In fact, the FD in question is an example of what's called a *trivial* FD. In general, a trivial FD is one that can't possibly not apply.[5]

Another point that's illustrated by Fig. 5.1 has to do with employee numbers and names. In that figure, each employee happens to have a unique name (ENAME) as well as a unique employee number (ENO). As a consequence, the "double dependency"

```
ENO ↔ ENAME
```

---

[5] Trivial FDs aren't very interesting from a practical point of view because they're, well, trivial. But if we're going to try to construct a proper *theory* of FDs, then we're going to have to take all FDs into account, trivial ones as well as nontrivial.

applies. So, of course, do the FDs:

```
ENAME → SALARY
ENAME → DNO
ENAME → BUDGET
```

Note, however, that the "double dependency" and these latter FDs are all a fluke, in a sense—they apply only because the employee names happen to be unique in the figure. If it's possible for two different employees to have the same name, then the situation would be different.[6]

Here finally for completeness are a few examples of "↛" in connection with relation R of Fig. 5.1:[7]

```
DNO     ↛ SALARY
SALARY  ↛ ENO
BUDGET  ↛ DNO
```

Collections of Attributes

After the text quoted earlier, the normalization paper continues thus:

> The definition given above can be extended to collections of attributes. Thus, if D, E are distinct collections of attributes of R, E is functionally dependent on D if, at every instant of time, each D value has no more than one E value associated with it under R. The notation →, ↛ introduced for individual attributes is applied similarly to collections of attributes.[8]

By way of illustration, consider the relation R shown in Fig. 5.2—a modified form of the shipments relation SP from Fig. 1.1 in Chapter 1 or Fig. 3.1 in Chapter 3—which has to do with shipments of parts (PNO) by suppliers (SNO):

SNO	PNO	QTY	SCITY
S1	P1	300	London
S1	P2	200	London
S2	P1	300	Paris
S2	P2	400	Paris

Fig. 5.2: A relation concerning shipments

---

[6] Of course, here we're running smack up against the fact that there's a logical difference between relation values and relation variables, a difference that really ought to be faced up to right at the outset. However, I'm still trying—perhaps mistakenly—to stick with the style of the normalization paper as such, until further notice.

[7] Note the difficulties of phrasing here—we can't say, for example, that "the FD DNO → SALARY doesn't apply," because (according to the definitions in the paper) if it doesn't apply, then it's not an FD in the first place! A hint here, then, that something needs to be done about tidying up those definitions.

[8] So too is the double dependency notation "↔", presumably.

Attribute QTY of this relation gives the shipment quantity and attribute SCITY gives the supplier city, and the following FD applies:

```
SNO → SCITY
```

(i.e., each supplier is located in just one city). Note, however, that the following FD, in which the left side is a "collection of attributes," also applies:

```
( SNO , PNO ) → QTY
```

Note: If the quantity for the shipment of part P2 by supplier S1 happened to be 400 instead of 200, the following FD would also apply:

```
PNO → QTY
```

Like the ones out of ENAME in the relation of Fig. 5.1, however, this latter FD would just be a fluke.

Redundancy and Further Normalization

The examples of Figs. 5.1 and 5.2 can be used as a lead-in to the concept of *levels of normalization*. To fix our ideas, let's consider the relation in Fig. 5.1. As you can see, that relation suffers from some *redundancy*; to be specific, the fact that a given department has a given budget appears several times, in general. That redundancy is due precisely to the fact that BUDGET is functionally dependent on DNO, and it can be eliminated by replacing the original relation R by two of its projections—one on ENO, ENAME, SALARY, and DNO, and the other on DNO and BUDGET. Fig. 5.3 shows the result of this replacement on the relation R from Fig. 5.1:

ENO	ENAME	SALARY	DNO
E1	Adams	50K	D3
E2	Boyd	60K	D2
E3	Cope	45K	D1
E4	Davis	75K	D2
E5	Eliot	80K	D3

DNO	BUDGET
D1	800K
D2	900K
D3	800K

Fig. 5.3: Replacing the relation of Fig. 5.1 by two of its projections

Note that the FD from DNO to BUDGET still applies, but now it does so within one of the two projections. Note too that no information is lost in the replacement, because the relation of Fig. 5.1 can always be recovered by joining the projections back together again (on DNO). So the suggestion is that in order to avoid the redundancy under discussion, it would be better for the database to be designed in such a way as to contain the two relations of Fig. 5.3 rather than the single relation of Fig. 5.1.

Turning to the relation in Fig. 5.2, the situation is rather similar: That relation too suffers from some redundancy; to be specific, the fact that a given supplier has a given city appears several times, in general. That redundancy is due to the fact that SCITY is functionally dependent on SNO, and it can be eliminated by replacing the original relation by two of its projections, one on SNO, PNO, and QTY, and the other on SNO and SCITY (see Fig. 5.4):

SNO	PNO	QTY
S1	P1	300
S1	P2	200
S2	P1	300
S2	P2	400

SNO	SCITY
S1	London
S2	Paris

Fig. 5.4: Replacing the relation of Fig. 5.2 by two of its projections

The FD from SNO to SCITY still applies, but now it does so within one of the two projections. Also, no information is lost in the replacement, because the relation of Fig. 5.2 can always be recovered by joining the projections back together again (on SNO this time). So, again, the suggestion is that in order to avoid the redundancy under discussion, it would be better for the database to be designed in such a way as to contain the two relations of Fig. 5.4 rather than the single relation of Fig. 5.2.

Now, in both of the foregoing examples, it's the *nonloss decomposition* of the original relation into projections that constitutes the "further normalization" of the normalization paper's title.[9] The general idea is that the original relation is necessarily already in some "normal form" (possibly just first) and the projections are in some higher normal form (either second or third, as far as the normalization paper is concerned).

Note: I deliberately omit the formal definitions here (I'll give them later, but there's a lot more territory I need to cover first). As promised earlier, however, I do want to say something about the paper's title, which I frankly think is quite misleading. That title is, to repeat, "Further Normalization of the Data Base Relational Model." But it's not the model that's being normalized!—rather, it's the particular relations (relvars, really) that happen to appear in the logical design of some particular database. In fact, the relational model as such doesn't *and can't* require relations (or relvars) to be in any particular normal form other than first.

---

[9] The decomposition is said to be "nonloss"—sometimes "lossless"—because, as already explained, the original relation can be recovered by joining the projections back together again. A decomposition that's not nonloss is said to be "lossy."

"Update Anomalies"

To follow on from the previous subsection: It's an odd fact that the normalization paper never actually mentions the problem of redundancy as such;[10] instead, it merely points out certain undesirable consequences of that more fundamental problem. The consequences in question are described in the paper as follows (the following text is based on text in the paper but is modified here to apply to the example of Figs. 5.2 and 5.4[11]):

> In Fig. 5.2, if supplier S1 relocates from London to Athens (say), more than one tuple has to be updated. Worse still, the number of tuples to be updated can, and usually will, change with time. It just happens to be two tuples at this instant.[12] [*And the paper subsequently refers to this situation as an example of an "update dependency."*]
>
> Now suppose supplier S1 ceases to supply parts P1 and P2, but may in the future supply some other parts. Accordingly, we wish to retain the information that supplier S1 is located in London. Deletion of one of the two tuples does not cause the complete disappearance of the association of S1 with London, but deletion of both tuples does. This is an example of a *deletion dependency* ... It is left to the reader to illustrate a corresponding *insertion dependency* using this example[13] ...
>
> Note how [*after replacing the relation of Fig. 5.2 by the two projections of Fig. 5.4*] the undesirable insertion, update, and deletion dependencies have disappeared.

Note: In a subsequent paper, Codd talked about insertion, deletion, and update *anomalies* rather than dependencies, and it's as "anomalies" that the concepts have gone into the literature. The paper in question is:

- E. F. Codd: "Normalized Data Base Structure: A Brief Tutorial," Proc. 1971 ACM SIGFIDET Workshop on Data Description, Access and Control, San Diego, Calif. (November 11th-12th, 1971)

---

[10] It does use the *term* redundancy (or nonredundancy, rather), but it does so in a very different context and it means something quite different by it. See the section "Keys," later.

[11] The text applies to the example of Figs. 5.1 and 5.3 as well, of course, mutatis mutandis.

[12] I can't resist pointing out here that anyone who talks about "updating tuples" in this way is already in a state of sin—for at least two different reasons, in fact.

[13] Leaving this latter to the reader is really a little unfair, because it relies on a notion that hasn't yet been discussed—not to mention the fact that the notion in question is one that, to say the very least, is somewhat suspect and raises a whole host of further issues. What Codd has in mind is as follows. Suppose we know that some supplier is located in Athens, but the supplier in question—supplier S5, say—doesn't supply any parts yet. Given the design of Fig. 5.2, then, we can't insert the fact that S5 is in Athens. Why not? *Answer:* Because the combination of SNO and PNO is the pertinent primary key, and (to quote the paper) "no tuple is allowed to have an undefined value for any of the primary key components." Again, why not? The only answer the paper gives is: "This restriction is imposed because of the vital role played by primary keys in search algorithms." I find this answer quite strange, and think we need to be told more.

I remark in passing that this latter paper seems to be the first in which Codd suggested that relations might conveniently be depicted not as arrays—see Chapters 2 and 4—but rather as tables.

TOWARD A MORE FORMAL TREATMENT

I'd like to begin my more formal treatment by taking a closer look at some of the text previously quoted from the normalization paper. I'll do so piecemeal.

Attribute B of relation R is functionally dependent on attribute A of R if, at every instant of time, each value in A has no more than one value in B associated with it under R. I have two comments here:

- First, note the phrase "at every instant of time." As noted earlier, the normalization paper makes fairly frequent use of this phrase, or other qualifiers of the same general nature (*at any time, change with time, time-independent, time-varying, instantaneous tabulation, data base state*, and possibly others). All of these phrases and qualifiers represent an attempt to get at the relation vs. relvar distinction, and they would be quite unnecessary if only that distinction were recognized right at the outset and then rigidly adhered to—and that's what I plan to do throughout the remainder of this chapter.

- My second comment is this: The text says (paraphrasing considerably) that the FD $R.A \rightarrow R.B$ means that within any relation r that's a legitimate value for relvar R, each value of $r.A$ is associated with *at most* one value of $r.B$. Throughout the rest of the paper, however, it's taken to mean that each value of $r.A$ is associated with *exactly* one value of $r.B$ (and indeed FDs have always been understood subsequently, in the database world in general, in this latter and more demanding sense). Now, I suspect that what was going on in Codd's mind here was the idea that certain values of $r.B$ might be missing or "undefined"... but, of course, such considerations open up an enormous set of problems that I certainly don't want to get into here. For the remainder of the present chapter, therefore, I propose to assume the "exactly one" interpretation.[14]

In other words, the projection of R on A and B is at every instant of time a function from the projection of R on A to the projection of R on B (this function can be, and usually will be, time-varying). Again note that phrase *at every instant of time* and that *time-varying*. (I have to say in passing that I don't think *time-varying function* makes any more sense than *time-varying relation* does. In fact, of course, a function *is* a relation—it's a special case.) But at least this

---

[14] Indeed, every tuple of r must contain exactly one A value and exactly one B value (because if it doesn't, then it's not a tuple of r, by definition)—so in fact it's *impossible* for some value of $r.A$ to be associated with less than one value of $r.B$.

text does explain the origin of that qualifier "functional" in the term *functional dependence*. It would have been nice, however, to introduce some terms for the left and right sides in an FD, which the normalization paper never actually does. In what follows, I'll use *determinant* for what appears on the left side and *dependant* for what appears on the right.

By the way, if we accept that *R* here is really a relvar and not a relation, we need to give a slightly extended meaning to phrases such as "the projection of *R* on *A*." By definition, projection is an operator that applies to relation values specifically. In particular, of course, it applies to the values that happen to be the current values of relvars. It thus clearly makes sense to talk about, e.g., the projection of relvar *R* on attribute *A*, meaning the relation that results from taking the projection on *A* of the current value of *R*. In the present context, however, it's convenient to use expressions like "the projection of *R* on *A*" in a slightly different sense. To be specific, we might say, loosely but very conveniently, that some *relvar*, *RA* say, is the projection of relvar *R* on *A*—meaning, more precisely, that the value of *RA* is equal at all times to the projection of the value of *R* on *A* at the time in question. In a sense, therefore, we can talk in terms of projections of relvars per se, rather than just in terms of projections of current values of relvars. Analogous remarks apply to join, of course, and in fact to all of the relational operators (but projection and join are the most relevant ones in the present context).

We write R.A → R.B if B is functionally dependent on A in R, and R.A ↛ R.B if B is not functionally dependent on A in R. This sentence touches on what was to become (in my own mind, at least, but I think in many other people's minds also) a major point of confusion. The confusion in question is between an FD as a semantic construct vs. an FD as a purely syntactic construct.[15] Let me elaborate.

I've already pointed out, in a footnote, the awkwardness involved in trying to say that some FD doesn't apply to some relation, because if it doesn't apply then—at least as far as the definitions given in the normalization paper are concerned—it isn't an FD in the first place. Well, the way to get around that awkwardness is as follows:

- First, to recognize that, formally speaking, an FD is just a piece of text (in other words, it's what I've called a purely syntactic construct);

- Second, to understand that (a) when that piece of text is interpreted with respect to some specific relation, it becomes a proposition, and then (b) by definition, that proposition evaluates to either TRUE or FALSE—where TRUE means the FD applies to the relation in question and FALSE means it doesn't.

By way of example, consider the following FD:

---

[15] The first paper to discuss FDs as a purely syntactic construct (and hence the first to show how they could be manipulated formally, without any regard for how they're meant to be interpreted) was "Dependency Structures of Data Base Relationships," by W. W. Armstrong (Proc. IFIP Congress, Stockholm, Sweden, 1974).

```
SNO → SCITY
```

This FD is just a piece of text. Interpreted with respect to the shipments relation R of Fig. 5.2, however, it means "For one value of R.SNO, there's exactly one corresponding value of R.SCITY," which is a proposition that evaluates to TRUE, and so the FD in question does apply to that relation. Now consider the FD:

```
SNO → QTY
```

This FD also is just a piece of text; interpreted with respect to the shipments relation R of Fig. 5.2, it means "For one value of R.SNO, there's exactly one corresponding value of R.QTY," which is a proposition that evaluates to FALSE, and so the FD in question doesn't apply to that relation.

In similar fashion, constructs of the form $A \nrightarrow B$ are also best thought of as pieces of text that, interpreted with respect to a particular relation, evaluate to either TRUE or FALSE.

If both R.A → R.B and R.B → R.A hold, then at all times R.A and R.B are in one to one correspondence, and we write R.A ↔ R.B. My only comment here is that, in practice, we almost never make use of this "double arrow" notation, though there's no particular reason why we shouldn't.

The definition given above can be extended to collections of attributes; thus, if D, E are distinct collections of attributes of R, E is functionally dependent on D if, at every instant of time, each D value has no more than one E value associated with it under R. I have three comments here. The first is just the rather trivial observation that there's no need to require D and E to be distinct (though if they're not, the FD R.D → R.E is indeed trivial), and the second is just a repeat of my previous comment regarding that phrase *no more than one*. My third comment is more significant, though. The fact is, given the FD $X \rightarrow Y$, the determinant X and the dependant Y are much better thought of as *always* being "collections," or sets, of attributes.[16] The case where such a set contains a single attribute is just a special case. Thus, from this point forward I'll express (e.g.) the FD from SNO to SCITY not like this—

```
SNO → SCITY
```

—but rather like this:

```
{ SNO } → { SCITY }
```

Note: I use braces rather than parentheses (which the normalization paper uses) because braces, not parentheses, are traditionally used in this way in connection with sets.

---

[16] The attributes in question must all be part of the same heading, though. See the formal definition of what an FD is in the section "Functional Dependency Precisely Defined," later.

Here's another example, one in which the determinant isn't a singleton set:

```
{ SNO , PNO } → { QTY }
```

This FD applies to the relation of Fig. 5.2, of course, also to the projection of that relation on SNO, PNO, and QTY (Fig. 5.4).

INTEGRITY CONSTRAINTS

Consider the relation R shown in Fig. 5.1 once again and the following FD:

```
{ DNO } → { BUDGET }
```

("whenever two tuples of R have the same value for DNO, they also have the same value for BUDGET"). Let's assume, reasonably enough, that this FD is supposed to evaluate to TRUE, not just for the relation of Fig. 5.1, but in fact for all relations that are legitimate values for a relvar called EMP for which Fig. 5.1 shows what the normalization paper would call "an instantaneous tabulation." In that case, the FD in question represents an *integrity constraint* on that relvar EMP. Here's a deliberately loose definition:

> **Definition (integrity constraint):** A boolean expression, or something equivalent to such an expression, that's required to evaluate to TRUE at all times. The DBMS must reject any attempt to perform an update that would otherwise cause some integrity constraint to evaluate to FALSE. *Note:* Integrity constraints effectively constrain update operations— and since database update operations apply, by definition, to relvars specifically (i.e., not to relations as such), it follows that such constraints can be thought of as applying to relvars specifically too. In other words, anything constrained by an integrity constraint must be a relvar, not a relation, by definition.

> *More terminology:* In the interest of clarity we draw a distinction between an integrity constraint *holding* and its being *satisfied*. To be specific, if integrity constraint *IC* mentions relvar *R*, we say that *IC holds* (or is required to hold) for *R*, and we say that every relation *r* that can successfully be assigned to *R satisfies* (or is required to satisfy) *IC*. For example, if the FD

```
{ DNO } → { BUDGET }
```

holds for relvar EMP,[17] then it must be satisfied by every relation (such as the one shown in Fig. 5.1) that can successfully be assigned to EMP. Here are the definitions:

---

[17] You might object here that the FD in question doesn't mention relvar EMP! True enough—but that's because I haven't shown yet how FDs might be defined in concrete syntax. I'll get to that in a few moments.

Definition (hold): Integrity constraint *IC* holds for relvar *R*—equivalently, relvar *R* is subject to constraint *IC*—if and only if every relation *r* that can successfully be assigned to *R* satisfies *IC*. *Note:* If integrity constraint *IC* fails to mention relvar *R*, it can sometimes be convenient to regard *IC* as holding for *R* trivially.

Definition (satisfy, violate): Let *IC* be an integrity constraint that mentions relvars *R1*, *R2*, ..., *Rn* ($n \geq 0$) and no others. Then relations *r1*, *r2*, ..., *rn* (in that order) satisfy *IC* if and only if evaluating *IC* with *R1* equal to *r1*, *R2* equal to *r2*, ..., and *Rn* equal to *rn* yields TRUE. *Note:* Relations *r1*, *r2*, ..., *rn* (in that order) violate *IC* if and only if they fail to satisfy it—i.e., if and only if evaluating *IC* with *R1* equal to *r1*, *R2* equal to *r2*, ..., and *Rn* equal to *rn* yields FALSE.

For simplicity, let's agree from this point forward to abbreviate the term *integrity constraint* to just *constraint*. Of course, any constraint that's supposed to hold in database *DB* needs to be declared as part of the definition of *DB*, and this observation is true of those constraints that happen to be FDs in particular. However, the normalization paper has little or nothing to say about FDs as constraints, and it doesn't explicitly discuss how "FDs as constraints" might be declared. If the system supports the arrow syntax, of course, it might be possible just to write something like this—

```
VAR EMP BASE RELATION
   { ENO ENO , ENAME NAME , DNO DNO , SALARY MONEY , BUDGET MONEY }
     KEY { ENO }
     CONSTRAINT { DNO } → { BUDGET } ;
```

—though personally I prefer a style that separates constraints out into declarations of their own, because they (the constraints) don't always refer to just one relvar.[18] Declaring the foregoing FD as a separate statement, without using the arrow syntax, might look like this:

```
CONSTRAINT FD1 COUNT ( EMP { DNO } ) = COUNT ( EMP { DNO , BUDGET } ) ;
```

(FD1 here is a constraint name. The subexpressions of the form EMP{...} denote projections of EMP on the specified attributes.)
    Note: Another, perhaps logically cleaner, way of declaring the constraint—one that doesn't rely on counting as such—is this:[19]

```
CONSTRAINT FD1 EMP = EMP { ALL BUT BUDGET } JOIN EMP { DNO , BUDGET } ;
```

---

[18] Though constraints that are FDs do.

[19] Note how this alternative formulation directly reflects the nonloss nature of the decomposition of EMP into its projections on {ENO, ENAME, SALARY, DNO} and {DNO,BUDGET}.

To repeat, the normalization paper doesn't explicitly discuss how FD constraints might be declared. In particular, it doesn't mention the fact that the higher the normal form a given relvar is in, the easier it is to declare FD constraints on that relvar. Let me therefore spell out the following specific (and important) point: If relvar *R* is in what later came to be called Boyce/Codd normal form (BCNF), then it's sufficient just to declare the keys of *R*, and all FD constraints on *R* will in effect then be declared automatically (because if *R* is in BCNF, then all FDs that hold in *R* are implied by the keys of *R*).[20] All of which serves as a lead-in to my next topic, keys.

KEYS

The normalization paper was the first of Codd's papers to provide reasonably precise definitions of the terms *candidate key* and *primary key*, as follows:

- Each *candidate key* K of relation R is ... a combination of attributes (possibly a single attribute) of R with properties P1 and P2:

    P1:   (*Unique Identification*) In each tuple of R the value of K uniquely identifies that tuple; i.e., R.K → R.Ω [holds in R,] where Ω denotes the collection of all attributes of [R].

    P2.   (*Nonredundancy*) No attribute in K can be discarded without destroying property P1.

    Obviously, there always exists at least one candidate key, because the combination of all attributes of R possesses property P1. It is then a matter of looking for a subset with property P2 ...

- For each relation R in a data base, one of its candidate keys is arbitrarily designated as the *primary key* of R. The usual operational distinction between the primary key and other candidate keys (if any) is that no tuple is allowed to have an undefined value for any of the primary key components, whereas any other components may have an undefined value.

Now, I've explained elsewhere why I think it's a mistake, at least from a formal perspective, to draw a distinction between primary keys and other keys (and in what follows, therefore, I won't make that distinction, other than in quotes from the normalization paper, but will instead refer to them all just as keys). I've also commented earlier in the present chapter (in a footnote) on that business of undefined values ... But at least it's good to see that keys are

---

[20] I note in passing that this characterization can actually be taken as a *definition* of BCNF (i.e., *R* is in BCNF if and only if every FD that holds in *R* is implied by the keys of *R*). Of course, the normalization paper doesn't actually discuss BCNF as such, it only goes as far as third normal form (3NF). BCNF was discussed in a later paper by Codd ("Recent Investigations into Relational Data Base Systems," Proc. IFIP Congress, Stockholm, Sweden, 1974). Confusingly, however, this latter paper referred to the new normal form as an "improved" version of *third* normal form! But other writers subsequently renamed it Boyce/Codd normal form, in honor of the definers. (Interestingly, a definition of "3NF"—actually BCNF—was given three years earlier in a paper by Heath (see Appendix B), so BCNF ought by rights to be called Heath normal form. But it isn't. In this connection, though, it's relevant to note that Heath's paper is referenced in Codd's normalization paper.)

explicitly defined to be *sets* ("combinations") of attributes. Here for the record is my own preferred definition (of course, it's not all that different from Codd's, but note my use of the term *irreducibility* in preference to Codd's *nonredundancy*):[21]

> **Definition (key):** Let K be a subset of the heading of relvar R; then K is a key for, or of, R if and only if (a) no possible value for R contains two distinct tuples with the same value for K (the uniqueness property), while (b) the same can't be said for any proper subset of K (the irreducibility property).

Note that, by definition, keys are sets of attributes (and key values are therefore tuples); however, if the set of attributes constituting some key K contains just one attribute A, then it's common, though strictly incorrect, to speak informally of that attribute A per se as being that key. Note further that if K is a key for relvar R, then the functional dependency $K \rightarrow X$ necessarily holds in R for all subsets X of the heading of R.

FIRST NORMAL FORM

The normalization paper defines first normal form (1NF) thus:[22]

> A relation is in *first normal form* if it has the property that none of its domains has elements which are themselves sets. An *unnormalized relation* is one which is not in first normal form.

Well, I'm on record elsewhere as disagreeing with this definition quite strongly—see the paper "What First Normal Form Really Means," in my book *Date on Database: Writings 2000-2006* (Apress, 2006)—but I'm prepared to overlook my objections for present purposes.[23] However, the point I do want to make is that Codd is quite right (though perhaps unintentionally so) in defining 1NF to be a property of a *relation*—by which I mean, specifically, a relation *value*, not a relvar.[24] By contrast, all higher normal forms, including 2NF and 3NF in particular, are very definitely properties of relvars and not relations, because (unlike 1NF) they're defined

---

[21] Note too that my definition allows a key to be empty, which Codd's definition appears not to.

[22] The paper doesn't actually make use of the convenient abbreviations 1NF, 2NF, 3NF, but I will. More important, the paper nowhere states categorically that the relational model actually *requires* all relations to be in 1NF! However, subsequent writings by Codd most certainly did—see his paper "Extending the Database Relational Model to Capture More Meaning," *ACM Transactions on Database Systems 4*, No. 4 (December 1979), for example. See also the remarks concerning "nonhierarchic relations" in Chapter 6.

[23] Just for the record, though, I believe that 1NF can usefully be defined (and indeed should be defined) in such a way that *all* relations are in 1NF—and if it is, then the phrase "an unnormalized relation" becomes a pure contradiction in terms.

[24] I suppose we might say a relvar is in 1NF if and only if all of its possible values are 1NF relations—but such a definition would be vacuous, because all relvars would then be in 1NF. (Well, I suppose they are. So I guess such a definition is at least harmless, and there's not much point in objecting to it.)

in terms of certain constraints—in fact FD constraints specifically, in the case of 2NF and 3NF (also BCNF) in particular—that are required to hold.

SECOND NORMAL FORM

The normalization paper's definition of second normal form relies on two further concepts, viz., *prime attributes* and *full FDs*. To quote:

■   [Any] attribute of R which participates in at least one candidate key of R [is] a *prime attribute* of R. All other attributes of R are ... *nonprime*.

■   Suppose D, E are distinct subcollections of the attributes of a relation R and R.D → R.E [holds]. If, in addition, E is *not* functionally dependent on any subset of D (other than D itself), then E is said to be *fully dependent* on D in R.

Once again I have some quibbles over terminology ... To be specific, I think *key attribute* is more apt than *prime attribute*, and I think *irreducibly dependent* is more apt than *fully dependent*. Here are my own definitions of these preferred terms:

Definition (key attribute): An attribute of a given relvar that's part of at least one key of that relvar. A nonkey attribute is an attribute that's not a key attribute.

Definition (irreducible FD): The FD $X \to Y$ is irreducible with respect to relvar R (or just irreducible, if R is understood) if and only if it holds in R and $X' \to Y$ doesn't hold in R for any proper subset X' of X.

Here now is the normalization paper's definition of 2NF:[25]

A relation R is in *second normal form* if it is in first normal form and every nonprime attribute of R is fully dependent on each candidate key of R.

Of course, the term *relation* in this definition should definitely be understood to mean a relvar. Tweaking the text to use my own preferred terminology gives the following revised definition:

---

[25] Although being in 2NF obviously doesn't preclude being in the next higher normal form (3NF) as well, the term *2NF* is often used loosely to refer to a relvar that's in 2NF and not in 3NF (and similarly for 3NF and higher normal forms, mutatis mutandis).

Definition (second normal form): Relvar R is in second normal form, 2NF, if and only if every nonkey attribute A of R is such that the set $\{A\}$ is irreducibly dependent on every key of R.[26]

Actually there's an alternative definition of 2NF that I tend to prefer over the foregoing. It does however rely on two further concepts, *superkey* and *subkey* (but then those concepts can be useful in their own right in other contexts). Here are the definitions:

Definition (superkey): Let X be a subset of the heading of relvar R; then X is a superkey for, or of, R if and only if no possible value for R contains two distinct tuples with the same value for X. In other words, a superkey is a superset of a key (loosely speaking)—it has the uniqueness property of keys but not necessarily the irreducibility property. Note that the heading of any given relvar R is necessarily a superkey for R, and so is every key of R. Note too that if SK is a superkey for R, then the FD $SK \rightarrow Y$ necessarily holds for all subsets Y of the heading of R.

Definition (subkey): Let X be a subset of the heading of relvar R; then X is a subkey for, or of, R if and only if there exists some key K for R such that X is a subset of K. In other words, a subkey is a subset of a key (loosely speaking). Note that the empty set $\{\ \}$ is necessarily a subkey for all possible relvars R.

Now I can give my alternative (and preferred) definition of 2NF:[27]

Definition (second normal form): Relvar R is in second normal form, 2NF, if and only if, for every nontrivial FD $X \rightarrow Y$ that holds in R, (a) X is a superkey or (b) Y is a subkey or (c) X isn't a subkey.

And just for completeness, here's a precise definition of a trivial FD:

Definition (trivial FD): An FD that can't possibly be violated. The FD $X \rightarrow Y$ is trivial if and only if Y is a subset of X. A nontrivial FD is one that's not trivial.

---

[26] Note that my definition differs from Codd's in that it makes no mention of 1NF as such. I do think it desirable in general that the definition of any given normal form make no mention of any other (and my preferred definitions as given in this chapter do all comply with this desideratum). In fact, there's never any need in any of those definitions to mention 1NF in particular (at least as far as I'm concerned), because as explained in footnote 24 it's my position that relvars are always in 1NF anyway.

[27] Proving that the definitions are equivalent is left as an exercise!

THIRD NORMAL FORM

Here's the normalization paper's definition of 3NF:

> A relation R is in *third normal form* if it is in second normal form and every nonprime attribute of R is nontransitively dependent on each candidate key of R.

This definition relies on the concept of a transitive FD, which I've already discussed briefly but which the normalization paper defines (somewhat informally) as follows:

> Suppose that A, B, C are three distinct collections of attributes of a relation R ... Suppose that all three of the following time-independent conditions hold:
>
> ```
> R.A → R.B
> R.B → R.C
> R.B ↛ R.A
> ```
>
> From this we may conclude that two other conditions must hold:
>
> ```
> R.A → R.C
> R.C ↛ R.A
> ```
>
> ... In such a case we say that C is *transitively dependent* on A under R.[28]

By contrast, my own preferred definition separates syntactic and semantic issues:

Definition (transitive FD): The FDs $X \to Y$ and $Y \to Z$ together imply the transitive FD $X \to Z$; thus, if the FDs $X \to Y$ and $Y \to Z$ hold in relvar R, then the transitive FD $X \to Z$ necessarily also holds in R.

But my preferred definition for 3NF doesn't mention transitive FDs anyway! Nor does it mention 2NF (at least, not explicitly). Here it is:

Definition (third normal form): Relvar R is in third normal form, 3NF, if and only if, for every nontrivial FD $X \to Y$ that holds in R, (a) X is a superkey or (b) Y is a subkey.

And now perhaps it's clear why I prefer my 2NF and 3NF definitions: They make crystal clear exactly what the differences are between 2NF and 3NF (also between 3NF and Boyce/Codd

---

[28] In case you're wondering, here's a proof that those "two other conditions" hold (I'll drop the "R." qualifiers for simplicity):
1. A → B and B → C both hold (given), so A → C holds by transitivity. 2. B → C holds (given), so if C → A holds as well, then B → A holds by transitivity; but B ↛ A holds (given), and so we have a contradiction; thus C ↛ A holds.
By the way, it's not clear why Codd insists that B → A mustn't hold. Certainly it mustn't hold if C → A is required not to hold, but I don't see why Codd insists on that condition either. Of course, it's true that if B → A does hold, then A → C holds "directly" as well as transitively (because if B → A holds then A is a key), but I don't see why that matters.

normal form, BCNF), as I now explain. (They also make it clear that any BCNF relvar is necessarily in 3NF and any 3NF relvar is necessarily in 2NF.) Here again is my preferred definition of 2NF:

> **Definition (second normal form):** Relvar R is in second normal form, 2NF, if and only if, for every nontrivial FD $X \rightarrow Y$ that holds in R, (a) X is a superkey or (b) Y is a subkey or (c) X isn't a subkey.

Dropping possibility (c) gives a definition of 3NF (repeated to facilitate comparison):

> **Definition (third normal form):** Relvar R is in third normal form, 3NF, if and only if, for every nontrivial FD $X \rightarrow Y$ that holds in R, (a) X is a superkey or (b) Y is a subkey.

And dropping possibility (b) gives a definition of BCNF:

> **Definition (Boyce/Codd normal form):** Relvar R is in Boyce/Codd normal form, BCNF, if and only if, for every nontrivial FD $X \rightarrow Y$ that holds in R, X is a superkey.

To get back to the normalization paper per se: Remarkably, the paper actually gives an example of a relation (or relvar, rather) that's in 3NF but not in BCNF, though of course it doesn't describe the example in those terms. The example is headed "Nonremovable Transitive Dependence." Here's the pertinent text in its entirety (attributes A and B are underlined in this extract to show that together they constitute the primary key for R):[29]

> It is not always possible to remove *all* transitive dependencies without losing information. This is illustrated by a relation R(<u>A,B</u>,C) in which [the following conditions hold]:
>
> ```
> R.(A,B)  →  R.C
> R.C      →  R.B
> R.C      ↛  R.(A,B)
> ```
>
> Thus, B is transitively dependent on the primary key (A,B).

Frankly, I don't find either this example or the accompanying discussion (what little there is!) very clear. It's true in the example that B is transitively dependent on (A,B), but of course it's also true that the transitive FD in question is trivial. In other words, I think the discussion of transitive dependencies, as such, in this example is kind of off base. What's really going on here is that R is an example of a relation (relvar) *that can't be nonloss decomposed into BCNF*

---

[29] In the present section (at least until further notice) I use the notation of the normalization paper instead of my own preferred notation, thereby writing, e.g., R.(A,B) → R.C, or sometimes just (A,B) → C, instead of what I'd really prefer to write—viz., {A,B} → {C}.

projections without "losing" an FD. For example, suppose R looks like this (note carefully that this relation does indeed satisfy the given FDs):

A	B	C
a1	b1	c1
a1	b2	c2
a2	b1	c1
a2	b2	c3

Observe that this relation has exactly eight distinct projections—three on just one attribute, three on a pair of attributes, one on all three attributes (the identity projection), and one on no attributes at all (the nullary projection).[30] For present purposes, however, we can ignore all except the three binary projections,[31] viz., the ones on (A,B), (B,C), and (C,A):

A	B
a1	b1
a1	b2
a2	b1
a2	b2

B	C
b1	c1
b2	c2
b2	c3

C	A
c1	a1
c2	a1
c1	a2
c3	a2

If we now consider these projections taken pairwise, we see that:

- R isn't equal to the join of the projections on (A,B) and (B,C). Of course, that join does produce every tuple of R (necessarily so); unfortunately, however, it produces some additional tuples as well. Given just those two projections, therefore, we've lost information, because R as such can't be recovered from them. Hence, decomposition of R into those two projections isn't nonloss (it's an example of what's sometimes called a *lossy* decomposition).

- The remarks of the foregoing bullet item apply to the projections on (C,A) and (A,B) also, mutatis mutandis.

- However, they *don't* apply to the projections on (B,C) and (C,A); that is, decomposition of R into those two projections is nonloss, because R is equal to the join of those two projections. *However, the FD (A,B) → C is "lost" in that decomposition.* What do I mean

---

[30] In fact, it's axiomatic that a relation of degree n always has exactly 2^n distinct projections.

[31] Why, exactly?

by "lost" here? In order to answer this question properly, I really have to switch back to my preferred terminology and notation, and so I will.

Suppose, then, that R is a relvar—not just a relation—with attributes A, B, and C, and suppose the following FDs hold in R (meaning among other things that {A,B} is a key for R):

```
{ A , B } → { C }
{ C }       → { A }
```

Now consider the first of these FDs in particular, and observe that it can be regarded as an integrity constraint that refers to just a single relvar. Because of this latter fact, monitoring updates to ensure that the constraint is never violated is a comparatively straightforward matter. But note what happens if R is nonloss decomposed into its projections—call them RBC and RCA—on {B,C} and {C,A}, respectively (note that these projections are both in BCNF). The constraint in question now looks like this:

```
CONSTRAINT FDR WITH ( R := RBC JOIN RCA ) : R = R JOIN R { A , B _} ;
```

The significant point about this revised constraint is that it refers to two distinct relvars, RBC and RCA. As a consequence, monitoring updates to ensure that the constraint is never violated is likely to be rather more complicated than it was before (before the decomposition, that is). And precisely for that reason, the decomposition might not be desirable in practice, even though the original relvar R isn't in BCNF and thus suffers from certain redundancies and hence certain update anomalies.

What the foregoing discussion shows, therefore, is that the twin objectives of

a. Decomposing into BCNF projections, and

b. Not losing any FDs while doing so,

can sometimes be in conflict.[32] And perhaps it was Codd's recognition of the existence of such problem cases that prevented him from taking the next step in his further normalization paper and defining BCNF as such.[33]

---

[32] It also shows that "losing FDs" isn't a very good way of characterizing the situation! What actually happened in the example was that an FD that applied to a certain relvar before the decomposition became an FD that applied to the result of joining two relvars after the decomposition. So it wasn't really a case of "losing" an FD—rather, it was a case of replacing one FD by another, one that was (in a sense) more complicated than the original one.

[33] This discussion touches on another point, though: There's no suggestion in the normalization paper that 3NF is somehow "the end of the normalization road," and I'm quite sure Codd didn't think it was. But some people in the industry certainly seemed to think it was at the time, and there might be those who still think so today. For the record, therefore, I give here an incomplete list of further normal forms that have been defined since Codd's original paper—fourth (4NF); essential tuple (ETNF); superkey (SKNF); fifth (5NF); and sixth (6NF). For definitions and explanations, I refer you to my book *Database Design and Relational Theory: Normal Forms and All That Jazz* (O'Reilly, 2012). Here I'll just note that 6NF *is* "the end of the normalization road," so long as we limit our attention to projection as the decomposition operator and join as the corresponding recomposition operator.

FUNCTIONAL DEPENDENCY PRECISELY DEFINED

Most people probably consider the idea of levels of normalization—in particular the introduction of 2NF and 3NF—as the major contribution of the normalization paper. Personally, however, I regard FDs as the more fundamental contribution. For that reason, I'd like to conclude the "formal" part of the present chapter with my own preferred (precise, and somewhat extended) definition of the FD concept as such:

> **Definition (functional dependence):** Let H be a heading; then a functional dependency (FD) with respect to H is an expression of the form $X \rightarrow Y$, where X (the determinant) and Y (the dependant) are both subsets of H. (The qualifying phrase "with respect to H" can be omitted if H is understood.) The expression $X \rightarrow Y$ is read as "Y is functionally dependent on X," or as "X functionally determines Y," or, more simply, just as "X arrow Y."
>
> Let relation r have heading H, and let $X \rightarrow Y$ be an FD, F say, with respect to H. Then r satisfies F if and only if all pairs of tuples $t1$ and $t2$ of r are such that whenever the projections of $t1$ and $t2$ on X are equal, then the projections of $t1$ and $t2$ on Y are also equal; otherwise r violates F.[34]
>
> Let relvar R have heading H. Then the FD F holds in R—equivalently, R is subject to the FD F—if and only if every relation r that can successfully be assigned to R satisfies that FD F. The FDs that hold in relvar R are the FDs of R, and they serve as integrity constraints on R.

Points arising from this definition:

1. Note that FDs are defined with respect to some heading, not with respect to some relation or some relvar.

2. Note too that from a formal point of view, an FD is just an expression (what earlier I called "a piece of text"): an expression that, when interpreted with respect to some specific relation, becomes a proposition that, by definition, evaluates to either TRUE or FALSE. (It's common informally to define $X \rightarrow Y$ to be an FD only if it actually holds in the pertinent relvar, but that definition leaves no way of saying a given FD fails to hold in some relvar, because, by that definition, an FD that fails to hold isn't an FD in the first place.)

3. By definition, every relvar R is always subject to all possible FDs of the form $K \rightarrow Y$, where K is a key—or, more generally, a superkey—for R and Y is an arbitrary subset of the

---

[34] Note the appeals here to the operation of tuple projection. Tuple projection is defined in Chapter 3.

heading of R. In other words, there are always "arrows out of superkeys," and it's "arrows not out of superkeys" that are the interesting ones, in a sense (because if R is subject to any such FDs, then it's not in BCNF, which is "the" normal form with respect to FDs).

4. X and Y in the FD $X \rightarrow Y$ are *sets* of attributes. Informally, however, it's common (though strictly incorrect) to speak of the attributes in X as if Y were functionally dependent on those attributes per se, instead of on the set X that contains those attributes. Likewise, it's common (though strictly incorrect) to speak of the attributes in Y as if those attributes per se, instead of the set Y that contains those attributes, were functionally dependent on X. *Note:* The foregoing remarks apply with special force in the common case where either X or Y is a singleton set.

What's more, many of the ideas that apply to FDs in particular can be extended to apply to integrity constraints in general. For example, it's true in general that:

- Some constraints are trivial.

- Some constraints imply others.

- The question of whether a certain constraint is implied by some given set of constraints is an interesting theoretical and practical problem.

- Given some set of constraints, finding a subset of the given set such that every constraint in the given set is implied by that subset is an interesting theoretical and practical problem.

What makes FDs in particular much more tractable than integrity constraints in general is the existence of a sound and complete set of inference rules for FDs,[35] rules that allow questions such as those sketched above to be addressed. Now, I don't know whether, when he wrote the normalization paper, Codd had in mind the possibility of such rules someday being found, but it wouldn't surprise me at all if he did.

"ADMISSIBLE STATES"

Consider Fig. 5.2 once again. Suppose the relation shown in that figure is in fact a sample value for a relvar SPC, with attributes SNO, PNO, QTY, and SCITY and sole key {SNO,PNO}. Suppose further that the FD

---

[35] In this connection, see the paper mentioned in an earlier footnote, "Dependency Structures of Data Base Relationships," by W. W. Armstrong. For a tutorial discussion of such matters, see Chapter 11 ("Functional Dependencies") of my book *An Introduction to Database Systems* (8th edition, Addison-Wesley, 2004).

```
{ SNO } → { SCITY }
```

holds in that relvar. Then the relvar isn't in 2NF, and decomposition ("further normalization") is therefore recommended: decomposition, that is, into projections SP and SC, where SP has attributes SNO, PNO, and QTY and SC has attributes SNO and SCITY (see Fig. 5.4). These projections are both in 2NF, and the decomposition eliminates some redundancy and thereby avoids certain update anomalies. But there's another point too: *Those projections are capable of representing certain information that can't be represented using just the original relvar SPC.* To be specific, we can represent the fact that (e.g.) supplier S5 is in Athens, even if supplier S5 doesn't supply any parts yet (see Fig. 5.5, which is a slightly revised version of Fig. 5.4):

SP

SNO	PNO	QTY
S1	P1	300
S1	P2	200
S2	P1	300
S2	P2	400

SC

SNO	SCITY
S1	London
S2	Paris
S5	Athens

Fig. 5.5: A revised version of Fig. 5.4

The normalization paper characterizes such a state of affairs by saying that the design illustrated in Fig. 5.5 has more "admissible states" than the design illustrated in Fig. 5.2. It also observes, quite correctly, that (a) if we form the join of the relations of Fig. 5.5 then we get back to the relation of Fig. 5.2, but that (b) information is lost in that process. Paraphrasing:

> Clearly, the design of Fig. 5.5 permits insertions and deletions not permitted by the design of Fig. 5.2. It is accordingly reasonable to say that these designs are not insertion-deletion equivalent.

All of which is true enough. But I think the paper should have gone on to say that if it's possible for a supplier to have a city even if the supplier in question currently supplies no parts, then the design of Fig. 5.2 is simply incorrect, because it doesn't faithfully reflect the true state of affairs in the real world. Or to put it another way: If the design of Fig. 5.2 did faithfully reflect the state of affairs in the real world, then relvars SP and SC would be subject to the following integrity constraint ("Every supplier number in SP appears in SC and vice versa"):

```
CONSTRAINT EQDX SP { SNO } = SC { SNO } ;
```

But this constraint—which is an example of what elsewhere I've called an *equality dependency* or *EQD*—obviously doesn't hold if it's possible for some supplier to exist without currently supplying any parts.

In brief, therefore, further normalization really addresses two rather different problems (and it would have been nice if the normalization paper had spelled that fact out explicitly):

1. It can be used to fix a logically incorrect design, as in the example above.

2. It can be used to reduce redundancy in an otherwise logically correct design.

Moreover, I tend to think the first of these is more important in practice than the second, though I also think the second has received rather more attention in the database world in general.

LOGICAL DATA INDEPENDENCE

In the introduction to this chapter, I said the normalization paper "helped lay the groundwork for what subsequently became known as *logical data independence*." Of course, it's well known now that views are the mechanism for achieving such independence (to the extent it can be achieved, that is). Now, the normalization paper never mentions the term *view* as such, but what it does have to say on the subject is tantamount to saying that views need to be supported:

> Now we wish to consider ... what happens to the application programs when the collection of [relvars] is ... changed to conform to a new [design] ... The really interesting type of change is replacement of a [relvar] R by two or more of its projections such that R may be recovered by taking the natural join of these projections ... We first examine a query and then an insertion. Each is expressed in the data base sublanguage ALPHA ...

I'll replace Codd's own sample query by one based on relvar SPC (sample value in Fig. 5.2) and its decomposition into projections SP and SC (sample values as in Fig. 5.4 or Fig. 5.5). The query is "Get the city for suppliers of part P1":

```
RANGE SPC SPCX

GET W ( SPCX.SCITY ) : ( SPCX.PNO = 'P1' )
```

The normalization paper continues as follows, except that I've revised the text to talk in terms of the foregoing example:

> When SPC is replaced by the two projections SP and SC, queries on SPC must undergo a transformation to make them work as before.[36] If the data base system were supplied with a suitable set of substitutions it could make this transformation automatically. We do not propose to go into the details here, but merely state that the resulting transformed query would be:

---

[36] Note in particular the implication that the relvar name SPC must still be available to the user and still be recognized by the system—but that name, which previously referred to a base relvar, must now refer to a view instead.

```
RANGE SP SPX
RANGE SC SCX

GET W ( SCX.SCITY ) : ∃SPX ( ( SCX.SNO = SPX.SNO ) ∧ ( SPX.PNO = 'P1' ) )
```

The real difficulty arises with insertion and deletion. [*And the paper goes on to explain some of the problems. It has little to say regarding solutions to those problems, however, so I won't bother to reproduce the pertinent text here.*]

Another remark that also touches on the subject of views appears later in the paper:

[If database relvars are all in 3NF as recommended, then] some queries will ... need to employ more join terms for cross referencing ... than might otherwise be the case. This potential burden on the user can be eased by user declared (and possibly pooled) cross referencing for heavily used types of queries.

MISCELLANEOUS COMMENTS

This final section consists of a few further general comments on the normalization paper that don't belong neatly in any of the foregoing sections and yet I don't want to lose.

■ On page 32, the paper says, in effect, that projecting a relation *r* on no attributes at all returns *r*, but this is wrong. In fact, the result of such a projection is TABLE_DUM if *r* is empty (i.e., contains no tuples), TABLE_DEE otherwise.[37]

■ There are a couple of places in the paper where Codd says, in effect, "Don't decompose too much." For example, after the decomposition illustrated in Fig. 5.3, the projection on ENO, ENAME, SALARY, and DNO is in 3NF, and probably shouldn't be decomposed any further, even though it could be. The justification given for this recommendation isn't all that convincing, though; basically, it's just "to keep the user from being confused by unnecessary [relvar] names (and to keep the system catalog from getting clogged by such names)." I would have thought a better rationale would be simply that such further decomposition just doesn't seem to buy us anything.[38]

In connection with the foregoing recommendation, Codd uses the terms *optimal second normal form* and *optimal third normal form*. A set of relvars is said to be in optimal

---

[37] Here Codd is simply repeating a mistake from his relational completeness paper. See Chapter 3, and footnote 17 in that chapter in particular.

[38] It would buy us something, though, if the name or the salary or the department number could ever be "missing" for some given employee. It's relevant to note here that relvar EMP is not just in 3NF but in fact in 5NF as well. By contrast, its projections on {ENO,ENAME}, {ENO,SALARY}, and {ENO,DNO} are all in 6NF, which—as noted in footnote 33—is in fact the "final normal form" with respect to projection and join. PS: Don't be misled by this example into thinking that 6NF relvars are always binary, nor that binary relvars are always in 6NF!

2NF if and only if (a) each relvar in the set is in 2NF and (b) the set contains the minimum number of relvars consistent with condition (a)—and likewise for optimal 3NF, mutatis mutandis. However, that "optimal" terminology never really caught on.[39]

- The paper is a little cavalier in its use of the labels "second normal form" and "third normal form" as qualifiers. What exactly is it that such labels actually apply to? Well, first of all, I've already complained that the paper suggests in its title that they apply to the relational model as such, but of course they don't. Second, the definitions given in the paper make it clear that they *do* apply to an individual relation (or relvar, rather). But then on page 12, and again on page 28, we find them being used to apply to *sets* of relvars (e.g., page 12 says "Both C1 and C2 are in second normal form," where C1 and C2 are definitely sets of relvars and not individual relvars as such). And then on pages 22 and 26 we find them being applied to the entire database!

  Of course, I'm not denying that it might be useful, as a shorthand, to talk about (e.g.) "a 3NF database," meaning a database in which all of the relvars are in 3NF. However, I do think an appropriate definition should be given, if only to head off at the pass objections like mine.

- Following on from the previous point, on page 28 we find this:

  > Thus, a relational model in second normal form, and more especially one in third normal form, is likely to be more readily understood by people who are not everyday users of the data.

  Note that indefinite article ("a" relational model)! No wonder there's so much confusion (confusion that persists to this very day) over the two rather different meanings of the term *data model*—or the term *relational model*, come to that.

- My final point is this. That business of 2NF or 3NF being "more readily understood" in the foregoing quote actually touches on another issue, one that I'd like to address by quoting at some length from my book *Database Design and Relational Theory: Normal Forms and All That Jazz* (O'Reilly, 2012):[40]

  > A glance at [*Fig. 5.2 in the present chapter*] is sufficient to show what's wrong with the design: It's *redundant*, in the sense that every tuple for supplier S1 tells us S1 is in London, every tuple for supplier S2 tells us S2 is in Paris, and so on. And normalization theory tells us that not designing the database in the obvious way will lead to such redundancy, and tells

---

[39] Codd actually goes on to say "It is ... conjectured that physical records in optimal third normal form will prove to be highly economical in [storage] space consumed." As noted in footnote 4, I find this remark rather unfortunate, suggesting as it does a "direct image" style of implementation (something I complained about in Chapter 2).

[40] As usual I've edited the quote lightly in order to make it fit better into the context of the present chapter.

us also (albeit implicitly) what the consequences of such redundancy will be. In other words, that theory is largely about reducing redundancy ... (As an aside, I remark that—partly for such reasons—the theory has been described, perhaps a little unkindly, as *a good source of bad examples.*)

Now, if normalization theory really does just bolster up your intuition, then it might be (and indeed has been) criticized on the grounds that it's really all just common sense anyway. By way of example, consider relvar SPC again. As I've said, that relvar is obviously badly designed; the redundancies are obvious, the consequences are obvious too, and any competent human designer would "naturally" avoid such a design, even if that designer had no explicit knowledge of design theory at all. But what does "naturally" mean here? What principles are being applied by that human designer in opting for a more "natural" (and better) design?

The answer is: They're exactly the principles that normalization theory talks about. In other words, competent designers already have those principles in their brain, as it were, even if they've never studied them formally and can't put a name to them or articulate them precisely. So yes, the principles are common sense—but they're *formalized* common sense. (Common sense might be common, but it's not always easy to say exactly what it is!) What normalization theory does is state *in a precise way* what certain aspects of common sense consist of. In my opinion, that's the real achievement—or one of the real achievements, anyway—of the theory: It formalizes certain commonsense principles, thereby opening the door to the possibility of mechanizing those principles (that is, incorporating them into computerized design tools). Critics of the theory often miss this point; they claim, quite rightly, that the ideas are mostly just common sense, but they don't seem to realize it's a significant achievement to state what common sense means in a precise and formal way.

Chapter 6

The Essentiality Paper

essential adj. absolute, basic, cardinal, characteristic, complete, constituent, constitutional, constitutive, crucial, definitive. elemental, elementary, formal, fundamental, ideal, important, indispensable, inherent, innate, intrinsic, key, main, necessary, needed, perfect, principal, quintessential, required, requisite, typical, vital

—Chambers Twentieth Century Thesaurus (1980)

The paper I'm calling "the essentiality paper" is the last of E. F. Codd's early papers on relational matters that I regard as really important. Here's a citation:

■ "Interactive Support for Nonprogrammers: The Relational and Network Approaches," IBM Research Report RJ1400 (June 6th, 1974)

Actually this paper was one of a pair. The other was:

■ "The Relational and Network Approaches: Comparison of the Application Programming Interfaces," IBM Research Report RJ1401 (June 6th, 1974)

The first of these two papers is attributed to "E. F. Codd and C. J. Date" and the second to "C. J. Date and E. F.Codd." Let me quickly explain! The truth is, Codd wrote the first paper and I wrote the second, but (for reasons that might possibly become clear in a few moments) Codd insisted on both of our names appearing on both. However, the first paper was far and away the better of the two.[1] The one by myself was merely a summary from an application programmer's point of view of the differences between the relational and network approaches, as those approaches were understood at the time; it was useful, perhaps, but it wasn't in any sense deep. By contrast, Codd's paper *was* deep; in fact, I now regard it as one of the best papers he wrote, though it seems to be have been very much overlooked by the community at large. Certainly it isn't much referenced in the literature. For such reasons, I'd like to give an overview of what I regard as the paper's major contributions. Before I do that, however, I should explain why we

---

[1] My contribution to that paper was limited to providing Codd with a few very minor technical details having to do with DBTG as an example of the network approach. (I also reviewed the draft, of course, but as I recall I had no comments on it at the time except positive ones.)

wrote the papers in the first place. In fact, they constituted our contribution to "The Great Debate" between proponents of the relational and network approaches,[2] which was held in May 1974 as part of that year's SIGMOD conference (or workshop, rather, since that was how it was described at the time). Of course, they were published in the conference proceedings:

- Randall J. Rustin (ed.), Proc. ACM SIGMOD Workshop on Data Description, Access, and Control, Volume II ("Data Models: Data-Structure-Set vs. Relational"), Ann Arbor, Michigan (May 1st-3rd, 1974)[3]

Now let me spell out what I regard as the essentiality paper's major contributions:

- First, it defined the notion of *essentiality*, an extraordinarily insightful and helpful notion that (a) went to the heart of the matter of The Great Debate, but (b) is actually of much wider and more general applicability and is still highly relevant today.

- Using that notion, it defined exactly what was meant (or ought to be meant) by the term *network database*—a term much used in discussions at the time, albeit one whose meaning certainly wasn't completely clear.

- It then raised a whole string of pertinent questions regarding the relational approach vs. others—questions that are even more pertinent today, given the current interest in such things as graph databases, key-value databases, XML databases, NoSQL databases, object databases, and on and on (not to mention SQL databases!).

HISTORICAL BACKGROUND

There were, of course, no mainstream relational products at the time of the debate; however, there was a great deal of interest in the possibility, or likelihood, that such products might materialize in the not too distant future. If I might be permitted a personal anecdote here ... In mid 1974, during the GUIDE 39 meeting in Anaheim, California,[4] I attended a working meeting

---

[2] I take this title from a report on the debate by Robert L. Ashenhurst that appeared the following month (i.e., in the June issue) of *Communications of the ACM*, of which Ashenhurst was Editor in Chief at the time.

[3] The workshop was held in May, but Volume II of the proceedings, which covered the debate, didn't appear until many months later, well after the date of publication of the papers as IBM Research Reports. To quote from the editor's foreword to that volume (viz., Volume II): "This volume is appearing much later than Volume I, and in fact much later than desired. This was due to unforeseen difficulties in transcription, editing, and organization ... What appears finally is a combination of submitted papers, heavy editing of some talks, and deletion of some material considered extraneous ... Special thanks must go to Susan Brewer for her part in reconstructing Charles Bachman's talk from a hopelessly garbled transcript." (Bachman was the principal proponent on the network side of the debate. "Data structure set" was his terminology; I think he used it as a way of avoiding the "network" label, which he seemed to be averse to for some reason.)

[4] GUIDE was one of the two major IBM user groups in the U.S. at the time (the other was SHARE).

of the GUIDE Database Programming Languages Project. The meeting was held just a few weeks after The Great Debate, possibly even in the same month—at this distance I don't recall precisely. My attendance was at the invitation of the IBM representative to the project, and I was there in order to answer questions about this new thing called relational database. Participants in the project had defined a set of five sample problems, and individual members had coded solutions to those problems using a variety of existing database products (IMS, TOTAL, IDS, and others), which they took turns to present to the rest of the group. Needless to say, the solutions were all quite complicated, each of them involving several pages of detailed code. So then I got up and was able to demonstrate that the five problems—which I'd come to cold (I mean, I'd never seen them before that afternoon)—could each be formulated as *a single line of code* in relational calculus. Well, I can assure you that everyone in the group was impressed, and indeed pretty excited at the possibilities.

As I say, then, there was a lot of interest—but there was competition, too. The CODASYL Data Base Task Group (DBTG) had published its *Report* in April 1971, proposing what became known as the network approach,[5] and of course that approach had its advocates too. Not only that, but the network approach had the advantage that commercial products did already exist— indeed, had existed for some time. So the likelihood of there being, sooner or later, some kind of confrontation between advocates of the two approaches was probably fairly high. When it came to the point, though, I was the one who caused it to occur ... Here's how it happened.

In July 1973, when I was still working for IBM in England, I had attended (again by invitation) a conference in Montreal, Canada: viz., the SHARE Working Conference on Data Base Management Systems (July 23rd-27th, 1973). I remember an awful lot of nonsense being talked at that event!—a state of affairs that made me realize that the database field was most certainly still in its infancy at the time. What made the conference interesting, though, was that Charles Bachman had just been named the 1973 ACM Turing Award winner, and he did a dry run for us of his Turing Award lecture "The Programmer as Navigator."[6]

Now, Charlie was the lead designer behind a system called IDS, which was the origin of the DBTG proposals mentioned above, and so Ted Codd and I—Ted was at the conference too, of course—already had a good idea of what he, Charlie, was going to say.[7] We also knew that the "navigational" (i.e., IDS or DBTG) ideas he was going to be describing were *not* the way to go—Ted's relational approach was. So of course Ted wanted to engage Charlie, and the audience, in an argument on the relative merits of the two schemes, right then and there. I

---

[5] By the way, I think it's fair to say that the widespread perception, which persisted for many years, that there were three broad approaches to "the database problem"—viz., the relational, hierarchic, and network approaches—was due largely to my own book *An Introduction to Database Systems* (1st edition, Addison-Wesley, 1975). In writing that book, I felt that for pedagogic reasons I needed to impose some kind of structure on what might otherwise have seemed to be just one giant disorganized mess. The structure I chose was inspired by a throwaway remark in the abstract to Codd's 1970 paper ("Existing ... data systems provide users with tree-structured files or slightly more general network models of the data"), and I divided the bulk of my book into three parts accordingly. Other books and publications then followed suit.

[6] His paper of that title was published in *Communications of the ACM 16*, No. 11 (November 1973).

[7] Forgive the familiarity here, but "Charlie" and "Ted" were how I knew and referred to Bachman and Codd, respectively, at the time, and the original notes I'm basing these explanations on weren't written to be all that formal.

wasn't too happy about that idea, though, because I knew that to do the job properly (a) we would need more time to prepare our position, and in any case (b) we would need more time to present that position, too—certainly more time than we could reasonably expect to be given, or would even be appropriate, in that SHARE conference environment. So I suggested to Ted that he not attempt to hold a proper debate with Charlie then and there, but rather that he issue a challenge to hold such a debate at some future event, perhaps at the next ACM SIGFIDET conference, which was due to be held in Ann Arbor, Michigan, the following May.[8] And Ted agreed.

So Charlie gave his talk. I could feel Ted almost quivering with anticipation in his seat next to me, waiting to leap up to the microphone the second Charlie finished. Of course, Ted and I both knew that the whole audience expected him to jump up and say *something*—probably offering some detailed technical criticism of what Charlie had presented. But what Ted actually did say was as follows, more or less: "First let me congratulate Charlie on his Turing Award. It couldn't happen to a nicer guy" (and so on and so forth) ... Then he continued: "But none of that alters the fact that on this issue Charlie is, unfortunately, *dead wrong*." And he went on to say that a Q&A session following a presentation wasn't the right forum for the kind of discussion that was really needed on these matters, and therefore that he and Chris Date would like to issue a challenge (etc., etc.). And so that was the origin of what came to be called The Great Debate, which was indeed held in Ann Arbor, Michigan, the following May, and was regarded by many people as one of the defining moments in the ongoing battle between the old way of doing things and Ted's new relational way.

Now, Ted and I took this debate very seriously, and we prepared a couple of detailed technical papers to support the arguments we planned to make: viz., the two papers already mentioned. The idea was that during the debate Ted would present the first paper and I would present the second. Unfortunately, however, the dates of the conference (May 1st-3rd, 1974) exactly clashed with the date of my move from England to California to start my California assignment for IBM, which was May 2nd. (As I recall, there was some complication or delay in my getting the necessary visas.) As a consequence I was unable to be present for the debate as such, and my presentation was given in my absence by Dionysios (Dennis) Tsichritzis, of the University of Toronto. But I don't think my absence mattered very much—Ted was clearly the man people wanted to hear, and what he had to say was far more important, as well as being much more innovative, than any contribution of mine could possibly have been.

---

[8] SIGFIDET stood for Special Interest Group on File Definition and Translation. By 1974, however, that name was beginning not to make much sense, and so that year the name was changed to SIGMOD (Special Interest Group on Management of Data).

ESSENTIALITY

Note: This section is heavily based on Chapter 11 ("Essentiality") of my book Relational Database Writings 1991-1994 (Addison-Wesley, 1995).

Of course, the battle between relations and networks is now ancient history (the good guys won). This fact notwithstanding, Codd's paper—even though it was written well over 40 years ago—is still worth reading today as a beautiful example of clear thinking. Indeed, it's quite remarkable to see how, on a topic where muddled thinking was the norm at the time, Codd was able to do such a good job of cutting through the confusion and focusing on the real issues. Let me elaborate.

- First of all, Codd realized that a comparison between the very concrete DBTG specifications and the much more abstract relational model would be an apples and oranges comparison and would involve numerous distracting irrelevancies.

- Hence, it would be necessary first to define an abstract "network model." The comparison could then be done on a level playing field, as it were, in a fair and sensible manner.

- Codd therefore proceeded to define an abstraction of the DBTG specifications that might reasonably be regarded as such a model (and then, of course, he went on to compare that abstraction with the equally abstract relational model).

As an aside, I note that Codd therefore has some claim to being the first person to give an abstract definition, not just of the relational model (of course), but also of a network model! Certainly none of the original IDS or DBTG proponents had ever attempted such a thing.

Anyway, Codd then went on to introduce the notion of essentiality, a notion that's critical to a proper understanding of data models in general and relations vs. networks in particular. To be specific, it's essentiality that allows us to pinpoint the crucial difference between relational databases and other kinds. And yet it's my experience that few database professionals really seem to be familiar with it; so let me take a few moments to discuss the basic idea.

To begin with, "everyone knows" that the only data structure available in the relational model is the relation itself.[9] To understand the significance of this point, however, it's necessary to know something about at least one other data structure: for example, the link structure found in hierarchic and network systems. So let's look at an example. Fig. 6.1 overleaf shows (a) a relational design for a simple departments-and-employees database, together with (b) a network analog of that design. (Actually the example is so simple that the network design degenerates to a mere hierarchy, but the differences between networks and hierarchies aren't important for

---

[9] This is Codd's well known *Information Principle*, of course (see Chapter 1).

present purposes. Hierarchies and networks are much more like each other than either one is like relations.)

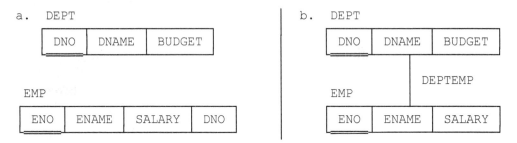

Fig. 6.1: Departments and employees–(a) relational design; (b) network design

The network design involves what the essentiality paper calls an *owner-coupled set* (not to be confused with a mathematical set—the two concepts are quite different). Each occurrence, or instance, of that owner-coupled set consists of one DEPT row (the owner); a set of corresponding EMP rows (the members); and one occurrence of a link ("DEPTEMP") that connects those DEPT and EMP rows together.[10] Within a given owner-coupled set occurrence, the corresponding link can be thought of as a chain of pointers—in the case at hand, a pointer from the owner DEPT row to the first member EMP row for that DEPT row, a pointer from that EMP row to the next EMP row for the same DEPT row, and so on, and finally a pointer from the last EMP row back to the original DEPT row.[11] *Note:* Those pointers don't need to be physically represented in storage by actual pointers, but the user can always think of them as actual pointers. That's the network model.

Observe now that the EMP rows in the network design don't include a DNO column. Thus, to find what department a given employee is in, we have to traverse the DEPTEMP link from the applicable EMP row to the corresponding DEPT row; likewise, to find the employees in a given department, we have to traverse the DEPTEMP link from the applicable DEPT row to the corresponding EMP rows. In other words, the information that was represented by a foreign key in the relational design is represented by a link in the network design. Links are the network analog of foreign keys (speaking *very* loosely).

Now let's consider a couple of sample queries against these two designs. For each one, I'll show a relational (or at least SQL) formulation and a network counterpart, using a hypothetically extended version of SQL that caters for links.

---

[10] I use the (comparatively!) neutral term *row* here rather than *record* (the network term) or *tuple* (the relational term) in order to avoid distractions caused by mere terminological differences between the two approaches. (Note too that I use the term *row* to mean a row *occurrence* specifically, not a row *type*.) Similarly, I use the comparatively neutral term *column* rather than *field* (the network term) or *attribute* (the relational term).

[11] In other words, the member rows within a given owner-coupled set occurrence don't just constitute a set as such, they constitute "a set with ordering," or in other words a list or sequence. But it's usual to refer to them as a set, even though such talk is really rather sloppy.

Q1: Get employee numbers and names for employees with salary greater than 20K.

```
Relational                          Network

SELECT  ENO , ENAME                 SELECT  ENO , ENAME
FROM    EMP                         FROM    EMP
WHERE   SALARY > 20K                WHERE   SALARY > 20K
```

Q2: Get employee numbers and names for employees with salary greater than 20K in department D3.

```
Relational                          Network

SELECT  ENO , ENAME                 SELECT  ENO , ENAME
FROM    EMP                         FROM    EMP
WHERE   SALARY > 20K                WHERE   SALARY > 20K
AND     DNO = 'D3'                  AND   ( SELECT  DNO
                                            FROM    DEPT
                                            OVER    EMP ) = 'D3'
```

For query Q1 the two formulations are obviously identical; for query Q2, however, they're obviously not. The relational formulation for Q2 still has the same basic form as for Q1 (SELECT – FROM – WHERE, with a simple restriction condition in the WHERE clause); the network formulation, by contrast, has to use a new language construct, the OVER clause (which is my hypothetical SQL representation of a link-traversing operation).[12] The WHERE condition in that formulation is certainly not just a simple restriction condition.

Query Q2 thus illustrates the point that networks fundamentally require certain additional data access operators. Note too that those operators *are* additional; the relational operators are still needed as well, as query Q1 shows. Note moreover that this point applies not only to manipulative operations (including updates as well as retrieval) but also to definitional ones (including security constraints, integrity constraints, and so on). Thus, the links of the network data structure certainly add *complexity*; however, they don't add any *expressive power*. To be specific, there's no data that can be represented by a network that can't be represented by relations, and there's no query that can be answered from a network and not from relations.

Now, it's sometimes suggested that the complexity in question can be reduced by reinstating the DNO column (the foreign key) in the EMP "table," as shown in Fig. 6.2 overleaf. This redesign allows query Q2 (network version) to be formulated without using the OVER construct; in fact, the formulation becomes identical to its relational counterpart. The reason is, of course, that DEPT and EMP in that revised design are identical to their relational analogs; the

---

[12] An UNDER clause is probably desirable too, if only for ergonomic reasons. For example, here's a hypothetical network formulation of the query "Get department numbers and names for departments with total employee salary greater than 200K": SELECT DNO, DNAME FROM DEPT WHERE (SELECT SUM (SALARY) FROM EMP UNDER DEPT) > 200K. (The reason I say "if only for ergonomic reasons" is that the same query could presumably also be formulated, albeit more clumsily, in terms of OVER, thus: SELECT DNO, DNAME FROM DEPT AS DX WHERE (SELECT SUM (SALARY) FROM EMP WHERE DEPT OVER EMP = DX) > 200K.)

database is now identical to its relational equivalent, except for that DEPTEMP link. But that link is now wholly redundant—it doesn't represent any information that isn't also represented by the foreign key, there's no logical need to use it, and in fact we can totally ignore it without losing any logical functionality.

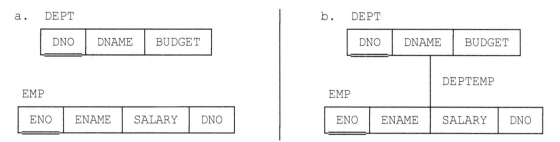

Fig. 6.2: Departments and employees—(a) relational design;
(b) network design with foreign key reinstated, link now inessential

So now I can explain the notion of essentiality. Basically, a data construct is *essential* if its loss would cause a loss of information—by which I mean, very precisely, that some relation would no longer be derivable. For example, in the relational version of departments and employees, all data constructs (in other words, all tables) are essential in this sense. Likewise, in the original network version of Fig. 6.1, all data constructs (that is, all "tables" and all links) are again essential. In the revised network of Fig. 6.2, however, the "tables" are essential, but the link is inessential: There's no information that can be derived from that network that can't be derived from the "tables" alone, and there's no logical need for the link at all.[13]

So now we can pin down the crucial difference between a relational database and any other kind, say a network database. In a relational database—and switching back now to proper relational, as opposed to SQL, terminology—the only essential data construct is the relation itself.[14] In other databases, *there must be at least one additional essential data construct* (typically an essential link, in the specific case of a network database). For if there isn't, then the database is really a relational database that happens to contain certain additional constructs[15]— and then the obvious question arises as to why those additional constructs are there anyway,

---

[13] Some have argued that the opposite could be the case (i.e., that it could be the link that's essential, and we don't need the foreign key). But that argument misses the point, which is that, since some tables—and hence (in effect) some rows and some columns—*must* be essential, and nothing else need be, then why have anything else?

By the way, it might help to point out that Codd's notion of essentiality can be seen as an application of Occam's Razor. (Thanks to François de Sainte Marie for this observation.) Occam's Razor, also known as the law, or principle, of parsimony, can be formulated in numerous different ways, but the one that I tend to prefer goes like this: Entities must not be multiplied beyond necessity (*Entia non sunt multiplicanda praeter necessitatem*).

[14] Codd's *Information Principle* again (see footnote 9). In fact, I believe it was Codd's work on essentiality that led him to formulate that principle. At least it's true that he had never stated it explicitly in any of his previous writings.

[15] If you try to defend the existence of those additional constructs, you'll eventually but inevitably be led to the point where you find yourself claiming that they somehow provide better performance. So why should those particular performance-oriented constructs be exposed to the user when others (e.g., indexes) aren't?

since there's no logical reason for the user to use them. And it's those additional essential constructs that lead to much (not all) of the complexity of nonrelational databases.

Note: In the case of DBTG specifically, there are at least four additional constructs that can also be used to carry information essentially. To get into details of those other DBTG constructs here would take us much too far afield, however, so for present purposes I simply propose to ignore them (for the most part, anyway).

A Remark on Ordering

The concept of essentiality helps explain why it's significant that relations have no ordering to their tuples: viz., that in an "ordered relation" or file, the ordering itself might be essential in the sense discussed above. For example, a file of temperature readings might be kept in the chronological order in which those readings were taken; the ordering itself might thus carry information, which would be lost if the records of the file were rearranged—just as, back in the old days, information could be lost if someone dropped a box of punched cards, if those cards didn't include a sequence field.[16] And essential ordering, like an essential link, requires additional operators to deal with it—"get the nth record," "insert a record between records n and $n+1$," "move the nth record to the mth position," and so on. For that reason it's not permitted in the relational model.

In contrast to the foregoing, it's sometimes suggested that *in*essential ordering might be acceptable. A file is inessentially ordered if its records are ordered on the basis of the value(s) of certain field(s); for example, the employee file might be ordered by employee number, but no information would be lost if the records were shuffled around. Some early "relational" systems did in fact support ordering in this sense. Note, however, that relations per se are unordered by definition; it would really be better to regard an "ordered relation" as a totally different kind of thing—perhaps as, precisely, a sequential file. Thus, e.g., the SQL ORDER BY operator is best thought of as converting a relation into such a file, rather than as "ordering a relation."

In any case, even inessential data constructs can cause problems, because they do still carry information. For example, they might represent a security risk. Suppose a file of employee records is ordered, inessentially, by increasing salary; then the fact that your manager's record appears in the file after your own certainly tells you something, even if you're not authorized to see actual salary values.

---

[16] If you're too young to know what boxes of cards and sequence fields are all about, then I envy you, and you can ignore this example.

STRUCTURE OF THE PAPER

Codd's essentiality paper consists of six main sections and a conclusion, together with a "historical footnote" and an appendix.[17] Here's a quote from the introductory section:

> Our objective in this paper is to explore the similarities and differences between the relational and network approaches to database management, with special emphasis on the topic of online interaction by nonprogrammers. To explain the marked differences between these two approaches ... we must raise the key question:
>
> ■ Do owner-coupled sets (see definition below) really belong in the principal schema;[18] and, if so, what is their role?
>
> The CODASYL DBTG proposal ... is used as an example of the network approach, because it has been widely publicized and because several implementations are being developed. However, we do not wish to dwell on the already well known (and as yet, in the literature, unanswered) shortcomings of DBTG in the matter of data dependence and overly implicit cursor controlled [update] and retrieval ... We agree with these criticisms as far as they go, but feel we must probe further in the interest of better understanding of both the relational and network approaches.[19]

I have two broad comments on this text. First, the implicit criticisms (i.e., regarding owner-coupled sets) in what Codd calls "the key question" are equally applicable to all and any constructs other than relations that bear information essentially. And the same goes, mutatis mutandis, for all of the arguments the paper subsequently makes, and all of the questions it subsequently raises, regarding owner-coupled sets specifically; all of them can and should be generalized to apply to those other constructs. Of course, Codd was well aware of this state of affairs; he limited his attention in his paper to owner-coupled sets specifically only because the primary purpose of the paper, at the time, was to argue against the network approach specifically. But I'd like to suggest, as you read either the original paper or the commentary on that paper in the present chapter, that whenever it makes sense to do so you mentally replace the term

---

[17] The "historical footnote" consists simply of a brief explanation of the fact that the relational approach was developed independently of, and in fact earlier than, the DBTG proposals (and thus was definitely not developed as just "a response to" those proposals). Here's a lightly edited quote: "The first report on the relational approach as currently understood appeared in August 1969, some two months prior to publication of the first DBTG report. In addition, public lectures on the relational model were presented in Europe and the U.S. during October and November 1969." As for the appendix, I'll discuss that toward the end of the present chapter.

[18] *Principal schema* was Codd's term for what others have referred to as the conceptual schema, the logical schema, the community schema, and a variety of other things. *Schema* in turn is just a fancy term for a data definition or set of data definitions.

[19] Later, Codd adds the following (very lightly edited here): "The reader is cautioned to avoid comparing approaches solely on the basis of differences in data structure. An adequate appreciation of the differences must entail consideration of the operators also." And still later he adds: "Discussions on the relational approach often become riveted on the data structure component to the neglect of other components. To do justice to the relational approach, all components must be considered as a package."

owner-coupled set by the phrase "owner-coupled set (or any other data construct, apart from relations, that might be used to bear information essentially)."[20]

My second general comment is this. I believe that all, or almost all, of the features of the relational approach that Codd goes on to claim as being advantageous from the point of view of the nonprogrammer are actually advantageous from the programmer's point of view as well. Now, Codd's argument (and of course I agree with him) is that nonprogrammer access to the database actually *requires* the relational features in question; however, it would be a pity if the essentiality paper was therefore regarded as a paper for nonprogrammers only and not for programmers.

OBJECTIVES AND STRATEGIES

To repeat, Codd wants to "explain the marked differences between," and to "probe further in the interest of better understanding of," the relational and network approaches. To that end, in Section 2 of his paper ("The Two Approaches"), he first introduces his concept of essentiality, and then he goes on to examine the two approaches in the light of that concept. In particular, he considers the respective objectives and strategies of the two approaches, because "it is not enough to take note of where these approaches stand today—we must also be clear about where they are going." Here then is Codd's definition of essentiality:

> **Definition (essentiality per Codd):** A data structure declaration D is *essential* (from an information standpoint) in a schema U if there is an instantaneous database B conforming to U such that removal from B of the structure specified by D causes loss of information from B (i.e., some relation is no longer derivable).

I do have a quibble here, though. To be specific, I note that the things that can be either essential or inessential according to Codd's definition are *declarations in schemas*. I think it would be clearer to consider the essentiality notion as applying to the *data constructs themselves*—i.e., the data constructs that are defined by those declarations in schemas. For example, consider the schema corresponding to part (a) of Fig. 6.1 (or Fig. 6.2, it doesn't matter which). That schema might look something like this in **Tutorial D**:

```
VAR DEPT BASE RELATION
  { DNO DNO , DNAME NAME , BUDGET MONEY }
    KEY { DNO } ;

VAR EMP BASE RELATION
  { ENO ENO , ENAME NAME , SALARY MONEY , DNO DNO }
    KEY { ENO }
    FOREIGN KEY { DNO } REFERENCES DEPT ;
```

---

[20] Sorry, yes, I know it's clunky, but I think you take my point.

Codd would say that both of these definitions (VAR statements) are essential; I would prefer to say that it's the DEPT and EMP relvars per se—i.e., the variables defined by those statements—that are essential.

Similarly, consider the schema corresponding to part (b) of Fig. 6.1. To invent some syntax on the fly—specifically, syntax that allows the definition of an owner-coupled set—that schema might look something like this:

```
VAR DEPT BASE RELATION
   { DNO DNO , DNAME NAME , BUDGET MONEY }
     KEY { DNO } ;

VAR EMP BASE RELATION
   { ENO ENO , ENAME NAME , SALARY MONEY }
     KEY { ENO } ;

VAR DEPTEMP OCSET
     OWNER DEPT
     MEMBER EMP ;
```

Here Codd would say that all three VAR statements are essential; I would prefer to say that it's the DEPT and EMP relvars per se, plus the DEPTEMP link per se,[21] that are essential.

For completeness, here's a possible schema corresponding to part (b) of Fig. 6.2 (note the foreign key that's been added to relvar EMP and the corresponding specification MATCHING DEPT in the definition of the owner-coupled set):

```
VAR DEPT BASE RELATION
   { DNO DNO , DNAME NAME , BUDGET MONEY }
     KEY { DNO } ;

VAR EMP BASE RELATION
   { ENO ENO , ENAME NAME , DNO DNO , SALARY MONEY }
     KEY { ENO }
     FOREIGN KEY { DNO } REFERENCES DEPT ;

VAR DEPTEMP OCSET
     OWNER DEPT
     MEMBER EMP MATCHING DEPT ;
```

In this example Codd would say that the first two VAR statements are essential and the third is inessential, but I would prefer to say that it's the DEPT and EMP relvars per se that are essential and the DEPTEMP link per se that's inessential.

Anyway, the paper continues:

---

[21] Or, rather, the DEPTEMP owner-coupled set per se. As previously in this chapter (and subsequently as well), I focus on the link, synecdochically, because of course it's the link that's the crucial—I'm tempted to say essential—aspect of any given owner-coupled set.

It is in the principal schema that we find one of the important distinctions between the relational and network approaches.

- In the relational approach the principal schema employs only one type of data aggregate to represent the entire information content of the database—namely, the nonhierarchic, *n*-ary relation. Ordering may be used, but only *inessentially* ... [22]

- In the network approach there is at least one owner-coupled set in the principal schema bearing information *essentially*.

Objectives

Under this heading the paper first cites some objectives for the relational approach:[23]

1. Provide a high degree of data independence

2. Provide a community view of the data of spartan simplicity, so that a wide variety of users in an enterprise (ranging from the most computer-naïve to the most computer-sophisticated) can interact with a common model (while not prohibiting superimposed user views for specialized purposes)

3. Simplify the potentially formidable job of the database administrator

4. Introduce a theoretical foundation (albeit modest) into database management (a field sadly lacking in solid principles and guidelines)

5. Merge the fact retrieval and file management fields in preparation for the addition at a later time of inferential services in the commercial world

6. Lift data-based application programming to a new level—a level in which sets (and more specifically relations) are treated as operands instead of being processed element by element

It then invites consideration of certain remarks from Bachman's Turing Award paper:[24]

1. "The Integrated Data Store (IDS) system and all other systems based on its concepts consider their basic contribution to the programmer to be the capability to associate records into [owner-coupled]

---

[22] Personally I would prefer (a) to drop that "nonhierarchic" qualifier (it has to do with Codd's flawed definition, discussed in Chapter 5, of first normal form), and also (b) to drop the remark about ordering (it's a red herring at best). I would also like to make it clear that as far as data constructs in the database are concerned, we should really be talking about relvars, not relations. But these points are all somewhat irrelevant, or at any rate minor, in the present context.

[23] The objectives are repeated from Codd's paper "Recent Investigations into Relational Data Base Systems," Proc. IFIP Congress, Stockholm, Sweden (1974).

[24] Charles W. Bachman, "The Programmer as Navigator," *Communications of the ACM 16*, No. 11 (November 1973).

sets and the capability to use these sets as retrieval paths. All the COBOL DBTG systems fall into this class."

2. "My proposition today is that it is time for the application programmer to abandon the memory-centered view, and to accept the challenge and opportunity of navigation within an *n*-dimensional data space."

3. At the end of his paper Bachman specifically proposes to "provide the [application] programmer with effective tools for navigation."

And Codd's discussion of objectives for the two approaches finishes up as follows:

From these statements together with the significant role of owner-coupled sets in the DBTG data manipulation language, one can conclude that the network approach as exemplified by DBTG is primarily concerned with the provision of tools for *programmers* and, in particular, tools to enable programmers to do their own *navigating* or *searching* in the database. This objective is in sharp contrast to that of the relational approach ... The absence from the DBTG proposal of any specific objectives for the support of nonprogrammer interaction is especially noteworthy.

Strategies

Under this heading the paper first cites the following "four main components" of "the relational strategy":

1. Simplify to the greatest practical extent the types of data structure employed in the principal schema (or community view)

2. Introduce powerful operators to enable both programmers and nonprogrammers to store and retrieve target data *without having to "navigate" to the target*

3. Introduce natural language (e.g., English) with dialog support to permit effective interaction by casual (and possibly computer-naïve) users[25]

4. Express authorization and integrity constraints separately from the data structure (because they are liable to change)[26]

It then cites the following "two main components" of "the network strategy":

---

[25] In connection with this possibility, see E. F. Codd: "Seven Steps to Rendezvous with the Casual User," IBM Research Report RJ1333 (January 7th, 1974), republished in J. W. Klimbie and K. L. Koffeman (eds.), *Data Base Management*, Proc. IFIP TC-2 Working Conference on Data Base Management (North-Holland, 1974).

[26] I agree strongly with this point. In fact I've recently come to the conclusion that it was a mistake even for key definitions to be bundled in with relvar definitions.

1. Provide a rich set of alternative types of data structure in the principal schema

2. Provide numerous alternative tools for accessing and traversing these structures using a "level of procedurality...about equal to that of COBOL"

And it concludes:

> As yet, there is no published strategy for DBTG (and more generally, the network approach) to support online interaction by [nonprogrammer professionals] or casual users. There is merely the statement in [the DBTG report] that this problem is deferred, and the claim[27] that DBTG "provides a solid foundation for such self-contained capabilities."

QUESTIONS CONCERNING OWNER-COUPLED SETS

At the heart of the essentiality paper is a series of crucial questions concerning owner-coupled sets (questions, needless to say, that have never been satisfactorily answered in the open literature)—and here perhaps I should remind you of my suggestion to the effect that whenever it makes sense to do so, you should mentally replace the term *owner-coupled set* by the phrase "owner-coupled set (or any other data construct, apart from relations, that might be used to bear information essentially)."

Before getting into those questions, however, the paper first defines something it calls, rather clumsily, "the NP/ARC capability":

> [Part of] the relational approach is the concept of a *relationally complete data sublanguage*. Such a language has at least the retrieval power[28] of ... first order predicate calculus ... [Such] a capability is a basic one and should be augmented by a library of functions. For example, the functions COUNT, TOTAL, AVERAGE, MAXIMUM, MINIMUM, would be needed in almost any application environment ... For nonprogrammers (abbreviated NP) it is essential that such an augmented, relationally complete, retrieval capability (abbreviated ARC) be provided *without* branching, explicit iteration, and cursors.[29] When this condition is fulfilled, we refer to the retrieval capability as NP/ARC. A language [is] said to have the NP/ARC capability if it not only provides relational completeness without branching, explicit iteration, and cursors, but includes provision for function invocation to condition the selection of data and to transform the data selected from the database.

---

[27] Personally I would have said the *unsubstantiated* claim.

[28] I greatly prefer the term *expressive power* myself (i.e., rather than retrieval power), but then the ARC abbreviation wouldn't make sense. At least, it wouldn't make sense if the "RC" in that abbreviation stands for "retrieval capability"—but actually I think it stands for "relationally complete," though the cited text from Codd's paper isn't clear on the point.

[29] The reference to cursors here is intended, primarily, as a reference to the DBTG construct known as "currency indicators," not to cursors as understood in SQL. (SQL cursors do have problems of their own, but they're not nearly as complicated and error prone as DBTG currency indicators are.)

The first few questions then have to do with the importance of *closure* in connection with the foregoing:

■ In the relational model the union, intersection, or difference of any two union-compatible relations is a relation; every projection and every [restriction] of a relation is a relation; every join of two relations is a relation. These closure properties are important in realizing the NP/ARC capability. When part of the information in a database is carried in an essential way by owner-coupled sets, these closure properties do not apply to this part. For example, how do you define a union operation for owner-coupled set occurrences that retains ownership information for each member record *and* yields a result that is an owner-coupled set occurrence?

Or more generally:

■ Can the NP/ARC capability be supported while retaining the owner-coupled set as an essential information-bearing data [construct] in the principal schema?

Two subsidiary questions follow on from the foregoing:

■ If the owner-coupled set has to be relegated to the role of bearing information inessentially, what is its intended role in the principal schema?

■ If [that] role is to act as an inter-relation cross index in order to provide better performance, why is it not treated like other indexes and hidden from both programmers and nonprogrammers, so that their programs and interactions can become more data independent?

The paper then turns to what it calls "fidelity questions":

Claims have been made ... that the network approach and, in particular, the owner-coupled set permit more natural or faithful modeling of the real world than the relational model [does]. Such claims are not easy to support or refute, because our present knowledge of what constitutes a good data structure for solving a given class of problems is highly intuitive and unsystematic ... However, we can observe that many different kinds of geometry, topology, and graphs (or networks) are in use today for solving "real world" problems. Relations tend to be neutral toward these problem-solving representations and yet very adaptable to supporting any of them ... On the other hand, the owner-coupled set gives rise to a [very] specific kind of network, and is accordingly ... convenient in some contexts and ... awkward in others. It is convenient when the application involves collections of sets, each of which has both a descriptor and a simple total ordering of its elements. It is awkward when the application involves partial orderings (e.g., PERT charts), loops (e.g., transportation routes), values associated with network links (e.g., utility networks), many to many binary relations, relations of degree greater than two, and variable depth, homogeneous trees (e.g., organization charts) ... These considerations give rise to what we call the *separation question*:

■ Should we continue to enrich the variety of data [constructs] available for use in the principal schema so that it may model the real world more faithfully *or* should we make available only those data [constructs] that contribute to ease of control by the database administrator and by the system itself, together with ease of use by the majority of users who have only trivial interactions?

[Choosing the latter alternative] implies that the burden for providing support for specialized problem-solving representations is shifted from the principal schema to the user schemas and, hence, falls on specialized packages for the pertinent problem classes.

The paper also asks what it calls a psychological question:

■ Can [nonprogrammers] reliably retrieve information using the network model [*i.e., assuming the existence of essential owner-coupled sets*]? Can they update information using [that] model?

And the paper's "Conclusion" section raises still more questions and is, I think, worth quoting pretty much in its entirety:

In the past, many designers of software systems and languages have confused two quite distinct notions: enrichment of features on the one hand, and generality of application on the other. A crucial issue in database management systems is that of the richness (i.e., variety) of data [constructs] that should be supported in the principal schema. In the event that enrichment of these data [constructs] beyond the minimum one is proposed, we ask the following questions:

■ As far as the *system* is concerned, are not more retrieval operators ... needed? Are not the concurrency and authorization controls more complicated? Hence, is not the implementation more complicated and therefore less reliable?

■ As far as the *programmers* and *nonprogramming users* are concerned, are they not subjected to an increased burden in deciding which structures to access and which operators or commands to apply? Is there not an increased probability of error and, when errors are discovered, is there not an increased variety of remedial actions to consider?

■ As far as the *database administrator* is concerned, are there not too many structural choices with few, if any, dependable guidelines for making those choices? Are not the mappings between the logical and physical levels more complicated to define and maintain? Are not security and privacy constraints more complicated to specify?

And on that note the body of the paper, and my detailed review of it in this chapter, both conclude. I should mention, however, that the paper does have quite a bit more to say than I've suggested in my review. In particular, it proposes what it calls "a relational discipline" that might serve as "a way out for DBTG users." That way out consists in essence of including in the principal schema only those DBTG constructs that have a fairly close counterpart in the relational approach (basically a "system owned set" for each record type[30]). That said, however, Codd adds that "some words of caution are perhaps appropriate here." Here are some of them:

■   First, this discipline does little to reduce the programming complexities associated with DBTG [*and here Codd references the essentiality paper's companion paper*].

■   Second, attempts to impose a discipline on the use of a software package are likely to be ineffective unless the package itself provides automatic enforcement of this discipline.

■   Third, if the package was not originally designed to operate with this discipline as a normal mode, it may need some tuning to obtain the desired performance. In particular, some extra inter-relation indexing may be needed "beneath the covers" to compensate for owner-coupled sets that are dropped altogether from the principal schema.

Further, he also points out that:

Clearly, adoption of this relational discipline does not immediately yield the full relational approach. It merely places DBTG implementations on the bottom rung of the relational ladder [*this metaphor is explained in Fig. 3 of the essentiality paper, but what it primarily means is that "the NP/ARC capability" is still not supported*], with the potential handicap of concurrency controls, integrity controls, and logical to physical mapping designed more for the network than the relational context.

ESSENTIALITY REVISITED

Essentiality as originally defined by Codd has to do with the data constructs that appear in some specific database (or, more precisely, with the declarations of those constructs that appear in that database's schema). But I think the concept can usefully be generalized, such that we can say that (a) the relational model involves just one essential construct (viz., the relation itself), while (b) the network model involves at least two (viz., something vaguely like a relation, plus the owner-coupled set). The following definitions are aimed at this goal.

First of all, we need to recognize that, unfortunately, the term *data model* has historically been used (and still is used) to mean two rather different things in the database world. The first and more fundamental meaning is as follows:

Definition (data model, first sense): A data model in the first sense is an abstract, self-contained, logical definition of the data structures, data operators, and so forth, that

---

[30] Be aware, however, that there are numerous logical differences—far too many of them to enumerate here—between DBTG "system owned sets" in general, on the one hand, and relations (or relvars) on the other. In other words, using a system owned set to simulate a relation (or relvar) would require a great deal of additional discipline on the part of the database designer, and possibly the database user as well. Further details are beyond the scope of this chapter.

together make up the abstract machine with which users interact. This is the meaning we have in mind when we talk about "the relational model" in particular—or "the network model," come to that.

The second meaning is as follows:

Definition (data model, second sense): A data model in the second sense is a model of the persistent data of some particular enterprise. In other words, it's just a logical design for some particular database.

Now I can give my preferred and slightly generalized definition of the concept of essentiality:

Definition (essentiality, extended definition): Let *DM* be a data model in the first sense, and let *DS* be a data structure supported by *DM*. Let *dm* be a data model in the second sense, constructed in accordance with the features provided by *DM*, and let *dm* include an occurrence *ds* of *DS*. Let *db* be a database conforming to *dm*. If removal from *db* of the data corresponding to *ds* would cause a loss of information from *db*, then *ds* is essential in *dm* (and, loosely, *DS* is essential in *DM*).

By this definition, both of the following are true:

■ The owner-coupled set DEPTEMP is essential in the database corresponding to part (b) of Fig. 6.1.

■ Owner-coupled sets in general are essential in the network model.

Following on from the foregoing definition, I'd like to quote the following extract from my book *The New Relational Database Dictionary* (O'Reilly, 2016):[31]

[Network] and other nonrelational systems provide numerous different ways of representing data, any or all of which can be used "essentially"—links and pointers, record ordering, repeating groups, and so forth. By contrast, relational systems provide just one way (viz., relations themselves), and so relations themselves are the sole essential information carrier in relational systems. Now, if data model *DM* [*where DM is a data model in the first sense of that term*] provides *n* distinct ways, essential or inessential, of representing information, then it's axiomatic that *DM* must also support *n* distinct sets of operators. However, there's nothing useful that can be done if $n > 1$ that can't be done if $n = 1$ (and $n = 1$ is the minimum, of course). And for the relational model, we do have $n = 1$; that is, the relational model supports just one data structure, the relation itself, and that data

---

[31] Of course, the text quoted really just repeats (and elaborates on, somewhat) material from Codd's essentiality paper, and I've I've commented on some of that material already.

structure is clearly essential, since if it were removed that model would be incapable of representing anything at all. However, since the relational model is in fact capable of representing absolutely any data whatsoever, any data model that supports relations in some shape or form as well as some additional data structure *DS* must be such that either relations are inessential or *DS* is. But if relations are inessential, then *DS* must be effectively equivalent to relations anyway!—in which case it could be argued that it's really *DS* that's inessential, not relations. What's more, a data model that doesn't "support relations in some shape or form" is unlikely in the extreme; even SQL could be said to support relations if various SQL idiosyncrasies—nulls, anonymous columns, duplicate rows, etc.—are avoided. Thus, for example, pointers (object IDs), bags, lists, and arrays could all be removed from the so called object model without any loss of representational power. Indeed, the fact that they're not removed is prima facie evidence that "the object model" fails to distinguish properly between model and implementation issues.

THE COMPARATIVE EXAMPLE

As a kind of bonus, the essentiality paper includes an appendix giving a detailed example coded in (a) DBTG and (b) Codd's own ALPHA language (see Chapter 4). The following is a lightly edited version of the paper's own introduction to the example:

> In a recent tutorial paper[32] Frank and Sibley selected an example to illustrate the application of the DBTG proposal. The sample database includes information about persons (identification number, name, birthdate, and salary), medical histories (identification number of person, "absent from" date, "absent to" date, disease, and comment), education (person's identification number, degree, university name, university start date, university stop date), jobs (job number, identification number of person who did the job, actual start date, actual stop date, and performance rating), machines (machine number, machine type), schedules (job number, identification number of person assigned, scheduled start date, scheduled stop date), skills (skill number, skill description), the possession of skills by persons (person identification number, skill number), and alternative skills needed to operate machines (machine number, skill number) ... The sample application can be stated as follows: Given machine X, a job number Y, the desired start date A for the job, and the desired stop date B, find the identification number of a person who has a skill appropriate for the operation of machine X, and who is not scheduled at all between date A and date B; schedule this person, if one is located.

Comment: As is so often the case with such examples, this one is far more complicated than it need be. To be specific, all that's needed for the sample application in relational terms is one relation (or relvar, rather) showing who has which skills; another showing which skills are needed to operate which machine; and another showing who's available when (i.e., who's not already scheduled for some job, the details of which are irrelevant). I suppose the objective might be to show a database definition, or schema, that involves as many different DBTG

---

[32] R. L. Frank and E. H. Sibley: "The Data Base Task Group Report: An Illustrative Example," ISDOS Working Paper No. 71, U.S. National Technical Information Service Document AD-759-267 (February 1973).

features as possible; but then I observe that Frank and Sibley's schema raises all kinds of additional questions and seems to be incomplete anyway (e.g., it mentions various procedures but doesn't define them).[33] Anyway, here's Frank and Sibley's schema, for what it's worth:

```
SCHEMA NAME IS EMPLOYEE-BASE;
     PRIVACY LOCK IS SCHED-SCHEMA
          OR PROCEDURE SECURE-SCHEDULE;
     AREA NAME IS PANDJ-AREA.
     AREA MED-AREA;
     PRIVACY FOR UPDATE IS PROCEDURE MED-DEPT.
     AREA SECRET; ON OPEN CALL SECURE-PROC;
     ON CLOSE CALL LOCK-PROC.
     AREA REST; PRIVACY IS PROCEDURE SCHED-DEPT
          OR PROCEDURE SECURE-PROC.
     AREA XP; AREA IS TEMPORARY; PRIVACY TEMP-AREA.
RECORD NAME IS PERSON;
     LOCATION MODE IS CALC EMP-HASH USING
          IDENTIFICATION-NUM DUPLICATES ARE NOT ALLOWED;
     WITHIN PANDJ-AREA;
     ON DELETE CALL MICROFILM-RECORDER;
     PRIVACY LOCK FOR DELETE ONLY IS PROCEDURE EMP-LEFT.
          NAME; PICTURE IS "A(20)".
          IDENTIFICATION-NUM; PICTURE IS "9(6)".
          DATE-OF-BIRTH; PICTURE IS "99X99X99".
     1 AGE; PICTURE "99V9"; IS VIRTUAL RESULT OF
          AGE-CALC USING DATE-OF-BIRTH, TODAYS-DATE.
     1 SALARY; TYPE IS FIXED 7,2; CHECK IS RANGE OF
          8000.00 THRU 75000.00.
     1 EDUCATION; TYPE FIXED 2.
     1 EDUCATION-INFO; OCCURS EDUCATION TIMES.
          2 DEGREE; PICTURE "AA".
          2 START-DATE; PICTURE "99X99X99".
          2 COMPLETION-DATE; PICTURE "99X99X99", CHECK
               NOT-BEFORE USING EDUC-OK, START-DATE.
          2 DEGREE-RECEIVED-FROM PIC "A(20)".
RECORD NAME JOB;
     LOCATION IS VIA JOBSET SET;
     WITHIN PANDJ-AREA.
     1 JOB-CODE; PIC "X(4)".
     1 START-DATE; PIC "99X99X99".
     1 FINISH-DATE; PIC "99X99X99".
     1 PERFORMANCE-RATING; PIC "99V9".
RECORD IS MEDICAL;
     LOCATION MODE CALC USING DISEASE DUPLICATES
          ARE ALLOWED;
     WITHIN MED-AREA.
     1 ABSENCE-DATES; PICTURE "99X99X99X99X99X99".
     1 DISEASE; PICTURE IS "A(30)".
     1 NOTE-PAGES; TYPE IS REAL FIXED DECIMAL 2.
     1 NOTES; OCCURS NOTE-PAGES TIMES.
          2 NOTE-PAGE; PICTURE "A(500)".
```

---

[33] But then I've copied that schema from the essentiality paper, and Codd must have copied it in turn from the original, so it's possible that there could be transcription errors on my part or Codd's or both.

```
RECORD NAME IS MACHINE; LOCATION MODE IS CALC
     MACH-HASH USING MACH-NUMBER
     DUPLICATES NOT ALLOWED;
     WITHIN REST, SECRET AREA-ID MACH-LOCATOR;
     PRIVACY LOCK PROCEDURE IS-IT-SECURE.
     1 MACH-TYPE; PICTURE "999".
     1 MACH-NUMBER; PICTURE "9(5)".
     1 SCHEDULE; PICTURE "99".
     1 SCHEDULED-USE; OCCURS SCHEDULE TIMES.
          2 JOB-CODE; PICTURE "9(8)".
          2 SCHEDULE-COMPLETION; TYPE IS DATE.
          /* NOTE IMPLEMENTOR-TYPE DATE. */
          2 SCHEDULE-START; TYPE IS DATE.
          2 WORKER-IDENTIFICATION; PICTURE "9(6)".
     /* NOTE THERE WOULD BE OTHER ELEMENTS,
          BUT IRRELEVANT TO THIS EXAMPLE */
RECORD SKILL-LINK; LOCATION MODE IS CALC
     USING SKILL-CODE, DUPLICATES ALLOWED;
     WITHIN REST.
     1 SKILL-CODE; PICTURE "999".
     1 SK-SALARY;
          VIRTUAL SOURCE IS SALARY OF OWNER OF HAS-SKILL.
     1 JOB-RATE; PICTURE "9(2)V9(2)";
          IS VIRTUAL RESULT OF AVERAGE-RATE
          USING SK-SALARY.
     1 MACH-SK; VIRTUAL SOURCE IS MACH-TYPE
          OF OWNER OF NEEDS-SKILL.
RECORD NAME IS CHECK-PERSON;
     LOCATION MODE IS CALC USING CHECK-PERSON-ITEM
          DUPLICATES NOT ALLOWED;
     WITHIN XP.
     /* NOTE: THIS IS THE TEMPORARY AREA. */
     01 CHECK-PERSON-ITEM;
          TYPE IS DATABASE-KEY.
     /* NOTE: THIS ASSUMES THAT A CALC-KEY
          CAN BE A DATABASE-KEY. */
RECORD NAME IS CHECK-MACHINE;
     LOCATION MODE IS CALC USING CHECK-PERSON-ITEM;
          DUPLICATES NOT ALLOWED;
     WITHIN XP.
     01 CHECK-MACHINE-ITEM;
          TYPE IS DATABASE-KEY.
SET NAME IS JOBSET;
     ORDER IS NEXT;
     OWNER IS PERSON.
     MEMBER IS JOB, MANDATORY, AUTOMATIC;
     SET OCCURRENCE SELECTION IS THRU CURRENT OF SET.
SET NAME IS MEDSET;
     ORDER IS LAST;
     OWNER IS PERSON.
     MEMBER IS MEDICAL, OPTIONAL, AUTOMATIC,
     SET OCCURRENCE SELECTION IS THRU CURRENT OF SET.
```

```
SET NEEDS-SKILL;
     ORDER IS SORTED DUPLICATES ARE ALLOWED;
     OWNER IS MACHINE.
     MEMBER IS SKILL-LINK OPTIONAL MANUAL
          LINKED TO OWNER;
     DESCENDING KEY SKILL-CODE;
     SET SELECTION THRU CURRENT OF SET.
SET NAME IS HAS-SKILL;
     ORDER IS SORTED DUPLICATES ARE FIRST;
     OWNER IS PERSON.
     MEMBER IS SKILL-LINK OPTIONAL MANUAL
          LINKED TO OWNER;
     ASCENDING KEY SKILL-CODE;
     SELECTION IS LOCATION MODE OF OWNER.
SET NAME IS WORKING-ON;
     ORDER LAST;
     OWNER IS PERSON.
     MEMBER IS MACHINE OPTIONAL MANUAL LINKED TO OWNER
     DUPLICATES NOT ALLOWED FOR SCHEDULE-START;
     SEARCH KEY IS SCHEDULE-START, MACH-NUMBER USING INDEX
          NAME IS MACH-WORK-INDEX DUPLICATES ARE NOT ALLOWED;
     SET OCCURRENCE SELECTION IS THRU
          LOCATION MODE OF OWNER.
     /* NOTE THIS IS CALC. */
SET SYS-MACHINE;
     ORDER IS SORTED INDEXED NAME IS MACHINE-INDEX
     DUPLICATES ARE NOT ALLOWED;
     ON REMOVE CALL SINKING-FUND;
     PRIVACY LOCK FOR REMOVE IS PROCEDURE MACH-AWAY;
     OWNER IS SYSTEM.
     MEMBER IS MACHINE OPTIONAL AUTOMATIC;
     ASCENDING KEY IS MACH-NUMBER.
     /* NOTE NO SELECTION CLAUSE FOR SINGULAR SETS. */
```

Next (to quote from the essentiality paper):

Except for one or two very minor omissions (e.g., the calculation of age from birth date, privacy locks and keys), the following code sets up a relational schema for the sample database ...

And the paper goes on to define several domains and several relations (relvars) based on those domains. Here, however, I choose to show only those domains and relations (relvars) that are pertinent to the sample application:

```
DOMAIN JOBNO   PIC X(4)
DOMAIN PNO     PIC 9(6)
DOMAIN MACHNO  PIC 9(5)
DOMAIN DATE    PIC 99X99X99
DOMAIN SKILLNO PIC 999
```

```
RELATION SCHED ( JOBNO , PNO , MACHNO ,
                         SCHED_START_DATE , SCHED_STOP_DATE )
        KEY ( JOBNO )
RELATION PERSON_SKILL ( PNO , SKILLNO )
        KEY ( PNO ,SKILLNO )
RELATION MACH_SKILL ( MACHNO , SKILLNO )
        KEY ( MACHNO , SKILLNO )
```

Codd then shows what he calls "an ALPHA program" for the sample application[34] that consists of just three statements:

```
GET (into workspace) W (at most) (1) PERSON_SKILL.PNO : (such that)
     EXIST MACH_SKILL (with
            MACH_SKILL.MACHNO = X
      & MACH_SKILL.SKILLNO = PERSON_SKILL.SKILLNO
      & NOT EXIST SCHED (with
               SCHED.PNO = PERSON_SKILL.PNO
            & SCHED.SCHED_START_DATE < B
            & SCHED.SCHED_STOP_DATE > A ) )

MOVE W INTO SCHED_RECORD .....(host language)

PUT SCHED_RECORD (into) SCHED
```

The paper also includes Frank and Sibley's DBTG code for the same application:

```
IDENTIFICATION DIVISION.
     PROGRAM-ID. SCHEDULE-PERSON-TO-MACHINE.
     PRIVACY KEY FOR COMPILE IS 'START-SCHEMA';
     PRIVACY KEY OF REST AREA IS PROCEDURE 'DEPT-SCHED'.
     AUTHOR. R.L.FRANK AND E.H.SIBLEY.
     DATE-WRITTEN. JANUARY 1973.
ENVIRONMENT DIVISION.
DATA DIVISION.
SCHEMA SECTION.
     INVOKE SUB-SCHEMA
          SCHEDULE-ID OF SCHEMA EMPLOYEE-BASE.
FILE SECTION.

WORKING-STORAGE-SECTION.

PROCEDURE DIVISION.
     OPEN PANDJ-AREA, WITH-HOLD, REST.
     OPEN nonDBTG files.
FIND-MACHINE.
     OPEN XP.
     MOVE MACHINE-NUMBER TO MACH-NUMBER.
     FIND MACHINE RECORD VIA SYS-MACHINE USING
          MACH-NUMBER.
     IF ERROR-STATUS = 326 GO TO
          NOT-IN-DATA-BASE.
```

---

[34] There are some minor syntactic discrepancies between the dialect of ALPHA illustrated here and the dialect described in Codd's ALPHA paper (see Chapter 4), but the details are unimportant for present purposes .

```
FOUND-REC.
    MOVE CURRENCY STATUS FOR MACHINE RECORD TO
        SAVE-MACHINE.
GET-NEXT-SKILL.
    FIND NEXT SKILL-LINK RECORD OF NEEDS-SKILL SET.
    IF ERROR-STATUS = 326 OR = 307 GO TO NO-ONE-AVAILABLE.
    FIND OWNER IN HAS-SKILL OF CURRENT OF SKILL-LINK RECORD.
    IF ERROR-STATUS = 322 THEN GO TO GET-NEXT-SKILL.
    MOVE CURRENCY STATUS FOR PERSON RECORD
        TO SAVE-PERSON.
    MOVE CURRENCY STATUS FOR
        PERSON RECORD TO CHECK-PERSON-ITEM.
    STORE CHECK-PERSON.
    IF ERROR-STATUS = 1205
        GO TO GET-NEXT-SKILL.
CHECK-PERSONS-SCHEDULE.
    FIND NEXT SKILL-LINK RECORD OF HAS-SKILL SET;
        SUPPRESS NEEDS-SKILL CURRENCY UPDATES.
    IF ERROR-STATUS = 307 GO TO PERSON-IS-FREE.
    FIND OWNER IN NEEDS-SKILL OF CURRENT OF SKILL-LINK RECORD;
        SUPPRESS NEEDS-SKILL CURRENCY UPDATES.
    IF ERROR-STATUS = 322
        GO TO CHECK-PERSONS-SCHEDULE.
    MOVE CURRENCY STATUS FOR MACHINE RECORD TO CHECK-MACHINE-ITEM.
    STORE CHECK-MACHINE.
    IF ERROR-STATUS = 1205 GO TO CHECK-PERSONS-SCHEDULE.
    GET MACHINE.
    MOVE 1 TO AVAILABLE.
    PERFORM SEE-IF-SCHEDULED THRU SEE-EXIT VARYING
        SCHEDULE-COUNT FROM 1 BY 1 UNTIL SCHEDULE-COUNT
        IS GREATER THAN SCHEDULE.
    IF AVAILABLE = 0 GO TO GET-NEXT-SKILL.
    GO TO CHECK-PERSONS-SCHEDULE.
SEE-IF-SCHEDULED.
    /* NOTE: HERE WE WILL MARK AS NOT BEING AVAILABLE
        ANYONE WHO IS SCHEDULED FOR THAT TIME. */
    IF SCHEDULE-DATE-START IS GREATER THAN SCHEDULE-START
        IN MACHINE (SCHEDULE-COUNT) AND LESS THAN
        SCHEDULE-COMPLETION IN MACHINE (SCHEDULE-COUNT)
        GO TO PERSON-NOT-AVAILABLE.
    IF SCHEDULE-DATE-END IS GREATER THAN SCHEDULE-START
        IN MACHINE (SCHEDULE-COUNT) AND LESS THAN
        SCHEDULE-COMPLETION IN MACHINE (SCHEDULE-COUNT)
        GO TO PERSON-NOT-AVAILABLE.
    GO TO SEE-EXIT.
PERSON-NOT-AVAILABLE.
    FIND PERSON USING SAVE-PERSON,
        SUPPRESS ALL CURRENCY UPDATES.
    GET PERSON.
    IF IDENTIFICATION-NUM IN PERSON IS EQUAL
        WORKER-IDENTIFICATION IN MACHINE
        (SCHEDULE-COUNT) MOVE 0 TO AVAILABLE,
        GO TO SEE-EXIT.
    MOVE WORKER-IDENTIFICATION IN MACHINE
        (SCHEDULE-COUNT) TO IDENTIFICATION-NUM IN PERSON.
    FIND PERSON RECORD, SUPPRESS HAS-SKILL
        CURRENCY UPDATES.
```

```
        MOVE CURRENCY STATUS FOR PERSON RECORD
              TO CHECK-PERSON-ITEM.
        STORE CHECK-PERSON.
SEE-EXIT. EXIT.
PERSON-IS-FREE.
        /* NOTE: HERE WE GET THE MACHINE WE WANTED TO SCHEDULE. */
        FIND MACHINE USING SAVE-MACHINE.
        GET MACHINE.
        FIND PERSON USING SAVE-PERSON.
        GET PERSON.
        ADD 1 TO SCHEDULE IN MACHINE.
        MOVE IDENTIFICATION-NUM IN PERSON TO WORKER-IDENTIFICATION
              IN MACHINE (SCHEDULE IN MACHINE).
        MOVE SCHEDULE-DATE-START TO SCHEDULE-START IN MACHINE
              (SCHEDULE IN MACHINE).
        MOVE SCHEDULE-DATE-END TO SCHEDULE-COMPLETION IN MACHINE
              (SCHEDULE IN MACHINE).
        MOVE SCHEDULE-TASK TO JOB-CODE IN MACHINE (SCHEDULE IN
              MACHINE).
        MODIFY MACHINE.
        IF ERROR-STATUS = 803
              GO TO PERSON-IS-FREE.
        CLOSE XP.
        GO TO GET-NEW-MACHINE.
```

Well, the relative simplicity of the relational solution is very striking! What's more (although the essentiality paper doesn't mention the fact), the DBTG "solution" actually contains at least two currency errors[35]—by which I mean errors in logic, not just simple syntax errors, of which there does also seem to be at least one.

Anyway, what the essentiality paper does say is that "Some comparative statistics may be of interest":[36]

	DBTG	ALPHA
GO TO	15	0
PERFORM UNTIL	1	0
currency indicators	10	0
IF	12	0
FIND	9	0
GET	4	1
STORE / PUT	2	1
MODIFY	1	0
MOVE CURRENCY	4	0
other MOVEs	9	1
SUPPRESS CURRENCY	4	0
total statements	>60	3

---

[35] A "currency error" in DBTG occurs when the position in the database that's represented by one of the implicit currency indicators—see footnote 29—isn't what the application programmer thinks it is.

[36] For reasons not worth discussing in detail, the table of statistics as shown above differs in certain minor respects from that given in the essentiality paper.

And the paper adds:

These statistics should not be interpreted as a criticism of Frank and Sibley. Their objective was to provide a tutorial on the application of DBTG, and in this respect they succeeded rather well.[37] The important thing to note is the elimination (in the ALPHA code) of branching, explicit iteration, and cursor control—an essential step toward providing general support for the nonprogramming user, and a desirable step toward removing a large burden of irrelevant decision-making by the programmer.

Finally, I observe that Codd actually missed a couple of tricks in connection with the foregoing example. The first is that the "three statements" of the relational solution could actually be compressed into just one!—viz., a PUT (into SCHED); the GET and the MOVE aren't strictly necessary. I show such a solution below, but for reasons of familiarity I switch now to SQL instead of using Codd's ALPHA language:

```
INSERT INTO SCHED ( PNO , MACHNO , JOBNO , START , STOP )
       SELECT PNO , X , Y , A , B
       FROM   PERSON_SKILL
       WHERE  EXISTS
            ( SELECT *
              FROM   MACH_SKILL
              WHERE  MACHNO = X
              AND    SKILLNO = PERSON_SKILL.SKILLNO
              AND    NOT EXISTS
                   ( SELECT *
                     FROM   SCHED
                     WHERE  PNO = PERSON_SKILL.PNO
                     AND    START_DATE < B
                     AND    STOP_DATE > A ) ) ;
```

The second trick I think Codd missed (or perhaps he didn't miss it but simply thought the point was obvious, given the title of his paper) is that, given that a procedural program as such isn't needed for the problem at hand, the foregoing solution could actually be produced by a nonprogrammer!—at least so long as the nonprogrammer in question understands a little bit of elementary logic, an assumption that I think would be warranted in the case at hand.

In closing, I should point out in the interest of accuracy that there's a small semantic difference between the foregoing ALPHA and SQL solutions. To be specific, the ALPHA solution uses a quota query—see Chapter 4—to find *at most one* suitable candidate for the job and schedules that person. By contrast, the SQL solution finds all such candidates, not just one, and then attempts to schedule them all (an attempt that will fail on a key uniqueness violation if the number of candidates found is greater than one). But I don't think this comparatively minor discrepancy should be allowed to detract from the overall message, which is surely clear.

---

[37] Indeed they did, but of course Codd's comment can be interpreted in at least two ways. Myself, I think Codd meant *exactly* what he said here.

Part III

CODD'S LATER WRITINGS

This part of the book examines two of the more significant of Codd's later writings:

- A two-part paper published in *Computerworld*, "Is Your DBMS Really Relational?" and "Does Your DBMS Run By The Rules?"

- His book *The Relational Model for Database Management Version 2*

The first of these is discussed in Chapter 7 and the second in Chapter 8.

Chapter 7

The Relational Model Version 1

There is only one religion,
though there are a hundred versions of it.

—George Bernard Shaw:
Preface to *Plays Pleasant and Unpleasant*, Vol. II (1898)

Sometime in the late 1980s I wrote a paper with the title "Notes Toward a Reconstituted Definition of the Relational Model Version 1 (RM/V1)," and included it as a chapter in my book *Relational Database Writings 1989-1991* (Addison-Wesley, 1992). The abstract to that paper read as follows:

Codd's 1985 definition of the relational model is summarized and criticized, and an alternative definition suggested.

As you can see, that abstract was rather terse! I elaborated on it somewhat in the following additional preamble to the paper (lightly edited here):

In 1985, Codd published reference [5],[1] which contained among other things the latest in a succession of definitions of the relational model. As the foregoing abstract indicates, the purpose of this paper is, in part, to criticize that definition. Now, it's well known that I've been a relational advocate for many years, and I certainly don't wish to be thought of as criticizing the basic idea of the relational model per se; on the contrary, I felt at the time when Codd first introduced it, and I still feel now, that his original papers on the model [1,2] were a work of genius, and he fully deserves all of the recognition that has come his way as a result of that major contribution. But the 1985 definition bothered me in several respects—it extended the original ideas in what seemed to me to be some rather questionable ways—and I felt it necessary to offer a dissenting opinion. And indeed I did exactly that, articulating a variety of concerns, both in print and in live discussion, both with Codd himself and with other database professionals, on numerous occasions during the late 1980s. Until I wrote the present paper, however, I hadn't tried to draw all of my objections together into a single published document (although some of them did find their way, in somewhat muted form, into the fifth edition of my book *An Introduction To Database Systems*).

---

[1] Numbers in square brackets in this chapter refer to publications listed in the section "References and Bibliography," which is located near the end of the chapter, immediately before the appendix.

The paper that follows, then, originated as an attempt to identify various aspects of Codd's 1985 definition that bothered me. For each such aspect, the paper explains just why I felt there was cause for concern, or it gives a reference to some other publication that contains such an explanation, or both. But, of course, the very act of articulating my concerns gave rise, inevitably, to a proposal—or at least the beginnings of a proposal—for an alternative definition of my own. The emphasis of the paper thus changed in the writing; I now feel its significance (what significance it might have) lies not so much in the fact that it documents a dissenting opinion, but rather in the fact that it makes a set of explicit proposals for revision—in other words, it suggests a "reconstituted definition" of the relational model, offered in all humility as a replacement for the version of reference [5].

Note: In a recent book [6], Codd has described what he calls Version 2 of the model, referring to the previous version as Version 1.[2] The present paper is concerned with Version 1 only; however, since Version 2 is intended to be an upward compatible extension of Version 1, the criticisms it levels at Version 1 apply to Version 2 also. I do feel strongly that it's important to get the foundation (i.e., "Version 1") right first before attempting to extend that foundation to any kind of "Version 2."

All of that said, I have to say too that I now find my original critique of reference [5] deficient or inadequate in a variety of ways, some of them fairly nontrivial. Hence the present chapter, which consists essentially of a heavily revised and expanded version of the critique portion of that original paper.

OVERVIEW

The relational model was introduced by Codd in references [1] and [2] in 1969 and 1970, respectively. Refined and extended definitions were given by Codd in 1979 [3] and again in 1982 [4]. Then, in 1985, Codd revised his definition yet again [5]. According to that 1985 definition, the model consisted of the following "nine structural features, three integrity features, and 18 manipulative features":

■ Structural features:

S1	Relations	S6	Attributes
S2	Base tables	S7	Domains
S3	Query tables	S8	Primary keys
S4	View tables	S9	Foreign keys
S5	Snapshot tables		

---

[2] I'm assuming here that Codd is using the term "Version 1" to refer to the 1985 version specifically, although in fact reference [6] isn't clear on this point—on the one hand, it says (page vi) that Version 1 consists of "the total content of [a series of papers published prior to 1979]"; on the other hand, it also says (page 10) that Version 1 contains "approximately 50 features," whereas the 1985 version (which certainly has more "features" than the pre 1979 versions did) still contains only 30.

■ Integrity features:

I1   Entity integrity   I3   User defined integrity
I2   Referential integrity

■ Manipulative features:

M1   θ-select   M10   Relational assignment
M2   Project   M11   θ-select maybe
M3   θ-join   M12   θ-join maybe
M4   Outer θ-join   M13   Outer θ-join maybe
M5   Divide   M14   Divide maybe
M6   Union   M15   θ-select semantic override
M7   Intersection   M16   θ-join semantic override
M8   Difference   M17   Outer θ-join semantic override
M9   Outer union   M18   Divide semantic override

As I've said, however, I had a number of concerns regarding the foregoing definition when it first appeared; moreover, I still have those concerns (and more) now, and the purpose of this chapter is to explain the nature of those concerns in some detail.

Note: In order to forestall one possible criticism of what follows, I should make it clear that the definition of the relational model in reference [5] is quite informal: so much so, in fact, that some might claim that it's not really a definition at all, and hence that to criticize it as if it were is inappropriate. However, reference [5] is the only one of Codd's publications, so far as I know, that even attempts to define the scope of the model as he perceived it in the mid 1980s. What's more, his 1990 book [6] certainly builds on the material from reference [5]. I therefore feel it *is* appropriate to examine and analyze that material from a critical perspective.

Without further ado, then, let me proceed to examine the definition of the model as given in reference [5].

STRUCTURAL FEATURES

General Comments

I have to say at the outset that I have major reservations regarding the way Codd's list of structural features is itself structured, and so I'd like to start out by offering some general comments on that list as such.

First of all, the most important structural feature surely has to be the relation itself; the system simply *has* to support relations, for otherwise there's no way it can reasonably be called relational in the first place. But relations have attributes, so support for relations implies support for attributes; and attributes in turn are defined over domains (or as I would greatly prefer to call them, types), so support for attributes implies support for domains, or types, as well. What's more, relations contain tuples, so support for relations implies support for tuples too. With regard to Codd's list, therefore, Feature S1 ("relations") is clearly a sine qua non. However, I don't understand how it makes sense to treat Features S6 ("attributes") and S7 ("domains") as having equal weight with that feature, nor as having equal weight with each other;[3] nor do I understand, if Feature S6 does have to be included in the list, why there isn't a "tuples" feature as well, of equal weight.

Now, it's not my intention in this chapter to give my own preferred definition of the relational model in full and formal detail, but I do think it's worth giving my own preferred definition (or sequence of definitions, rather) for the term *relation* itself—partly to give some idea of what I think a full and formal definition of the relational model might look like, and partly because this particular definition, or sequence of definitions rather, is so obviously fundamental.[4] *Note:* I give these definitions more for interest than for anything else; I don't think you need to study them carefully, unless you want to. Do observe, however, how they rely on the definition (not included here) of the notion of *type*.

> **Definition (heading):** A *heading H* is a set, the elements of which are *attributes*. Let H have cardinality n $(n \geq 0)$; then the value n is the *degree* of H. A heading of degree zero is *nullary*, a heading of degree one is *unary*, a heading of degree two is *binary*, ..., and more generally a heading of degree n is *n-ary*. Each attribute in H is of the form $<Aj,Tj>$, where Aj is the *attribute name* and Tj is the corresponding *type name* $(0 < j \leq n)$, and the attribute names Aj are all distinct.

> **Definition (tuple):** Let heading H be of degree n. For each attribute $<Aj,Tj>$ in H, define a *component* of the form $<Aj,Tj,vj>$, where the *attribute value vj* is a value of type Tj. The set—call it t—of all n components so defined is a *tuple value* (or just a *tuple* for short) over the attributes of H. H is the *tuple heading* (or just the heading for short) for t, and the degree and attributes of H are, respectively, the degree and attributes of t.

> **Definition (body):** Given a heading H, a *body B* conforming to H is a set of m tuples $(m \geq 0)$, each with heading H. The value m is the *cardinality* of B.

---

[3] I can speculate, though. I suspect the reason why Codd wanted separate "domains" and "attributes" features was that—aware that he'd failed to do so adequately in references [4] and [5] (and then later criticizing others, myself included, for making that very same mistake!)—he wanted to make it clear now that domains and attributes were distinct concepts, and indeed to stress the fact that there was an important logical difference between them.

[4] These definitions are repeated from Chapter 2.

Definition (relation): Let *H* be a heading, and let *B* be a body conforming to *H*. The pair *<H,B>*—call it *r*—is a *relation value* (or just a *relation* for short) over the attributes of *H*. *H* is the *relation heading* (or just the heading for short) for *r*, and the degree and attributes of *H* and the cardinality of *B* are, respectively, the degree, attributes, and cardinality of *r*.

Aside: In a still more complete and formal definition, I would add the following among other things:

a. Every tuple is of some *tuple type*. Every relation is of some *relation type*.

b. Tuple types and relation types are types.

c. Two tuples are of the same type if and only if they have the same heading. Two relations are of the same type if and only if they have the same heading.

End of aside.

I haven't finished with my complaints about the overall structure of Codd's list of structural features; I turn now to Features S2 ("base tables"), S3 ("query tables"), S4 ("view tables"), and S5 ("snapshot tables").

■ First of all, I don't much care for the descent from the terminology of relations as used in Feature S1 to that of tables (and, accordingly, from the terminology of attributes and tuples to that of columns and rows) in these features, but let that pass.

■ Much more important, it's really difficult to talk about the concepts Codd is attempting to grapple with in Features S2-S5 without first introducing the all important distinction between relation *values*, or just *relations* for short, and relation *variables*, or *relvars* for short. Sadly, Codd never did accept that distinction, at least not properly (or if he did, he certainly never admitted as much in his writings). Never mind; for present purposes I'm going to assume that you at any rate do accept the distinction and indeed are familiar with it, and I'm going to change the text (though not the titles) of Codd's various features accordingly—Features S2-S5 in particular—by replacing "tables" by "relvars" or "relations" or both, as applicable, throughout what follows. For the most part, moreover, I'll make those replacements silently, in order to avoid an unsightly excess of square brackets in quoted text. Note, incidentally, that relvars are always explicitly declared and named; relations, by contrast, are neither.[5]

---

[5] Though in practice a system might, and indeed probably should, provide a way of declaring *relation constants*, and those constants will of course have names. You can think of a relation constant, *very* loosely, as a relation variable that's given a particular value—a relation value, of course—when it's declared and is never updated. In fact, TABLE_DEE and TABLE_DUM (see Chapter 3, footnote 17) are examples of such constants, and very important ones at that.

- Features S2, S4, and S5 all have to do with the distinction between base relvars and other kinds (Feature S3 is rather different, and I'll get to that in a moment). The "other kinds" in question—which I'll refer to generically as derived relvars—are views (Feature S4) and snapshots (Feature S5). Now, I certainly agree it's necessary—in some contexts but not all!—to make such a distinction. But surely the right way to do so is simply to say something like this: A derived relvar is one that's defined in terms of other relvars (its definition in terms of those other relvars is given by some relational expression that's specified when the derived relvar itself is defined), and a base relvar is one that's not derived (it corresponds, loosely, to what SQL means by a "base table").

- By contrast, Feature S3 is, as already noted, rather different in kind from Features S1-S2 and S4-S5. In fact it's hardly a "structural feature" as such at all, and it's really not clear what it's doing here. To be specific, the feature merely asserts (in essence) that the result of a query is a relation. Of course that's true; but note how important that business of distinguishing between relations and relvars becomes; the result is indeed a relation, not a relvar, but what reference [5] actually says is "the result is a *table*" (my italics), and of course the term *table* is ambiguous as we know. Note too that the result of evaluating *any* relational expression is a relation; queries as such have nothing to do with it,[6] and I don't really know why they're dragged into the discussion at all.

Finally, with respect to Features S8 ("primary keys") and S9 ("foreign keys"). My principal complaint here is simply that these features are in the wrong place—surely they belong in the integrity part of the model. But since Codd places them in the structural part, I'll have more to say about them, in the pertinent subsections, later in the present section.

Now I turn to some more detailed comments on individual structural features (i.e., Features S1-S9) from Codd's list. I'll consider them one by one.

S1 Relations

Feature S1 requires support for "relations of assorted degrees—or equivalently tables with unnumbered rows, named columns, no positional concepts, and no repeating groups." Some comments:

- "Assorted degrees" should include the case of degree zero, something that Codd's writings usually seem to omit (see, e.g., reference [6], page 2 and, more especially, page 20).

---

[6] I could be charitable to Codd here and assume he's adopting the deprecated but common usage according to which the term *query* is used to mean a relational expression. But if so, then I have to ask: What term does he use for a query? (Personally, I prefer to use the term *query* to mean the formulation of some retrieval request in English or some other natural language—e.g., "Get names and salaries of employees in department D8.")

■ I think it would be worth stating explicitly, at least in the context of an informal definition such as this one, that relations never contain duplicate tuples, and hence that operations such as projection (Feature M2) always eliminate duplicates from their result.

■ I think it would also be worth stating explicitly that if *r* is a relation in the database, then no attribute of *r* is allowed to contain any pointers. (I'm sure Codd would agree with this position, but he doesn't say as much explicitly in reference [5].)

■ By contrast, one thing Codd does say explicitly in reference [5] is "no repeating groups"— i.e., if *r* is a relation, then every value of every attribute of *r* must be "atomic." For reasons explained elsewhere, however (see, e.g., reference [15]), I don't agree with this one, mainly because it doesn't seem to be possible to give the term "atomic value" any very precise definition. In particular, I believe that "relation valued attributes" (RVAs) should be legal—i.e., it should be legal for a relation to have an attribute whose values are relations in turn.[7]

S2 Base Tables

Feature S2 requires support for "base relvars representing the stored data." But I've explained elsewhere that base relvars don't necessarily "represent the stored data," at least not directly (see reference [10] and, more especially, reference [13]).[8] And in any case, how in practice could a system possibly support relations (Feature S1) and not support base relvars?

S3 Query Tables

As already noted, Feature S3 states that the result of a query is a relation. Of course I agree, but I observe that this state of affairs is just one consequence (or, perhaps, one specific case) of the more general, and more fundamental, requirement of support for closure (see the "Manipulative Features" section later).

Note: Reference [5] also says the result of a query can be "saved and later operated on." Again I agree, but this state of affairs is just one consequence of the more general, and more fundamental, requirement of support for relational assignment (see Feature M10).

---

[7] Actually I might be persuaded to agree with "no repeating groups"—it all depends on what the term *repeating group* really means. But I definitely don't want to prohibit RVAs, and I believe Codd does.

[8] Indeed, I would argue that views "represent stored data" just as much as base relvars do. In fact, the real point here has nothing to do with "stored data," as such, at all; rather, it has to do with that business I mentioned a couple of pages back—viz., the need to draw a distinction between base and derived relvars—and I think Codd here was merely groping, unsuccessfully, for a way to make that distinction.

S4 View Tables

Feature S4 requires support for "virtual relvars that are represented internally by one or more relational commands, not by stored data." I'd prefer to say simply that the system must allow any relational expression to be used in a view definition.[9] *Note:* There was a time when certain products, and indeed the SQL standard itself, failed to abide by this requirement; for instance, they didn't allow UNION to appear in such a context. (The standard has since been fixed in this regard, however, and so have the leading products.)

Incidentally, Codd frequently uses the term *command* (not just in the wording of Feature S4 but elsewhere in reference [5], and indeed in many other writings also) when *expression* or *operator* would be much more appropriate. In the world of computing, the term *command* is usually taken to be synonymous with *statement*. Thus, use of the term in Feature S4 in particular suggests that a view definition might legitimately involve a sequence of several statements—in other words, a procedure—which of course isn't what was intended. Incidentally, I note in this connection that Feature S4 doesn't just talk in terms of commands as such, it explicitly talks about "*one or more* relational commands" (my italics).[10] Of course, I'm sure Codd didn't intend *commands* to be equated with *statements* in this particular case, but the possibility of such misinterpretation is there.

To pursue the point a moment longer: Talking in terms of operators instead of commands (or statements) stresses, or at least tends to stress, the idea that *expressions* are the proper basis for formulating queries, defining views and snapshots, and so on. Note that an expression is really nothing but a request for invocation of some operator, in which the operands if any are denoted by further expressions (subexpressions of the original expression). In my opinion, a system that's properly designed around the concept of expressions is much more likely to possess such desirable properties as closure, orthogonality, parsimony, generality, flexibility, and so on, than one that's designed around something else (commands, for example).

S5 Snapshot Tables

Feature S5 requires support for "relvars that are evaluated [*sic*] and stored in the database, together with an entry in the catalog specifying the date and time of their creation." I'd prefer to say simply that the system must allow any relational expression to be used in a snapshot definition.[11] As for that business of recording the date and time of creation in the catalog, surely that's better seen as a separate and subsidiary requirement. (In any case, why does Codd mention it in connection with snapshots and not in connection with views?) What's surely much

---

[9] Any relational expression, that is, that includes a relvar reference. (If there were no such references, then the expression would denote a constant value, and the view would thus not be a relation *variable*, as such, at all.)

[10] As Hugh Darwen has pointed out (in a private communication), this requirement, if taken literally, would imply that a statement of the form CREATE VIEW WORKER AS EMPLOYEE—which ought to be legal in SQL, though in fact it isn't—wouldn't be a valid view definition, because it involves no "relational commands" at all.

[11] If snapshots need to be mentioned in connection with the model at all, which is something I'm far from convinced about.

more important, at least as far as snapshots as such are concerned, is that the system should automatically "refresh" the snapshot at prescribed intervals—for otherwise the requirement can be trivially satisfied by means of relational assignment (see Feature M10).

S6 Attributes

Feature S6 says: "Each column of each relation and/or relvar is an attribute." [12] Now, reference [5] doesn't explicitly say as much, but I believe the term "attribute" here is intended to include the case of composite—also known as compound—attributes,[13] as discussed in Chapter 3 of this book. If so, then I have to disagree. (My reasons for taking this position are documented in detail in reference [12].) What we do want is proper type support (see the next item below), and then the "compound attribute" requirement—such as it is—will come out in the wash.

S7 Domains

Feature S7 requires the system to support domains, where a domain is "the set of values from which one or more attributes obtain their values." Well, every system must necessarily provide *some* kind of domain support, even if it's limited to nothing more than support for elementary data types such as numbers and strings; so in a sense the requirement as stated is vacuous. Much more important, however, is the question of what a domain really is, and hence what true domain support would consist of. It's my position—apparently very different from Codd's—that a domain is neither more nor less than a type, possibly (and often desirably) user defined.[14] And my concern with respect to Feature S7 as stated is that if an implementation treats domains just as "sets of values from which one or more columns obtain their values" *and nothing more*, then that implementation is likely to be "half baked [and] difficult to extend correctly in the future" (to quote reference [8]).

In the interest of precision, I note too that the phrase "one or more attributes" in Codd's statement of this feature ought really to be "*zero* or more attributes."

S8 Primary Keys

Feature S8 says: "Each base relvar has one or more attributes whose values identify each tuple of that relvar uniquely." I have several comments on this one:

---

[12] The wording here is actually quite odd. If *column* is replaced (as indeed it really ought to be) by *attribute*, it reduces to "Each attribute ... is an attribute" (?).

[13] It certainly is so intended in Version 2 of the model [6] (see Chapter 8 of the present book).

[14] Unfortunately I can't tell you exactly what Codd's position is on the matter of domains vs. types, because I don't understand it, and in fact I don't think it makes sense. But it's discussed in reference [6], if you want to try to understand it for yourself. It's also discussed briefly in Chapter 2 of the present book.

■ I firmly believe in keys in general—what we used to call *candidate* keys—but I no longer believe in primary keys specifically (at least, not in the context of the formal relational model as such, though they might have some pragmatic role to play in database design).

■ I also firmly believe that all relvars have keys, not just base relvars. To state the matter more precisely, (a) every relvar has a nonempty set of keys; (b) every such key consists of some subset—possibly the empty subset—of the set of attributes of the relvar in question; and (c) every such key should be declared (unless it can be inferred by the system, perhaps, which might possibly be the case for certain derived relvars).[15]

■ On the other hand, it's hard to know what support for keys of any kind could consist of in the absence of manipulative considerations. Merely being able to declare that some set of attributes of relvar *R* is a key for *R* isn't particularly useful in itself. In other words, as mentioned previously, I think that Feature S8 should be moved from the "structural" list to the "integrity" list (and there presumably relabeled).

■ In the interest of precision, I note that the phrase "one or more attributes" in Codd's statement of this feature ought really to be "zero or more attributes."

S9 Foreign Keys

Feature S9 requires the system to support foreign keys, where a foreign key is "any attribute ... that is [defined] on the same domain as the primary key of some base relvar." Again I have several comments:

■ As with keys in general (see Feature S8), I'm in favor of foreign key support, but it's hard to know what such support could consist of in the absence of manipulative considerations. Merely being able to declare that some set of attributes of relvar *R2* is a foreign key referencing relvar *R1* isn't particularly useful in itself. In other words, as mentioned previously, I think this feature, like Feature S8, should be moved from the "structural" list to the "integrity" list (and there presumably relabeled).

■ Contrary to Codd's wording of the text of this feature, it's not the case that "any attribute defined on the same domain as the primary key of some base relvar" is necessarily a foreign key. Counterexamples are easily provided (exercise for the reader).

■ Contrary to Codd's wording of the text of this feature, it's not the case that a foreign key has to consist of a single attribute. To state the matter more precisely, (a) every relvar has a possibly empty set of foreign keys; (b) every such foreign key consists of some subset—

---

[15] Of course, if it isn't declared (or perhaps inferred), then it isn't really a key at all as far as the DBMS is concerned.

possibly the empty subset—of the set of attributes of the relvar in question; and (c) every such foreign key should be declared (unless it can be inferred by the system, perhaps, which might possibly be the case for certain derived relvars).[16]

■ Contrary to Codd's wording of the text of this feature, the target relvar for a given foreign key doesn't have to be a base relvar specifically (nor does the "source relvar," come to that), and the target key doesn't have to be a primary key specifically.

Actually there's a huge amount more that could be said about foreign keys in general, but this isn't the place. See reference [14] for a much more extensive discussion.

INTEGRITY FEATURES

General Comments

I have a number of general comments on Codd's list of integrity features:

■ In various books and papers—see, e.g., reference [15]—I've described an important integrity feature known, perhaps not very aptly, as *type constraints*. In essence, the type constraint for a given type T is simply a definition of the set of values that constitute that type T. Reference [5] contains no mention of such constraints at all.[17]

■ The following is a fundamental integrity feature that applies to any system that supports types: If (a) V is a variable (i.e., something to which a value can be assigned), and if (b) an attempt is made to assign a value v to V, then (c) v and V must be of the same type; otherwise the assignment will fail (probably and preferably at compile time). Now, I'm quite sure Codd intended the relational model to abide by this familiar rule; in fact, I think it's part of what he meant by the term *domain integrity*, which he uses in reference [6], though it's hard to be sure.[18] What's clear, however, is that reference [5] nowhere spells the point out explicitly, though it should.

■ What I referred to in the previous bullet item as a "familiar rule" might better be regarded as a *metarule*: It implies among other things that any given database must be subject to certain individual rules that are specific to the database in question (e.g., a rule to the effect

---

[16] Footnote 15 applies here also, mutatis mutandis.

[17] But reference [6] does, though (albeit very briefly), on page 46 and then again on page 156. What it actually says in this connection is a little strange, though: "[A] domain declaration normally includes ... [a definition of] the range of values that spans the ranges permitted in all of the columns drawing their values from this domain" (page 156). That "normally" in particular raises some questions. PS: Page 46 says *frequently*, not *normally*, but the same questions arise.

[18] Actually "domain integrity" seems to cover both less than what's required in some respects and more in others (see Chapter 8).

that every value assigned to an attribute called COLOR must be a value of the associated type, perhaps also called COLOR). Those specific rules taken together then guarantee that the metarule in question isn't violated by that particular database.

■   Finally, I reject the entire notion of "nulls" (and three- and four-valued logic) as proposed by Codd in numerous writings, and I therefore have significant reservations, discussed in more detail below, regarding Features I1 and I2.

I turn now to some more specific criticisms of individual features.

I1 Entity Integrity

Reference [5] says the entity integrity rule "must be followed closely," but doesn't say exactly what that rule is![19] The following formulation is taken from reference [3]: "No primary key value of a base relvar is allowed to be null or have a null component." (And reference [6] adds the following: "[Also,] no component of a foreign key [value] is allowed to be [the missing-and-inapplicable null].") Some comments:

■   I reject any rule that treats primary and other keys differently.

■   I reject any rule that treats base and other relvars differently.

■   In any case I reject the entire notion of nulls; as a consequence, I regard the entity integrity rule as vacuous, and I believe it could be dropped without loss. I note, however, that if it were retained it would in fact be a metarule, not an integrity rule as such, since it would be requiring each individual database to be subject to an appropriate set of individual integrity rules that would be specific to that particular database.

I2 Referential Integrity

Reference [5] says the referential integrity rule "must [also] be followed closely," but again doesn't say exactly what the rule is ... The following formulation is taken from reference [6] (but is edited very slightly here): "For each distinct nonnull foreign key value there must exist an equal value of a primary key from the same domain." I agree with the broad spirit of this rule, but:

■   "Nonnull" should be deleted, since values are "nonnull" by definition. (Indeed, Codd and I both agree that the phrase *null value* is a contradiction in terms.)

---

[19] That "closely" is a little puzzling, too. Surely the rule is either followed or not? *Note:* This same comment applies to Feature I2 also.

- "A primary key from the same domain" should be "the applicable target key." By the way, "from the same domain" could be deleted without loss, since two values can't possibly be equal if they're not from the same domain.

- Codd's referential integrity rule as stated here tacitly (and deliberately) allows a given foreign key to have more than one target relvar associated with it. For reasons explained in detail in reference [14], I reject that possibility.

- Like the domain and entity integrity rules, the referential integrity rule is really a metarule.

I3 User Defined Integrity

"In addition to the [entity and referential integrity rules] that apply to every relational database, there is a clear need to be able to specify additional integrity constraints ..." [5]. I agree with the general sense of this statement. However:

- "Database specific integrity" would be a far more appropriate name for this feature than "user defined integrity." After all, *every* integrity rule that applies to *any* database is—in fact, must be—user defined, in the final analysis. *Note:* By "rule" here I mean a rule that's specific to some database, not a "metarule."

- As a consequence of the foregoing point, I categorically reject Codd's classification scheme for integrity constraints—which actually isn't described in reference [5], but is sketched, albeit very superficially, in reference [6] (see Chapter 8).

MANIPULATIVE FEATURES

Reference [5] doesn't in fact have all that much to say regarding the manipulative part of the model in general. What it does say is as follows (paraphrasing):

- The model doesn't require the DBA (i.e., the database administrator) "to set up any special access paths." I agree.

- The model doesn't require the user "to resort to iterative loops or recursion or cartesian product." Actually, from other writings of Codd's I'm pretty sure that what he really means here is, rather, that the model requires the user *not* "to resort to iterative loops or recursion or cartesian product." If so, then the requirement is too dogmatic—there are situations in which iterative loops and/or recursion and/or cartesian product are exactly what's needed. For example, given only the operators defined in reference [5], there's no way to compute a transitive closure without using loops and/or recursion.[20] As for cartesian product, I'll give an example later (in the subsection "Missing Operators") of where that operator categorically does need to be used.

■ The model doesn't require the system "to generate a cartesian product as an intermediate result." Actually, from other writings of Codd's I can state with confidence that what he really means here is, rather, that the model requires the system *not* "to generate a cartesian product as an intermediate result"—in which case the requirement is again too dogmatic, because there are situations in which generating such an intermediate result is in fact the best thing for the system to do (as work by others on "star joins" has made clear).[21]

After making the foregoing general points, reference [5] simply goes on to list "the 18 manipulative features" without any further discussion. In my opinion, however, there are many additional general points that could and should be made, which I'll discuss in the subsection "General Comments" immediately following.

General Comments

The manipulative part of the model consists of—or, I suppose I have to say, should consist of—(a) a set of read-only operators that together constitute the relational algebra (or something logically equivalent to the relational algebra), together with (b) a relational assignment operator that allows the result of evaluating any given relational algebra expression to be assigned to some given relvar. I'll discuss the algebra first. Overall, the algebra should:

■ Support proper relation type inference, meaning among things that it's properly closed (i.e., the result of every algebraic operation is itself a "proper relation," with a proper relation heading in particular)[22]

■ Be strongly typed, meaning among other things that it does *not* support any such suspect notion as "domain check override"

■ Be firmly based on traditional two-valued logic, meaning among other things that it does *not* support any such suspect notion as "null"—and meaning further, therefore, (a) that it

---

[20] Of course, I'm not saying an operator for computing transitive closure directly couldn't be added to the model—indeed, reference [6] does exactly that—but the model as defined in reference [5] includes no such operator.

[21] Bu surely it's not appropriate for the *model* to say what the *implementation* can and can't do? In any case, (a) generating a cartesian product is harmless if data volumes are small, and (b) what's more, "small" nowadays can actually be quite large.

[22] A scheme that guarantees such proper relation type inference is explained in many places (see, e.g., reference [15]). The scheme in question is based on the simple principle that whenever a correspondence needs to be established between relational attributes, as in, e.g., a union or join operation, then that correspondence is established by requiring the attributes in question to be, formally, one and the same (i.e., to have the same name and be of the same type).

doesn't support any special "maybe" operations and (b) that any "outer" operators it does support will require some redefinition

■ Ideally, be able, given declarations of functional dependencies (FDs) and keys for base relvars, to infer FD and key constraints that (a) are satisfied by the result of evaluating a given relational algebra expression and hence (b) hold in any derived relvar for which the expression in question is specified as the defining expression [7]

As for relational assignment: As noted under Feature M10 later, a properly defined relational assignment operator is in fact the only operator of an updating nature that's needed *in the model*. Of course, various INSERT, DELETE, and UPDATE operators are extremely useful in practice—but those operators are all, in the last analysis, just shorthand for certain relational assignments.

Now let me go on to offer some more specific comments on Codd's "18 manipulative features."

M1 θ-Select

The θ in "θ-select" stands for "any one of the comparators equal [to], not equal [to], greater than, less than, greater than or equal to, less than or equal to" [5]. But there's no need to limit the truth valued expression in a "θ-select" operation to just simple "θ-comparisons" (or logical combinations thereof); instead, such expressions should be allowed to be any expression whose truth value can be determined, for a given tuple, by examining just that tuple in isolation. (In other words, there should be no need to examine any other tuple in the pertinent relation, nor any other relation in the database, in order to determine the truth value of the expression in question for the tuple in question.) *Note:* Such an expression—i.e., a truth valued expression that can be evaluated for a given tuple by examining just that tuple in isolation—is usually called a *restriction condition*, and the generalized form of "θ-select" in which the associated truth valued expression is allowed to be any such condition is usually called a *restriction*. From this point forward, therefore, if I need to refer to these constructs again, I'll use these latter terms.[23]

M2 Project

No comment, except perhaps to note that it's highly desirable in concrete syntax to support two forms of this operator, one that specifies the attributes to be retained and one that specifies the attributes to be discarded.

---

[23] In a concrete language, of course, we would surely want to support expressions of the form *rx* WHERE *bx*, where *rx* is a relational expression and *bx* is a boolean expression and *bx* in particular isn't limited to being just a restriction condition as such but is allowed to be of arbitrary complexity. But there's no need for such generality *in the model*, since equivalent functionality can be obtained by other means.

M3 θ-Join

Loosely speaking, "θ-join" is defined to be a restriction (in fact a "θ-selection") of the cartesian product of the relations in question,[24] and the comments on "θ-select" under Feature M1 above thus apply here also, mutatis mutandis. In practice, however, *natural* join is vastly more important than any kind of θ-join (even when θ is "=")—so much so, in fact, that the term *join*, unqualified, is almost universally taken to mean the natural join specifically. As a consequence, I believe Feature M3 should be replaced by a requirement that natural join be supported, instead of θ-join. Indeed, I wouldn't think much of a system that provided direct support—i.e., explicit syntax—for θ-join but only a cumbersome, SQL-style circumlocution for natural join.

M4 Outer θ-Join

Since I reject nulls, I reject all "outer" operations (at least as defined by Codd) a fortiori. I would, however, accept a carefully defined "outer join"—meaning outer natural join, not outer θ-join—that generates actual values (specified by the user) instead of nulls in its result [11].

M5 Divide

I have several problems with this requirement:

- The first and most important is that if the system supported image relations [15], which I strongly believe it should, then divide becomes unnecessary—any relational expression involving divide can always be replaced by one that uses image relations instead, and is usually much easier to understand as well.[25]

- Second, there are at least seven distinct relational operators all having some claim to be called "divide." At the very least, therefore, Feature M5, if it's retained, will need to be stated very carefully. My own preference, however, would be to drop it entirely, since (with the best will in the world) any discussion of the divide operator is always going to be open to misinterpretation and misunderstanding, precisely because of this terminological state of affairs.

- Third, no matter which version of divide we're talking about, the operator isn't primitive anyway, and so it's not clear exactly what support for it would consist of. Let me illustrate.

---

[24] But the list of operators in reference [5] doesn't actually include cartesian product, though earlier definitions did (see, e.g., reference [3])—but in any case, in the version of the algebra that I advocate, cartesian product is nothing more than a degenerate special case of natural join, and "my" algebra most certainly does include a natural join operator.

[25] Actually image relations are only shorthand anyway. What's really needed is support for the EXTEND operator (see Chapter 1). However, using EXTEND to simulate Codd's divide operator becomes vastly more straightforward if image relations are supported as well. See reference [15] for further discussion.

Let's agree for the sake of the discussion to focus on the simplest version of the operator, and let me use the keyword DIVIDEBY to denote that version. Then an SQL analog of the relational expression[26]

```
SP { SNO , PNO } DIVIDEBY P { PNO }
```

is:

```
SELECT DISTINCT SPX.SNO
FROM   SP AS SPX
WHERE  NOT EXISTS
     ( SELECT DISTINCT PX.*
       FROM    P AS PX
       WHERE   NOT EXISTS
             ( SELECT DISTINCT SPY.*
               FROM    SP AS SPY
               WHERE   SPY.SNO = SPX.SNO
               AND     SPY.PNO = PX.PNO ) )
```

So do you think SQL can be reasonably said to support DIVIDEBY? No, I don't think so, either.[27]

M6 Union

Support for union is vitally important, of course. However, Codd says the union of relations *r* and *s* is defined if and only if *r* and *s* are "union compatible," which page 79 of reference [6] explains thus (paraphrasing slightly):

Relations *r* and *s* are *union compatible* if and only if (a) they're of the same degree and (b) it's possible to establish at least one mapping between the attributes of *r* and those of *s* with the property that, for every attribute *A* of *r* and every attribute *B* of *s*, if attribute *A* is mapped on to attribute *B*, then *A* and *B* draw their values from a common domain.

I reject this weak, ad hoc, and cumbersome notion;[28] in its place, I would require simply that *r* and *s* be of the same (relation) type—equivalently, that *r* and *s* have the same heading. (The result of the operation will then have the same heading as well.) *Note:* The same applies to intersection and difference also, of course (Features M7 and M8).

---

[26] The example is based on the familiar suppliers-and-parts database (see, e.g., Fig. 1.1 in Chapter 1), and the query (simplifying slightly) is "Get supplier numbers for suppliers who supply all parts." The braces denote projection over the specified attributes.

[27] Codd himself subsequently indicated (in reference [6], pages 86-87) that in his opinion such clumsy circumlocutions do *not* constitute "reasonable support," and I agree. (Please don't misunderstand me here, though! I'm *not* saying divide should be supported—I'm just saying I don't think SQL supports it.)

[28] Even the terminology could be criticized, since "union compatibility" certainly doesn't apply just to union but is in fact of much wider applicability.

M7 Intersection

Like divide and θ-join, intersection isn't a primitive operation, so again it's not clear exactly what support for the operation would consist of. To be specific, intersection is a special case of natural join; thus, a system that supports natural join will support intersection a fortiori. (On the other hand, a system that supported union explicitly but intersection only implicitly could fairly be criticized on ergonomic grounds if nothing else, so explicit intersection support is probably desirable in practice.[29])

M8 Set Difference

No comment, except to point out that *"relation* difference" would be a more accurate name for the operator—the operands must be relations, not just sets. This is a very minor point, of course, but I do feel we should strive for precision whenever possible, above all in a relational context. (And Codd certainly agrees with this objective—see reference [6], page v, where he says "[A] concern of mine has been, and continues to be, precision.")

M9 Outer Union

I reject this operation for reasons explained under Feature M4—though it's perhaps worth pointing out that the regular or "inner" union is a special case (actually the sensible special case) of outer union, so it's not entirely clear why both kinds of union should be needed anyway.

   By the way, it's also not clear why reference [5] calls for support for outer union but not for outer intersection or difference. Though of course I'd reject them if it did! More specifically, (a) I reject Codd's outer intersection and difference (and union) operators as originally defined in reference [3], and (b) I also reject Codd's revised outer intersection and difference (and union) operators as redefined in reference [6]. I note in passing that the definitions in reference [6] in particular seem to be quite complex; they're also, in my opinion, ad hoc, and indeed somewhat arbitrary.

M10 Relational Assignment

I had no objection to this operator when I first saw it included in reference [5]—but I most certainly did object to it when I saw it explained more fully in reference [6]. When I first saw it, I naturally assumed that Codd was talking about an operation of the form

```
R := rx
```

---

[29] Note that if relations *r1* and *r2* have different headings, then an expression of the form *r1* INTERSECT *r2* will certainly fail while an expression of the form *r1* JOIN *r2* might not—another ergonomic reason for providing explicit support for intersection. Compare footnote 34.

where R is a relvar name, rx is a relational expression, and the semantics are that the relation r denoted by rx is assigned to R. (Of course, R and r must be of the same type.) In other words, I assumed that Codd was talking about a mechanism for updating the database. But he wasn't. On page 87 of reference [6], he says this (paraphrasing somewhat):

> When querying a database, the user may wish to have the result of the query ... retained in memory ... [This requirement is] satisfied ... by relational assignment ... [In the] expression[30] $R := rx$ ... R denotes a user selected name for the relation that is specified by rx and that is to be retained in memory.

And that's the totality of what he has to say on the matter! In other words, Codd's relational assignment is intended merely for keeping the result of a query in some kind of local relvar.[31]

Well, I said I object to this operator—but that's too strong, of course. I don't object to the idea of keeping query results somewhere (of course not); but what I really want is support for proper relational assignment, and then the rather minor requirement articulated here by Codd will come out in the wash as a trivial special case.

M11 θ-Select Maybe

As previously noted, I reject all aspects of nulls and three- and four-valued logic support, and so I automatically reject all "maybe" operators. (See also my comments on Feature M1.) But I note in passing that in reference [6] Codd extends the "maybe" idea, and hence also the "maybe" operators, to incorporate an "unknown" maybe, a "does not apply" maybe, and an "either of the above" maybe as well. So Features M11-M14 must presumably each now exist in three different "flavors," in Codd's version of the model.

M12 θ-Join Maybe

See the comments under Feature M11 above, also the comments under Feature M3.

M13 Outer θ-Join Maybe

See the comments under Feature M11 above, also the comments under Feature M4.

---

[30] I can't resist pointing out that here for once Codd's term "command" might be appropriate, and here for once he chooses to use the term—highly *in*appropriate, in this context—"expression" instead.

[31] By "local relvar" here, I mean a relvar that's kept in local memory instead of being part of the database.

M14 Divide Maybe

See the comments under Feature M11 above, also the comments under Feature M5.

M15 θ-Select Semantic Override

Note: As mentioned in Chapter 2 of this book, the term "semantic override" was a renaming of the earlier and more specific term "domain check override," and I'll stay with that earlier term here.

As previously noted, I reject the notion of "domain check override" entirely, and so I automatically reject all "domain check override" operators. But I note in passing that Codd apparently limits the "domain check override" idea to just the following operations: restrict (or θ-select, rather), θ-join, outer θ-join, and divide. It's unclear why union, difference, and intersection are excluded from this list;[32] orthogonality would surely dictate that "domain check override" should be specifiable in all contexts in which it makes sense. I note too that presumably there should be support for "outer θ-join maybe domain check override" (etc., etc.), and furthermore that each such operator should exist in three versions, corresponding to the three types of "maybe" mentioned under Feature M11 above—and indeed Codd effectively makes just such a proposal in reference [6]. This proliferation of concepts (a combinatorial explosion, really) suggests rather strongly that something has gone seriously awry somewhere.

M16 θ-Join Semantic Override

See the comments under Feature M15 above, also the comments under Feature M3.

M17 Outer θ-Join Semantic Override

See the comments under Feature M15 above, also the comments under Feature M4.

M18 Divide Maybe

See the comments under Feature M15 above, also the comments under Feature M5.

Missing Operators

The list of manipulative features given by Codd in reference [5] is notable not only for what it includes but also for what it doesn't. Indeed, there are some rather important omissions. First of

---

[32] Actually I don't think the reason why these operators are excluded is unclear at all; rather, I think it's unfortunately all too clear. To be specific, I think it's because Codd couldn't figure out what the domains for attributes of the result would have to be in these cases.

all, there's the matter of *relational comparisons* (see Chapter 2). It's a generally accepted principle of language design—and after all, the relational model really is (among other things) just a kind of programming language, albeit one that's rather abstract—that, for each kind of object the system supports, there should be both (a) a means of assigning one object of that kind to another and (b) a means of comparing two objects of that kind. In the case of relational systems, therefore, there should be (a) a relational assignment operator—and Codd agrees here, though his version of that operator (see the discussion of Feature M10 earlier) is seriously deficient—and (b) a collection of relational comparison operators. The comparison operators in question should include all of the following: "=", "≠", "⊇" ("includes"), "⊃" ("properly includes"), "⊆" ("is included in"), and "⊂" ("is properly included in"). There should also be an operator ("∈") for testing whether a specified tuple is contained in a specified relation.[33]

Next, as noted in a footnote earlier, cartesian product is also omitted from reference [5]. In contrast to Codd, I do think this operator is worth including explicitly, even though in the version of the algebra I advocate it's just a degenerate case of natural join.[34] Here's a simple example of a query that needs it—"Find supplier-number / part-number pairs such that the indicated supplier doesn't supply the indicated part" (the database is suppliers-and-parts as usual):

```
( S { SNO } TIMES P { PNO } ) MINUS SP { SNO , PNO }
```

MINUS here denotes the relational difference operator, of course, and TIMES is the explicit cartesian product operator.

Here now is a list of other important operators that, though perhaps not all "fundamental," I do think should be included (I won't try to define or illustrate these operators here—such definitions and illustrations can be found in many places, including reference [15] in particular):

■ (Attribute) RENAME

■ EXTEND (two versions)

■ SUMMARIZE (though if EXTEND is supported, as I believe it should be, then SUMMARIZE becomes strictly unnecessary, especially if image relations are supported as well)

■ GROUP and UNGROUP

---

[33] There should also be (a) operators for extracting a tuple from a relation and extracting an attribute value from a tuple and (b) operators for building up a tuple from attribute values and building up a relation from tuples (speaking a trifle loosely in both cases).

[34] The difference between the explicit cartesian product and natural join operators is that with the former it's an error if the operand relations have any attribute names in common; with the latter, it's not, though attributes with the same name are required to be of the same type. Compare footnote 29.

- MATCHING and NOT MATCHING

- "Disjoint union" (D_UNION) and "included minus" (I_MINUS)

- "Exclusive union" (XUNION)

CONCLUDING REMARKS

This brings me to the end of my brief analysis of the relational model (meaning "Version 1" of that model) as defined, or at least sketched, by Codd in reference [5]. In presenting that analysis, moreover, I've effectively proposed a replacement for the model as defined in that reference. As you've seen, that proposed replacement differs rather radically from the reference [5] version, and I've given my reasons (or some of my reasons, at any rate) for preferring it.[35] So what should we conclude?

Well, there are clearly two broad options: We could just accept Codd's definition anyway; or we could try to agree on a set of changes to that definition, along the lines suggested in the foregoing. Naturally, I'd vote for the second option. But note that, given the current state of affairs, it no longer really makes sense to talk about "the" relational model; that is, I don't think we can even attach any unambiguous meaning to the phrase "the relational model" at this time. (In fact, it could be argued that such has been the case for some time anyway, given all of Codd's own definitions and redefinitions over the years—see the paragraph immediately following.)

It seems to me, therefore, that, for better or worse, we simply have to accept that there are indeed several different versions of the model, and the database community—users, vendors, researchers, standards bodies, and anyone else who might be interested—will just have to decide which version it wants to run with. After all, Codd himself has now described at least three "official" versions: namely, the original model (now referred to as RM/V1), the extended version RM/T [3], and "the relational model Version 2" (RM/V2) [6]. He has also described at least four different versions of RM/V1 [2,3,4,5] (some of them mutually incompatible, incidentally—for instance, the definition of "foreign key" has changed several times [9]).

Whichever way the community decides to go, however, there's one thing that seems to me certain: The model will continue to evolve. Indeed, in his book on RM/V2 [6], page vi, Codd indicated that he was already thinking about a "Version 3" (RM/V3), and hinted that he also intended to define further versions (RM/V4, RM/V5, etc.) at regular intervals. In fact, of course, Codd is, sadly, no longer with us, and none of those projected later versions ever saw the light of day; but others will surely pick up the torch and continue to run with it.

---

[35] Most, perhaps all, of the features proposed in "my" version of the model are now prescribed as part of *The Third Manifesto*. Indeed, the present rewrite of my original paper has benefited considerably from experience gained from work done by Hugh Darwen and myself on our *Manifesto* subsequent to publication of that original paper. See our book *Databases, Types, and the Relational Model: The Third Manifesto* (3rd edition, Addison-Wesley, 2007) for much further discussion.

ACKNOWLEDGMENTS

Note: What follows is essentially the "Acknowledgments" section from the original paper on which this chapter is based. It's no longer totally appropriate (especially since most of the persons mentioned haven't even seen the present rewrite!), but the sentiments expressed are still applicable, and I don't want to lose them. However, I've at least altered the wording to replace most uses of the present tense by now more appropriate uses of the past tense instead.

Among the numerous friends and colleagues who helped me crystallize and organize my thinking on the topics discussed in this chapter, there were a few whose influence was perhaps more significant than most. First of all, of course, there was Ted Codd himself, the prime mover in this field; I was (and still am) supremely grateful to him for his fundamental contribution, and I certainly didn't (and still don't) mean for my criticisms to be seen as any kind of personal attack. Second, I'm enormously indebted to Hugh Darwen for his support, and especially for his help in clarifying my thinking on many points. Adrian Larner also gave me much food for thought on several occasions; Adrian was probably more responsible than anyone else for making me realize the importance of getting the foundations right first, for which I was (and still am) most grateful to him. Discussions with David McGoveran and (especially) Charley Bontempo over the years have also proved very helpful. I'd also like to thank Charley, David, Hugh, and Chris Hultén and Colin White for their careful and helpful reviews of drafts of the original paper on which this chapter is based. Finally, I'd like to pay tribute to the designers of the Peterlee Relational Test Vehicle (PRTV), a relational prototype built in the early seventies at the IBM Scientific Centre in England [16]; they got so many things right that later systems got wrong, and it's a great pity, and certainly through no fault of theirs, that their ideas weren't more widely disseminated or accepted at the time.

REFERENCES AND BIBLIOGRAPHY

Note: Many of the books and papers listed below have effectively been superseded by later publications. In the interest of historical accuracy, I've decided to retain the references from the review as originally published; however, specifics of those more recent publications can be found (in most cases) in the "References and Bibliography" section of Chapter 8, q.v.

1. E. F. Codd: "Derivability, Redundancy, and Consistency of Relations Stored in Large Data Banks," IBM Research Report RJ599 (August 19th, 1969).

2. E. F. Codd: "A Relational Model of Data for Large Shared Data Banks," *Communications of the ACM 13*, No. 6 (June 1970).

3. E. F. Codd: "Extending the Database Relational Model to Capture More Meaning," *ACM Transactions on Database Systems 4*, No. 4 (December 1979).

4. E. F. Codd: "Relational Database: A Practical Foundation for Productivity," *Communications of the ACM 25*, No. 2 (February 1982).

5. E. F. Codd: "Is Your DBMS Really Relational?" (*Computerworld*, October 14th, 1985); "Does Your DBMS Run by the Rules?" (*Computerworld*, October 21st, 1985).

6. E. F. Codd: *The Relational Model for Database Management Version 2*. Reading, Mass.: Addison-Wesley (1990).

7. Hugh Darwen: "The Role of Functional Dependence in Query Decomposition," in C. J. Date and Hugh Darwen, *Relational Database Writings 1989-1991* (Addison-Wesley, 1992).

8. C. J. Date: "What Is a Domain?" in C. J. Date, *Relational Database Writings 1985-1989* (Addison-Wesley, 1990).

9. C. J. Date: "Referential Integrity and Foreign Keys Part I: Basic Concepts," in C. J. Date, *Relational Database Writings 1985-1989* (Addison-Wesley, 1990).

10. C. J. Date: "What Is a Relation?" in C. J. Date, *Relational Database Writings 1989-1991* (Addison-Wesley, 1992).

11. C. J. Date: "The Default Values Approach to Missing Information," in C. J. Date, *Relational Database Writings 1985-1989* (Addison-Wesley, 1990).

12. C. J. Date: "We Don't Need Composite Columns," in C. J. Date, Hugh Darwen, and David McGoveran, *Relational Database Writings 1994-1997* (Addison-Wesley, 1998).

13. C. J. Date: *Go Faster! The TransRelational^{TM} Approach to DBMS Implementation*. Frederiksberg, Denmark: Ventus Publishing (2002, 2011).

14. C. J. Date: "Inclusion Dependencies and Foreign Keys," in C. J. Date and Hugh Darwen, *Database Explorations: Essays on The Third Manifesto and Related Topics* (Trafford, 2010).

15. C. J. Date: *SQL and Relational Theory: How to Write Accurate SQL Code* (3rd edition). Sebastopol, Calif.: O'Reilly (2015).

16. P. A. V. Hall, P. Hitchcock, and S. J. P. Todd: "An Algebra of Relations for Machine Computation," Conference Record of the 2nd ACM Symposium on Principles of Programming Languages, Palo Alto, Calif. (January 1975).

APPENDIX: CODD'S TWELVE RULES

In the same two-part paper in which he defined his 1985 version of the relational model (viz., reference [5]), Codd also defined his famous—I'm tempted to say infamous—"twelve rules" for relational DBMSs. He then used those rules, together with the "nine structural, three integrity, and 18 manipulative features of the relational model," as a basis for an evaluation scheme to be used in assessing how relational a given DBMS might be, and went on to apply that scheme to three specific products: DB2 from IBM, IDMS/R from Cullinet, and Datacom/DB from Applied Data Research.[36]

Codd's evaluation scheme worked like this: For each of 42 items (the twelve rules, plus the nine structural, three integrity, and 18 manipulative features of the model), a DBMS scored one point if and only if it supported that item *fully*; anything less than full support got a zero. Then, if and only if the system achieved a score of 42 (the maximum), a bonus of eight was added; finally, the total was doubled to yield a percentage "fidelity rating." A system was then said to be "mid 80s fully relational" if and only if it got a fidelity rating of 100 percent. (The qualifier "mid 80s" reflected the fact that, to quote reference [5], "it is likely that there will be a few more requirements by the nineties.")

According to this scheme, Codd awarded DB2, IDMS/R, and Datacom/DB fidelity ratings of 46 percent, 8 percent, and 10 percent, respectively.

I didn't endorse the foregoing scheme at the time, nor do I do so now, and in this appendix I'd like to explain why.

Preliminary Remarks

There are a couple of points I'd like to make clear at the outset:

1. I'm not opposed to the idea of evaluating systems—far from it; on the contrary, the availability of an independent and objective evaluation scheme could be extremely beneficial to both users and vendors. But it's clearly desirable that any such scheme be very carefully thought out in order to be (as far as possible) impartial and above all reasonable criticism. In my opinion, Codd's scheme fails to meet this requirement.

---

[36] IDMS/R and Datacom/DB are both now marketed by CA Technologies (formerly known as Computer Associates International, Inc.).

2. We shouldn't lose sight of the fact that to measure how relational a system is only to measure that system along one of several possible axes. I would certainly agree that the relational axis is an extremely important and indeed fundamental one, but other axes are obviously possible, and relevant. For example, what about recovery support? What about concurrency control? How well does the system perform? What frontend subsystems are available, and how well are they integrated with the DBMS? And so on. A fair assessment of a given system would consist of some weighted sum of its ratings along each of these various axes. Again, I would certainly agree that the weighting assigned to the relational axis should be very high, but different users will surely want to assign different weights to different axes.

General Comments

The overall basis for the thinking behind Codd's twelve rules was that, first, satisfying those rules was by and large a technically feasible proposition;[37] second, there were clear practical benefits to the user if the system did in fact satisfy them. The rules were supposedly all based on a single "foundation rule" (*aka* "Rule Zero"):

> *For any system that is advertised as, or claimed to be, a relational database management system, that system must be able to manage databases entirely through its relational capabilities.*

There's no question that this rule could be a good, albeit informal, guiding principle. However:

■ It's not clear that all twelve of the rules were logical consequences of Rule Zero as stated (see, e.g., Rule 11).

■ It's not clear why Codd chose exactly the rules he did and not others that could be argued to be at least equally important (e.g., why not a "proper closure" rule?).

■ Although I agreed and still do agree with most of the rules in spirit, some of them seemed to be hard to justify other than in a purely intuitive manner (see, e.g., Rule 5).

■ The rules weren't all independent of one another (see, e.g., Rules 6 and 9).

■ Some of the rules were effectively just a restatement of certain aspects of the underlying relational model (see, e.g., Rule 2); why those particular aspects and not others?

---

[37] Though it turned out subsequently that at least one of the rules, and arguably as many as three or four of them, could not in fact be fully satisfied—at least not within the state of the art at the time, and possibly still not.

- Some of the rules were stated rather imprecisely and/or seemed to be hard to apply (see, e.g., Rules 3, 6, and 11).

- Some of the rules didn't seem to be particularly relational (see, e.g., Rule 11).

- Finally, the all or nothing scoring system was unduly harsh. For example, it seems very unfair to give (say) IBM's DB2 the same score, zero, on Rule 6 as a system that doesn't support views at all—yet zero is the right score if we follow the evaluation scheme faithfully.

Now I turn to more detailed comments on the individual rules. I'll consider them one by one. *Note:* The rule names are taken from reference [5]; however, the detailed statements and explanations of those rules are not—I've deliberately chosen to rephrase them, in most cases.

Rule 1 – The Information Rule: *All information in the database is represented explicitly in one and only one way—namely, by values in column positions within rows of tables.*[38]

This is a good rule, and I certainly have no objection to it, though personally I would prefer to phrase it thus:

> *The only kind of variable permitted in the database is, specifically, the relation variable or relvar.*

I note in passing, however, that Codd did say in an earlier paper[39] that *inessential ordering* could also be used in the database as a means of representing information—so I'm glad to see that by 1985 he had apparently had second thoughts on the matter.

Rule 2 – Guaranteed Access Rule: *Every individual data item in the database must be logically addressable by specifying the name of the containing table, the name of the containing column, and the primary key value of the containing row.*

I object to the idea that for each relvar in the database we're required to select one key out of possibly several such and make it primary, but otherwise have no objection to this rule—except to point out that it seems to be just a restatement of something that's already part of the model anyway (see Codd's Feature S8). I mean, could a DBMS possibly get different scores on Feature S8 and Rule 2? Surely independence among the rules is desirable, for exactly the same kinds of reasons that the rules themselves demand certain kinds of independence in relational systems.

---

[38] As its name suggests, this rule is of course basically just a reformulation of *The Information Principle* (see Chapter 1).

[39] The paper in question was Codd's essentiality paper (see Chapter 6).

(Though I certainly understand that it might be difficult to come up with a fully orthogonal set of rules—i.e., rules that are 100 percent independent of one another.)

Rule 3 – Systematic Treatment of Null Values: *The DBMS must support a representation of missing information and inapplicable information that's systematic, distinct from all regular values (for example, distinct from zero or any other number, in the case of numeric values), and independent of data type. Such representations must also be manipulated by the DBMS in a systematic way.*

Systematic treatment of missing information is clearly desirable, but "null values"—at least as that term is usually understood—are not. Thus, I reject this rule as stated.

Rule 4 – Dynamic Online Catalog Based on the Relational Model: *The DBMS must support an online, inline, relational catalog that's accessible to authorized users by means of their regular query language.*

This is a good rule. No additional comment.

Rule 5 – Comprehensive Data Sublanguage: *The DBMS must support at least one relational language*[40] *that (a) has a linear syntax, (b) can be used both interactively and within application programs, and (c) supports data definition operations (including view definitions), data manipulation operations (update as well as retrieval), security and integrity constraints, and transaction boundary operations (BEGIN TRANSACTION, COMMIT, and ROLLBACK).*

I feel intuitively that this is a good rule, but find it hard to justify in any precise and objective way. Codd's argument in reference [5] that "it should rarely be necessary to bring the database activity to a halt [and therefore] it does not make sense to separate the services listed above into distinct languages" isn't completely convincing. I certainly subscribe to the proposition that the same functionality should use the same syntax everywhere it appears in the system—but is that all there is to it? Also, is the list of services meant to be exhaustive? If we're going to include operations such as BEGIN TRANSACTION, COMMIT, etc., then what about concurrency control operations (e.g., LOCK and UNLOCK)? What about load and unload operations? What about database reorganization? Auditing? Other utility functions? (etc., etc.). All of these items surely have as much—or as little—right to be included as do BEGIN TRANSACTION, COMMIT, etc., in a list of "relational" requirements. (My point, in case it's not obvious, is that such matters really have nothing to do with the question of whether a given DBMS qualifies as relational or not.)

---

[40] Note that I say "language" here, not "sublanguage." I've never subscribed to the idea that there must necessarily be a sharp separation between the database language and the host language, and in fact I think there are strong arguments against it.

Rule 6 – View Updating: *All views that are theoretically updatable must be updatable by the system.*

Codd goes on to say that "a view is theoretically updatable if there exists a time-independent algorithm for unambiguously determining a single series of changes to the base [relvars] that will have as their effect precisely the requested changes in the view." Again, I agree with the general intent of this rule, but I have at least two problems with the detailed statement:

a. First, the rule clearly implies that the system must support the *definition* of all updatable views. (Note that a system could fail on this requirement alone; for example, certain early SQL systems prohibited the use of UNION in a view definition, and yet it's clearly possible to perform, e.g., DELETE operations on a union view.) But is there an implication that we know exactly what it is that characterizes the class of theoretically updatable views? Is the "time-independent algorithm" always known? I'm not aware of any documented definition of that class or of such an algorithm. And if those definitions in fact don't exist (or at least aren't yet known), then this part of the rule is rather hard to apply, to say the least.[41]

b. Compliance with this rule is a logical consequence of compliance with Rule 9; i.e., if a system satisfies Rule 9, it must satisfy this rule also. As noted under Rule 2 above, surely independence among the rules is desirable, for exactly the same kinds of reasons that the rules themselves demand certain kinds of independence in relational systems.

Rule 7 – High Level Insert, Update, and Delete: *The system must support set level INSERT, UPDATE, and DELETE operators.*

I certainly approve of and agree with the emphasis on set level operators in general. I also agree with and approve of the idea that set level INSERT, UPDATE, and DELETE operators be supported in particular. But I'd like to see support for explicit relational assignment also, and I'd like it to be recognized that INSERT, UPDATE, and DELETE are all in the final analysis just shorthand for certain relational assignments.

Rule 8 – Physical Data Independence: *(I assume you're familiar with this concept and won't bother to define it here.)*

Once again this is a good rule in principle. But the problem is that physical data independence is not an absolute; in fact, it's probably true to say that every system should get a "Partial" score on this one. In particular, the rule doesn't seem to have been fairly applied in the cases considered

---

[41] I subsequently wrote a book myself—*View Updating and Relational Theory: Solving the View Update Problem* (O'Reilly, 2013)—that addresses such questions. What it doesn't do, though, is answer them definitively! I do believe the book has a positive contribution to make, but I also believe the questions as such are still somewhat open.

by Codd in his paper—DB2 is given a "Yes" (score one point) while IDMS/R and Datacom/DB are both given a "No" (score no point), yet DB2 fails to provide full physical data independence in at least the following ways:[42]

- Creating or dropping a UNIQUE index can affect the logic of existing queries or programs (this is partly a lack of integrity independence as well as a lack of physical data independence—see Rule 10)

- Columns of type LONG VARCHAR (equivalently, VARCHAR(n) with $n > 254$) are subject to numerous restrictions (e.g., they can't be used in WHERE or GROUP BY or HAVING or ORDER BY or DISTINCT or PRIMARY KEY or FOREIGN KEY, and probably elsewhere also)

- Partitioning columns can't be updated

- The meaning of "SELECT *" can change if the physical representation of the table in storage is changed

- The meaning of INSERT with an implicit list of column names can change if the physical representation of the table in storage is changed

Note too that the rule doesn't explicitly mention such matters as changes in column width or data type or units, etc., though some systems (not DB2) do provide a measure of independence in such areas also. The problem is, to repeat, there are really different degrees of physical data independence. Even a system like IMS provides a certain amount of such independence. Thus, I don't think such independence can be a simple "Yes" or "No" item.

Rule 9 – Logical Data Independence: *(I assume you're familiar with this concept and won't bother to define it here.)*

Codd goes on to say that "the DBMS must be capable of handling inserts, updates, and deletes on *all views* that are theoretically updatable" (emphasis in the original)—in other words, Rule 9 implies Rule 6, as previously claimed.[43] Note too that, like the previous rule, this rule really is not a simple "Yes" or "No" item. (Come to think of it, in fact, almost none of Codd's rules is a simple "Yes" or "No" item.)

---

[42] This claim was valid at the time I wrote the original paper. I don't know to what extent it still is.

[43] I might add here that the DBMS also needs to be capable of handling *retrievals* on all views—another area in which certain early SQL systems, including early versions of DB2, failed.

Rule 10 – Integrity Independence: *Integrity constraints must be specified separately from application programs and stored in the catalog. It must be possible to change such constraints as and when appropriate without unnecessarily affecting existing applications.*

I have no objection to this rule as such, but note that:

a. First, Codd actually violates the rule himself, in his ALPHA language!—at least with respect to <u>KEY</u> specifications (see Chapter 4).

b. Second, the requirement has effectively already been specified as part of Rule 5 (the comprehensive data sublanguage rule).

c. Third, it's stated (or at least implied) again later as one of "the three integrity features" of the relational model.

Note that points b. and c. demonstrate once again that the requirements aren't as independent of one another as they might be.

Rule 11 – Distribution Independence: *Existing applications should continue to operate successfully (a) when a distributed version of the DBMS is first introduced; (b) when existing distributed data is redistributed around the system.*

This seems to be another rule that's hard to apply in practice, since it has to do with future possibilities. An argument could be made that *any* database language (e.g., IMS's DL/I) could be implemented in a transparent fashion over distributed data; in fact, I believe IBM's CICS/ISC "data request shipping" feature did provide a measure of distribution independence for DL/I as far back as 1985. It's also not clear that distribution independence has anything to do with relational technology per se. Of course, I do agree that relational technology is the best basis for a distributed system, but that seems to me to be a quite separate point.

Rule 12 – Nonsubversion: *If the system provides a low level (record level) interface, then that interface can't be used to subvert the system by (e.g.) bypassing a relational security or integrity constraint.*

While this might be a very desirable property of systems in practice, it does appear as if it was included in the list primarily in order to disqualify "born again" relational systems (meaning systems like IDMS/R and Datacom/DB that consist of a relational layer on top of an older, nonrelational DBMS). The low level interface in such systems is certainly an Achilles heel, and it's legitimate to warn users of the potential dangers inherent in the existence of such an interface. But to make this requirement one of the basic "twelve rules," when there are so many other candidate rules that are much more genuinely relational, doesn't seem very objective to me.

Conclusion

Despite the many criticisms outlined in the foregoing, it's undeniable that Codd's "twelve rules" did have a major influence on the database marketplace for many years (in fact they probably still do, to some extent). What's more, Codd subsequently incorporated versions of those rules into RM/V2 (see Chapter 8). By now, therefore, the whole business is probably beyond redemption. Nevertheless, it still seems to me that it would be good to improve the rules before they become cast any further into concrete—improve them, that is, to a point where they were less arbitrary, better structured, and less open to criticism, and hence could serve as a fairer and more balanced basis for assessing systems. It also seems to me that a more scientific rating scheme could surely be constructed. In other words, a methodology for performing scientific, independent, and objective DBMS product evaluations is still needed. Codd's rules might form a basis from which such a methodology could be developed, but in their original form they weren't even close to satisfactory (and therefore, obviously, they still aren't). At least, that's my opinion.

Chapter 8

The Relational Model Version 2

Second thoughts are best (or are they?)
— 16th century proverb, somewhat modified

I first wrote a paper with the same title as this chapter well over 25 years ago, and published it as a chapter in my book *Relational Database Writings 1989-1991* (Addison-Wesley, 1992). The abstract to that paper read as follows:

> Codd's 1990 definition of the relational model ("The Relational Model Version 2") is summarized and briefly criticized.

As you can see, that abstract was rather terse! I elaborated on it somewhat in the following additional preamble to the paper (lightly edited here):

> In the previous chapter [*i.e., of that same book, viz., Relational Database Writings 1989-1991*], I examined Codd's 1985 definition of the relational model ("Version 1"), found it wanting in a number of respects, and proposed a reconstituted definition. In the present chapter, I turn my attention to Version 2.
>
> Now, it goes without saying that the publication in 1990 of Codd's book on Version 2 was an event of considerable importance in the database world, and one that was eagerly anticipated. When I was finally able to obtain a copy, however, I regret to say I found it quite disappointing in a number of respects. First, for a variety of reasons, it seemed to be quite difficult to read; second, I was surprised to find there was almost nothing in it that was genuinely new; third (and much the most important, of course), I found there was much that I disagreed with at the technical level—so much so, that I began to be seriously concerned about the impact the book might have if it were allowed to go unchallenged. Hence this review.[1]

That said, I now need to say too that for a variety of reasons (space reasons among them, but not just space reasons), my original review omitted a lot of material that I really would have preferred to include. As a consequence, the idea of rewriting and extending my original review to include that extra material has been nagging at me for years (over a quarter of a century, in fact); however, it wasn't until comparatively recently that a couple of incidents occurred that

---

[1] And here let me acknowledge the helpful comments of Charley Bontempo, Hugh Darwen, and David McGoveran on earlier drafts of that review.

made me think I really needed to get down to producing that rewritten and extended review, and that's what this chapter is.

Here then is what I plan to do:

- First, I'll repeat my original review, more or less as it appeared in its original published form, but with a few purely cosmetic revisions and a certain amount of additional technical annotation, or commentary. The cosmetic changes are silent. By contrast, the technical annotation—usually in the form of added footnotes—isn't silent but is preceded by the tag *"Note added in this rewrite:"* in order to highlight it.

- Then I'll add a lengthy postscript, divided up into several subsections and consisting of material that was omitted for one reason or another from the original review.

A note on the references: Many of the books and papers listed in the "References and Bibliography" section in the original review (and referenced in the body of this chapter by numbers in square brackets) have effectively been superseded by later publications. In the interest of historical accuracy, I've decided to retain the references from the review as originally published; where one of those original references might better be replaced by something more recent, however, I've so indicated by means of appropriate annotation in that section.

OVERVIEW

The 1990 publication of Codd's book *The Relational Model For Database Management Version 2* [2] was almost by definition a highly significant event in the world of database management. As the originator of the relational model, on which (at least to a first approximation) virtually all modern databases are founded,[2] Codd was and is clearly someone whose ideas deserve the courtesy of close, careful, and widespread attention. It's thus perhaps a little surprising to find that the book has received only one serious review in the literature, so far as I'm aware [24]. Moreover, what follows isn't intended as a review of the book as such either—at least, not primarily. Rather, it's intended as a review of the ideas the book propounds: namely, the relational model, Version 2 (which, following Codd and reference [2], I refer to hereinafter as RM/V2).

Clearly, the first question we need to ask is: What exactly *is* RM/V2? It's a little difficult to answer this question in any very succinct manner (indeed, as far as I can tell, reference [2] doesn't even attempt to provide any kind of "one liner" definition). But the following might help. RM/V2, whatever else it might be, is obviously meant as an extension (a compatible extension, of course) of Version 1 of the model ("RM/V1"). And the essential difference between the two is as follows: Whereas RM/V1 was intended as an abstract blueprint for just

---

[2] *Note added in this rewrite:* Excluding various application-specific databases.

one particular aspect of the total database problem—essentially the user language aspect—RM/V2 is intended as an abstract blueprint for the entire system. Thus, where RM/V1 contained just three parts (structure, integrity, and manipulation), RM/V2 contains 18; and those 18 parts include not only the original three (of course), but also parts having to do with views, the catalog, authorization, naming, distributed database, and various other aspects of database management. Here for reference is a complete list of the 18 parts:

A	Authorization	M	Manipulation
B	Basic operators	N	Naming
C	Catalog	P	Protection
D	Principles of DBMS design	Q	Qualifiers
E	Commands for the DBA	S	Structure
F	Functions	T	Data types
I	Integrity	V	Views
J	Indicators	X	Distributed database management
L	Principles of language design	Z	Advanced operators

Within each of these parts, or *classes* as Codd calls them, Codd defines a set of *features*. For example, the first feature in Class A (authorization) is as follows (italics and boldface as in the original):

RA-1 Affirmative Basis All authorization is granted on an affirmative basis: this means that users are explicitly *granted permission* to access parts of the database and parts of its description instead of being explicitly *denied access*.

Each feature has a label (RA-1 in the example—R for relational and A for authorization); [3] a descriptive tag or name (Affirmative Basis, in the example); and a prescriptive or occasionally proscriptive elaboration. RM/V2 includes a total of 333 such features, of which (according to Codd) 130 are "fundamental, and hence top priority," while the remainder are merely "basic" (?).

As already mentioned, what follows is intended primarily as a review of RM/V2 per se, rather than as a review of the book that describes it. But the following list of chapter titles from the book might be helpful in giving some indication of RM/V2's, as well as the book's, scope and structure:

1. Introduction to RM/V2
2. Structure-oriented and data-oriented features
3. Domains as extended data types
4. The basic operators
5. The advanced operators

---

[3] Actually, every feature label begins with an R.

6. Naming
7. Commands for the DBA
8. Missing information
9. Response to technical criticisms regarding missing information
10. Qualifiers
11. Indicators
12. Query and manipulation
13. Integrity constraints
14. User defined integrity constraints
15. Catalog
16. Views
17. View updatability
18. Authorization
19. Functions
20. Protection of investment
21. Principles of DBMS design
22. Principles of design for relational languages
23. Serious flaws in SQL
24. Distributed database management
25. More on distributed database management
26. Advantages of the relational approach
27. Present products and future improvements
28. Extending the relational model
29. Fundamental laws of database management
30. Claimed alternatives to the relational model

There are also two appendixes:

A. RM/V2 feature index
B. Exercises in logic and the theory of relations

Finally, there's a list of references and an index.[4] Regarding that list of references, incidentally, one overall criticism that could be leveled at RM/V2 is that it pays comparatively little attention to—often, in fact, it doesn't even mention—the great deal of prior work by other workers in the field: work, that is, not on RM/V2 per se (of course not), but on just about every one of the problems that RM/V2 is intended to address. (Reference [24] makes the same point.) Specific instances of such omissions would be out of place at this juncture, but I'll give a few examples later.

---

[4] Speaking as someone who has compiled many indexes over the years, I know what a challenging and tedious task it can be—— but I have to say the index in the book under discussion is one of the worst I've ever encountered. In fact I've found it to be almost entirely useless. I suppose your experience might differ.

And while I'm on the subject of overall criticisms, there's another aspect of RM/V2 that I find a little disturbing: namely, its generally prescriptive tone. (Again reference [24] makes the same point.) Many of the specific ideas within RM/V2—for example, its approach to naming, Features RN-1 through RN-14—are somewhat controversial, to say the least; in some cases, they're clearly wrong. And it doesn't seem appropriate to state categorically that the system *must* adopt (for example) a particular naming scheme, when that scheme is demonstrably flawed and superior schemes have already been described in the literature. (Again, see later for more specifics.) And even where the ideas aren't wrong or controversial, it still seems undesirable to be excessively prescriptive, for fear of stifling invention.

GENERAL QUESTIONS

There are some obvious general questions that need to be raised and at least briefly discussed before we get into too much detail—namely:

■ What's truly new in RM/V2?

■ What's good about it?

■ What's bad about it?

■ What's its likely impact?

What's Truly New?

By "new" here, I mean new as compared with RM/V1 as defined by Codd in reference [1].[5] In the preface to his book [2], Codd claims that the most important new features of RM/V2 are as follows (paraphrasing slightly):

■ Extension of support for missing information from three- to four-valued logic, to deal with "inapplicable" as well as "unknown" information

■ Extended support for integrity constraints, especially "user defined" constraints

■ "A more detailed account of view updatability"

■ Some "relatively new" DBMS and language design principles

---

[5] I have some criticisms of Codd's RM/V1 too, but this isn't the place to air them. They're discussed in detail in reference [17]. *Note added in this rewrite:* That reference is superseded by Chapter 7 of the present book.

■ Details of the catalog

■ Support for distributed database management

■ A definition of "some of the fundamental laws" underlying the relational model

And a few more items might be added to the foregoing list—for example, there are some new relational operators, and certain existing ones have been redefined (see various discussions later). Referring back to the original question, however ("What's truly new?"), I'd have to say the answer is "Not very much" ... Of the seven items in Codd's list above:

■ The first, having to do with missing information, *is* new, but I don't agree with it (see the section "Major Areas of Concern," later).

■ The last, having to do with "fundamental laws," is arguably new too, but it's not really part of the model as such (see the appendix to the present chapter).

■ The others might be new from the point of view of the relational model per se, but they're certainly not new from the point of view of relational technology in general, at least as that technology is perceived by most workers in the field. To be a little more specific:

    a. The area of integrity constraints has been previously addressed by many people. For instance, Eswaran and Chamberlin proposed a set of requirements for integrity support as far back as 1975 [20], and a more extensive and comprehensive set of such requirements appeared in a subsequent paper of my own [12]. Furthermore, there are products on the market today—DEC's Rdb/VMS is a case in point[6]—that already go quite a long way toward supporting that "more extensive and comprehensive set of requirements."

    b. The area of view updating likewise has received considerable attention over the years, and a variety of results have been formally proved by, e.g., Dayal and Bernstein in 1982 [19] and Keller in 1985 [23]. Reference [9] (published in 1986) presents a set of informal view updating rules very similar to those given by Codd.[7]

---

[6] *Note added in this rewrite:* DEC sold its Rdb division to Oracle Corporation in 1994, and the product is now known as Oracle Rdb.

[7] Except that it gives no rules for union, intersection, and difference views (but the extensions needed for these latter cases are essentially straightforward). *Note added in this rewrite:* My book *View Updating and Relational Theory: Solving the View Update Problem* (O'Reilly, 2013) contains a revised set of rules, much more extensive and (in my opinion) considerably less ad hoc than those given by either reference [9] or Codd's book.

c. The "DBMS design principles" are basically just a set of miscellaneous features that many of today's relational DBMSs already support (e.g., Feature RD-13, "Atomic Execution of Relational Commands"). The "language design principles" are likewise a set of miscellaneous features, some of them having to do with language design as such and some with implementation (e.g., Feature RL-2, "Compiling and Recompiling"). Once again, there's little that's truly new, at least in concept, regarding these language features as such; however, it's true that not all systems today support them all, partly because most systems today support SQL (which fails to satisfy the requirements on numerous counts), and partly perhaps because some of the requirements are controversial anyway (see later).

d. Concerning the catalog: Given that all existing relational or would-be relational systems already support a catalog of some kind (necessarily so, in fact), comment seems superfluous.

e. Finally, concerning distributed database: Again, research has been under way for many years (so has development, come to that). A good survey was published by Rothnie and Goodman as far back as 1977 [25], and prototypes implementing many of the features identified by Codd—at least the good ones—have been operational since the early eighties. And I published a paper in 1987 (reference [14]) that identified many of the same principles that Codd includes in RM/V2.

What's Good?

I find it difficult to answer this question other than in a rather general kind of way. Even if it's true as claimed above that there's little in RM/V2 that's truly new, I suppose it's useful to have all of the material collected together in a single place, and there's undoubtedly much food for thought in the 333 features. The 18 classes taken together do cover a large part of the database management problem (though there are still some omissions—utility support might be an example—and there's an observable and very unfortunate lack of orthogonality among the various features as stated). The emphasis on integrity is nice, and there's some recognition (though not enough, in my opinion) of the fact that systems these days need to have an open architecture—implying, among other things, that users need to be able to define their own data types and their own operators. *Now read on ...*

What's Bad?

I'm afraid I have to say I do find much in RM/V2 that's bad. Here I'll just list some major areas of concern (I'll give more specific criticisms later):

■ Naming

- Domains and data types

- Operators

- Support for missing information

- Orthogonality (or lack thereof, rather)

- Distributed database support

In addition, I have a large number of criticisms at a more detailed level. Some of these criticisms will also be covered later (especially in the section "A Survey of RM/V2").

What's the Likely Impact?

Another difficult question. I certainly think that database professionals ought to read the book; vendors (meaning DBMS product designers and implementers) should *definitely* read it.[8] But as I've already indicated, I do have a number of concerns:

- First, I'm concerned about the generally prescriptive tone.

- Second, I'm *very* concerned about those aspects I find to be bad, such as the prescribed support for missing information.

- Third, I'm also concerned about a lack of orthogonality in the requirements as stated.[9] Unorthogonal, piecemeal statement of the requirements is likely to lead to unorthogonal, piecemeal DBMS and language designs and implementations.

- Finally, I'm concerned about the amount of "adhocery" involved (to coin an ugly but convenient term).

For all of these reasons and more besides, I'm concerned that the overall impact could be negative, not positive. Certainly it's desirable that everyone who reads the book—vendors especially—do so with a critical eye, and with a clear understanding that for many of its recommendations there do exist alternative approaches that are at least worth considering.

---

[8] *Note added in this rewrite:* This sentence is repeated verbatim from my 1992 paper. I'm not sure I agree with it now.

[9] It's ironic, therefore, that two of Codd's "design principle" features for RM/V2 are, specifically, "Orthogonality in DBMS Design" (Feature RD-6) and "Orthogonality in Language Design" (Feature RL-8).

Note added in this rewrite: I was doing my best in my original review to be as diplomatic as I could with respect to the foregoing issues. As I've written elsewhere, however, it's my considered opinion now—and this opinion is shared by others—that, overall, Codd's RM/V2 and his book about it are both embarrassingly bad, and the best thing that could happen to them is for them to be quickly and quietly forgotten. The present rewrite of my original review might therefore be counterproductive!—but I still wanted to get my thoughts down all in one place, if only for ease of subsequent reference. And in any case, bad ideas do have a habit of surfacing again, long after one might have thought they'd been thoroughly debunked; thus, having this rewrite available, in all of its gory detail, might conceivably come in useful some day.

To summarize, then: As I've stated elsewhere (in reference [17] in particular), I do think it's crucially important to get the foundation—namely, RM/V1—right first before trying to build on that foundation to create any kind of Version 2. RM/V2 does nothing to correct what I regard as mistakes in RM/V1 (some of which are quite serious). In other words, if we're not careful, I think there's a real danger we could be building houses on sand.

A SURVEY OF RM/V2

In this section I'll give a more comprehensive overview of what's included in RM/V2. I'll use Codd's own classification scheme as a basis for structuring the discussion. However, I won't attempt to follow any particularly logical sequence but will simply present the classes alphabetically. *Note:* Perhaps rather surprisingly, the RM/V2 book [2] mostly—though not exclusively—uses the terminology of tables, columns, and rows in place of the more formal terminology of relations, attributes, and tuples. In what follows, therefore, I'll do the same.

Authorization (Class A)

The authorization features consist essentially of a minor variation on what SQL already does today. Thus, they include (a) the use of views to hide information, plus (b) the GRANT and REVOKE operators (and GRANT includes the grant option), plus (c) a few miscellaneous features.[10] There's little or no mention of other aspects of authorization, nor of other approaches or capabilities. Examples of such topics include:

- User identification

- Authentication (e.g., password checking)

---

[10] An example of such a "miscellaneous feature" is Feature RA-15, which requires that "authorization can be conditioned by the [terminal] from which a user is operating." However, that feature serves as a good example of the lack of orthogonality mentioned earlier. If authorization constraints—also known as security constraints—are specified by relational expressions (as they should be), and if an operator is available that returns the ID of the terminal in use (as it should be), then this feature is logically redundant, and there's no need for it to be stated as an explicit and separate requirement.

- Support for user groups

- CREATE and DROP PERMIT ("permits" are supported by at least one system today, viz., INGRES, and I for one think them superior to the use of views for security purposes)

- Mandatory vs. discretionary authorization

- Flow controls

- Statistical or inference controls

- The Data Encryption Standard

- Public key encryption schemes

This list isn't meant to be exhaustive.

Basic Operators (Class B)

The "basic operators" consist essentially of:

a. The relational operators—project, join, etc.—of RM/V1 (including a rather strange form of relational assignment), together with

b. A variety of INSERT, DELETE, and UPDATE operators,[11] some of them involving certain cascade effects.

Regarding the relational operators, RM/V2 unfortunately still treats truth valued expressions—specifically, in the context of "theta select, originally called theta restrict" (page 69)[12]—that are simple comparisons or logical combinations thereof as somehow special, a distinction that I find both unnecessary and undesirable [17]. And while I'm on the subject, I note that RM/V2 extends the usual set of scalar comparison operators ("=", "<", etc.) to include the new operators *least greater than* ("L>"), *greatest less than* ("G<"), etc. An example of a query using such an operator might be "Get parts whose weight is the least greater than 10":

---

[11] *Note added in this rewrite:* But how can INSERT, DELETE, and UPDATE be considered "basic" operators if—as it should be—relational assignment is properly supported? (Of course, as noted in Chapter 7 of the present book, it *isn't* properly supported in RM/V1, and reference [2] makes it clear that it isn't properly supported in RM/V2 either.)

[12] Unlike reference [1], reference [2] uses "theta" (thus spelled out) in place of the Greek letter "θ" in operator names, and thus talks about, e.g., "theta select" instead of "θ-select."

```
P WHERE WEIGHT L> 10
```

Here for comparison is an SQL formulation of this query:

```
SELECT   PX.*
FROM     P AS PX
WHERE    PX.WEIGHT =
       ( SELECT MIN ( PY.WEIGHT )
         FROM    P AS PY
         WHERE   PY.WEIGHT > 10 )
```

One interesting aspect of these new "scalar" comparison operators is that they're not!—not scalar, I mean, because their arguments aren't just simple scalar values. As a consequence, the expression WEIGHT L> 10, for example, isn't a restriction condition as such, because it can't be evaluated for a given row by examining just that row in isolation (as indeed the SQL version of the query makes clear).[13] These new operators thus violate Codd's own Feature RZ-38, which requires (in part) that "the truth value of [such expressions] must be computable for each row using only [column values within] that row."

> *Aside:* An interesting sidelight on these new operators is the following: Suppose view V is defined using the expression shown in the foregoing example (or its SQL counterpart). Then inserting a single row into table P or deleting a single row from table P or updating a single row in table P could change *the entire population* of view V "at a stroke." (Of course, the same is true for any view for which the view defining expression is more complex than a simple restriction—for example, a view that consists of just those rows of table P with WEIGHT equal to the current minimum WEIGHT value.) *End of aside.*

Regarding the "cascade" operators (see, e.g., Feature RB-36, "The Delete Operator with Cascaded Deletion"): First, I believe that CASCADE DELETE (and similar actions) should be specified declaratively, not procedurally.[14] Second, it's entirely possible that different referential constraints involving the same primary key will require different treatment when some given row is deleted (e.g., some might specify ON DELETE CASCADE while others specify ON DELETE NO CASCADE), in which case the procedural operator makes no sense. Third, Codd appears to ignore all of the work previously done on such matters by other people (see, e.g., my own work as reported in reference [5]).

---

[13] *Note added in this rewrite:* What's more, in the expression *rx* WHERE *A* L> *B*, *A* can be—indeed, probably is—the name of an attribute of the relation denoted by *rx* but *B* can't be (why not, exactly?).

[14] Though I might be persuaded that the declarative specification should be triggered only if the user uses the corresponding procedural operator, so that at least the user understands that cascading will or might occur. *Note added in this rewrite:* But what if the cascading in question affects some table that's hidden from the user in question? On reflection, I think I have to stand by my original position that cascading should be specified declaratively, not procedurally at all.

Catalog (Class C)

No real surprises, and no comments.

Principles of DBMS Design (Class D)

A somewhat miscellaneous collection of features. To give some idea of the scope of the features in question, I'll simply list them here by name:

1. Nonviolation of any fundamental law of mathematics[15]
2. Under-the-covers representation and access
3. Sharp boundary [*i.e., between logical and physical considerations*]
4. Concurrency independence
5. Protection against unauthorized long term locks[16]
6. Orthogonality in DBMS design
7. Domain based index
8. Database statistics
9. Interrogation of statistics
10. Changing storage representation and access options
11. Automatic protection in case of malfunction
12. Automatic recovery in case of malfunction
13. Atomic execution of relational commands
14. Automatic archiving
15. Avoiding cartesian product
16. Responsibility for encryption and decryption

A small comment regarding item 4 here, "Concurrency independence" (Feature RD-4): For some reason Codd discusses "intra command" concurrency (which refers to the possibility of evaluating distinct portions of a single expression in parallel), also "inter command" concurrency (which refers to the possibility of evaluating distinct expressions and/or statements in parallel), but not transaction concurrency, which is surely the kind of concurrency most commonly found in systems today.

---

[15] *Note added in this rewrite:* Ironically, however, Codd's own "marks" lead to exactly such violations! For example, $x + y - y$ doesn't reduce to just x, if y happens to be "marked."

[16] *Note added in this rewrite:* Personally, I don't believe locking as such should be mentioned at all as part of what's supposed to be an abstract model, because concurrency control doesn't have to be based on locking. And Codd appears to agree, because on page 19 of the RM/V2 book [2] he says "[when] locking as a form of concurrency control is mentioned ... it is accompanied by the phrase 'or some alternative technique that is at least as powerful as locking (and provably so)'." But Feature RD-5 for one doesn't abide by this practice.

Commands for the DBA (Class E)

These "commands" (as noted in reference [17], I vastly prefer either the term *operators* or—depending on the intended interpretation—the term *statements*) are basically the usual data definition operators (basically CREATE, ALTER, RENAME, and DROP operators for domains and base tables and columns), plus a LOAD operator, plus ARCHIVE and REACTIVATE operators, plus operators to create and drop indexes, etc.—plus a rather peculiar operator called CONTROL DUPLICATE ROWS (Feature RE-20).[17]

I have two broad comments on these "DBA commands." First, I don't think it's appropriate, in an abstract model of the kind I assume RM/V2 is meant to be, to suggest that any "command" is only for the DBA, or only for anyone else for that matter (the question of who uses a particular feature is surely a question that lies outside the scope of the model per se). Second, *indexes*? What on earth does creating and dropping indexes have to do with the *model*? (As an aside, I note that reference [2] has quite a lot to say about indexes, all of which in my opinion could be deleted without loss. For example, on page 92 we find this: "[Indexes] ... are automatically updated by the DBMS to reflect the requested update activity." Why, in this context, should it be necessary to say such a thing at all?)

Functions (Class F)

The required functions—incidentally, I much prefer the term *operators*, or more specifically *read-only* operators if the "functions" in question are indeed functions in the mathematical sense, but let that pass—include:

■ The usual scalar operators "+", "–", "*", "/", "**" (exponentiation), "| |" (string concatenation), and substring

■ The usual aggregate operators COUNT, SUM, AVG, MAX, and MIN, with and without duplicate elimination[18]

Support for user defined operators is also required.

Note: Codd unfortunately says the required operators must be "built into the DBMS." While such might be the user's perception, I've argued elsewhere (e.g., in reference [16]) that the operators in question shouldn't need to be built into the DBMS per se; i.e., the DBMS doesn't need to "understand" those operators—all it needs to know is how to invoke them.

---

[17] Incidentally, the text accompanying Feature RE-20 in reference [2] contains the following delightful remark: "The [resulting] column ... is named by the DBMS as column ZZZ or given some equally unlikely name."

[18] And with a suggested syntax, incidentally, that makes the same mistakes as SQL does with respect to argument specifications, in connection with both argument scope and duplicate elimination (see Chapter 4).

Integrity (Class I)

Codd requires support for "five types of integrity"—domain, entity, referential, column, and "user defined." I don't have any major objections to the requirement as such,[19] but I think a much better (i.e., much more systematic) classification scheme can be defined [12]—one that includes all of the features Codd discusses and more besides—and I also think this is an area where credit should be given to the very great deal of work that has already been done by other people (including the vendors of certain commercially available products, such as INGRES and Rdb/VMS). A couple of minor points:

- First, Codd does not permit "MAYBE qualifiers" to appear in integrity constraints, without offering any justification for this violation of orthogonality. (Of course, I'm assuming for the moment that support for such qualifiers is desirable, which I don't in fact believe.)

- Second, the discussion of constraints seems to have *true* and *false* back to front: It says on pages 263-264, and possibly elsewhere, that the specified response to an attempted integrity violation is carried out if the condition part of the constraint evaluates to *true*, but surely that *true* should be *false*.

Indicators (Class J)

Indicators are set to show that some exceptional situation has arisen during the execution of some operation. To give some idea of the scope of the proposed indicators, I'll simply list them here by name:

1. Empty relation
2. Empty divisor
3. Missing information
4. Nonexisting argument
5. Domain not declared
6. Domain check error
7. Column still exists
8. Duplicate row
9. Duplicate primary key
10. Nonredundant ordering
11. Catalog block

---

[19] Actually I do, if only to Codd's terminology. For one thing, as noted in Chapter 7, *every* constraint that applies to *any* database is—indeed, must be—"user defined," in the final analysis.

12. View not tuple insertible
13. View not component updatable
14. View not tuple deletable

I don't want to get into a detailed discussion of all of these indicators here; however, I remark that the class as a whole seems to involve a very great deal of adhocery. For example: Why is there an "empty divisor" indicator as well as an "empty relation" indicator (since after all a divisor, as that term is meant to be understood here, is certainly a relation)? Why are the "duplicate row" and "duplicate primary key [value]" indicators set by LOAD but not INSERT? Why is there a "domain not declared" indicator (which is set if a column definition mentions a nonexistent domain) but no "table not declared" indicator (which might be set if a foreign key definition mentions a nonexistent table)? Etc., etc.

Principles of Language Design (Class L)

As already noted in the section "General Questions" earlier, the "language design principles" are basically a set of miscellaneous features, only some of which have to do with language design as such (the rest have to do with implementation). None of them is truly new, in my opinion; however, some of them are certainly debatable. Here are some examples:

■ Feature RL-2: [Database] commands must be compilable separately from the host language context in which they ... appear. The DBMS must support the compilation of [such] commands, even if it also supports [interpretation] ... the DBMS must support automatic recompilation of [database] commands whenever any change in access paths [etc.] invalidates the code developed by a previous compilation.

I don't think it's appropriate, in an abstract model such as I assume RM/V2 is intended to be, to *require* a clear separation between database operations and the host language—i.e., to bless the "embedded data sublanguage" approach—even if you happen to think such separation is a good idea, which I don't [6]. I also don't think it's appropriate (again in an abstract model) to *require* that database operations be compiled, not interpreted, even though there might be good practical reasons to prefer compilation. Nor do I think it appropriate (yet again in an abstract model) to bless the System R approach of automatic recompilation, even though, again, it might often be a good idea.

■ Feature RL-9: [The relational language must be] more closely related to the relational calculus ... than to the relational algebra.

Very debatable!—even though I do tend to prefer the calculus myself.[20] The argument Codd gives to support this requirement—namely, that it improves optimizability—is specious (see reference [22], also Chapter 3 of the present book).

■ Feature RL-12: There must be a single canonical form for every request.

While I'm in sympathy with the objectives behind this requirement, I tend to doubt whether it's achievable as stated. Is there a proof somewhere?

■ Feature RL-16: Time-oriented conditions can be included in any condition specified in a [database] command.

Another example of lack of orthogonality in the requirements as stated: If temporal operators such as "time now," "date today," etc., are provided, as they obviously should be, then the feature is logically redundant—there's no need for it to be stated as an explicit and separate requirement.[21]

Incidentally, it seems to me that if RM/V2 is to lay down principles regarding language design, then it really ought to give some credit to, or at least pay some attention to, the achievements of the programming languages community in this connection over the last 30 years or so[22]—especially since the most visible "achievement" of the database community in this regard, namely SQL, in all of its various forms, is in so many ways the prize example of how not to do it. See, e.g., reference [7].

Manipulation (Class M)

Class M requires a "comprehensive data sublanguage" (this term is taken from Codd's original "twelve rules" [1]), including support for set level INSERT, DELETE, and UPDATE operators and support for three- and four-valued logic. It also requires or reemphasizes:

a. Transaction support (BEGIN, COMMIT, and ROLLBACK operators)

b. "Operational closure" (the result of a relational operation is always another relation)

---

[20] *Note added in this rewrite:* Well, maybe. I mean, it might still be true that I prefer the calculus, but I think it's less true now than it was when I wrote my original review in 1992. (Degrees of truth, anyone?)

[21] *Note added in this rewrite:* Hugh Darwen, Nikos Lorentzos, and I have published an entire book on the handling of time in a relational database (*Time and Relational Theory: Temporal Data in the Relational Model and SQL*, Morgan Kaufmann, 2014). I mention this point merely in order to make it clear that Codd is *not* proposing support here for any aspect of the temporal problem more sophisticated than the rather trivial one of supporting operators such as the ones mentioned ("time now," "date today," etc.).

[22] *Note added in this rewrite:* The phrase "the last 30 years or so" is as it appeared in my original review and thus refers to the period 1960-1990, roughly speaking.

c. "Dynamic mode" support (operations such as creating and dropping tables must be possible without halting the system)

d. An interface to record level languages such as COBOL

e. Domain constrained operators and support for "domain check override"

f. "Library checkout and return" operators (intended as a primitive level of support for version control)

Regarding a. here, Codd also requires a special kind of transaction called a "catalog block" for performing data definition operations, though it's not really clear why two distinct transaction mechanisms are necessary (another example of lack of orthogonality?). Regarding d., Codd goes out of his way to suggest that SQL-style cursors are *not* very satisfactory for the purpose, an opinion with which I concur. Regarding e., I disagree with Codd's approach to this whole area (see the section "Major Areas of Concern," later). I also disagree with his requirement for three- and four-valued logic support (again, see the section "Major Areas of Concern").

Naming (Class N)

Codd proposes a naming scheme for "domains and data types" [*sic!*], relations and columns (including result relations and columns), "archived relations," functions, and integrity constraints (though oddly enough not for security constraints[23]). And later he also proposes an extension of that scheme for use in the distributed database context (Class X).

As mentioned earlier, naming is one of the areas regarding which I have severe reservations, and so I'll defer further comment on this topic to the section "Major Areas of Concern."

Protection (Class P)

Protection here refers to protection of the user's investment. This class consists essentially of the physical data independence, logical data independence, integrity independence, and distribution independence features from Codd's original "twelve rules" [1] (see also reference [18]). No further comment.

---

[23] This omission is presumably due to the fact that security constraints in RM/V2 are unnamed, created as they are by an SQL-style GRANT statement instead of by some kind of CREATE operation. *Note added in this rewrite:* But the fact that security constraints are unnamed has certainly given rise to problems in SQL systems. Is Codd just blessing a particular style of implementation here simply because it's one he happens to be familiar with?

Qualifiers (Class Q)

Qualifiers are *statement modifiers*. They're used within a statement[24] "to alter some aspect of the execution of that [statement]." The available qualifiers are summarized below:

1. *A-MAYBE:* Consider the "statement" (actually it's not a statement but an expression)

   ```
   rx WHERE bx A-MAYBE
   ```

   Let *tv* be the truth value resulting from evaluation of the boolean subexpression *bx* for some specific row of the relation *r* denoted by *rx*. Then the effect of the A-MAYBE qualifier is as follows: (a) If *tv* is either "inapplicable" or *true*, it's replaced by *false*, and (b) if *tv* is "applicable but unknown," it's replaced by *true*. Thus, the given "statement" (expression) evaluates to a relation containing just those rows of *r* for which *bx* evaluates to the "applicable but unknown" truth value.[25]

2. *I-MAYBE:* Consider the expression

   ```
   rx WHERE bx I-MAYBE
   ```

   Let *tv* be the truth value resulting from evaluation of the boolean subexpression *bx* for some specific row of the relation *r* denoted by *rx*. Then the effect of the I-MAYBE qualifier is as follows: (a) If *tv* is either "applicable but unknown" or *true*, it's replaced by *false*, and (b) if *tv* is "inapplicable," it's replaced by *true*. Thus, the expression overall evaluates to a relation containing just those rows of *r* for which *bx* evaluates to the "inapplicable" truth value.

3. *MAYBE:* Consider the expression

   ```
   rx WHERE bx MAYBE
   ```

   Let *tv* be the truth value resulting from evaluation of the boolean subexpression *bx* for some specific row of the relation *r* denoted by *rx*. Then the effect of the MAYBE qualifier is as follows: (a) If *tv* is *true*, it's replaced by *false*, and (b) if *tv* is "applicable but unknown" or "inapplicable," it's replaced by *true*. Thus, the expression overall evaluates to a relation

---

[24] *Note added in this rewrite:* But what about modifying expressions rather than statements? In any case, the whole idea of modifying either statements or expressions in the manner proposed is fraught with all kinds of difficulties, problems, and traps for the unwary. The paper "An Overview and Analysis of Proposals Based on the TSQL2 Approach" (by Hugh Darwen and myself, but originally drafted by Hugh alone) in my book *Date on Database: Writings 2000-2006* (Apress, 2006), gives some idea of the kinds of difficulties that can arise.

[25] A-MAYBE is so called on page 208 of reference [2] but is called MAYBE_A on page 209 and elsewhere. Likewise, I-MAYBE is so called on page 208 of reference [2] but is called MAYBE_I on page 209 and elsewhere.

containing just those rows of *r* for which *bx* evaluates to either the "applicable but unknown" truth value or the "inapplicable" truth value.

4. *AR(x):* During evaluation of some aggregate operator invocation, replaces values marked "applicable but unknown" by *x*.

5. *IR(x):* During evaluation of some aggregate operator invocation, replaces values marked "inapplicable" by *x*.

6. *ESR(x):* During evaluation of some expression, replaces empty relations by a relation containing the single tuple *x*.[26]

7. *ORDER BY:* Imposes an order on the result of a retrieval operation.

8. *ONCE ONLY:* This qualifier applies only to some rather complex new operators called T-joins, details of which are beyond the scope of this chapter. For more information, I refer you to Codd's book [2].

9. *DCO:* "Domain check override." See the section "Major Areas of Concern."

10. *EXCLUDE SIBLINGS:* Another complex one, having to do with the "cascade" update operations in the case where several relations share a common primary key.[27] Again I refer you to Codd's book [2] for more information.

11. *DOD:* "Degree of duplication" (applies to projections and unions only). "For each row in the result, the DBMS calculates the number of occurrences of that row [that would have appeared in the result] if duplicate rows had been permitted ... This count is appended to each row in the actual result as ... the *DOD column*."

12. *SAVE:* Causes the result of a relational assignment to be saved in the database. (As noted in Chapter 7 of the present book, relational assignment in RM/V2 without this qualifier merely causes the expression on the right hand side of the assignment to be evaluated and the result to be saved, under a user specified name, "in memory" [2].)

---

[26] *Note added in this rewrite:* But how can this possibly make sense? The tuple *x* must have the same heading as the empty relation in question, and in general different relations have different headings—so what happens if evaluation of the expression in question encounters two or more distinct empty relations? In any case, pages 203 and 211 of reference [2] seem to contradict each other regarding the ESR qualifier.

[27] *Note added in this rewrite:* "Relations" here and elsewhere would more correctly be "relvars" (i.e., relation variables). And I reject the notion of primary keys anyway, believing rather that all keys (all "candidate" keys, that is) should be treated equally. (By the way, please note that I follow reference [2] in this chapter in talking in terms of relations (or tables) throughout. I leave it as an exercise for the reader to decide when "relvars" would really be more correct.)

13. *VALUE:* "When this qualifier is attached along with a value *v* to a command or expression[28] that (1) creates a new column in a relation (base or derived) and (2) would normally fill this column with marked values, it causes *v* to be inserted in this column instead of each of the marked values."

The foregoing thumbnail sketches should be more than sufficient to suggest that the "Qualifiers" class of features is quite ad hoc and not very orthogonal. To take two examples, almost at random: First, given proper orthogonal treatment for the aggregate operators (COUNT in particular), the DOD qualifier is totally redundant. Second, instead of an AR(*x*) qualifier—assuming for the sake of the discussion that we accept the idea that support for "applicable but unknown marks" (or nulls) is desirable in the first place—surely it would be preferable to support SQL's COALESCE operator (or DB2's VALUE operator, or ORACLE's NVL operator, or INGRES's IFNULL operator, or whatever), and then to allow that operator to be used completely orthogonally (i.e., to appear wherever a scalar literal of the appropriate type can appear).

Structure (Class S)

The only arguably new features in this class are those having to do with composite domains and columns[29] (see below). The other features are basically as expected—they have to do with relations, columns, prohibition of duplicate rows,[30] prohibition of "positional concepts," primary and foreign keys, "domains as extended data types," representation of missing information by "marks," and so on. (Note that Codd talks throughout reference [2] in terms of "marks" rather than "nulls," partly in order to make it clear that in RM/V2 the representation of the fact that a value is missing isn't itself a value.)

Regarding composite domains and columns, I have to say that I find RM/V2 extremely muddled in this area. For instance: "The sequence in which the component columns are cited in [the declaration of the composite column] is part of the meaning of the [composite column]." So (A,B) and (B,A) are *different*? I thought there was a "prohibition against positional concepts"? And arguably much worse: Codd says the expression C θ D, where C and D are composite columns with components (C1,C2,...,C*n*) and (D1,D2,...,D*n*), respectively, and θ is "a comparator such as LESS THAN (<)," is evaluated by performing the sequence of tests C1 θ D1, then C2 θ D2, and so on, and "the first test that fails causes the whole test to fail" (reference [2], page 39). So according to this definition we have—

---

[28] Note that "command or expression"! This is one of the few places where reference [2] actually mentions expressions as such, and it's also one of the places where such a mention doesn't really make sense.

[29] *Note added in this rewrite:* Called *compound* domains and columns by Codd in earlier writings.

[30] Incidentally, I lost count of the number of times I was told by reference [2] that duplication wasn't permitted.

(1,4) = (1,5) is *false* (of course)

(1,4) ≠ (1,5) is *false* as well (!)

(1,7) < (2,6) is *false*

(1,7) ≥ (2,6) is *false* as well

—and an infinite number of similar absurdities. Note in particular that by these rules—using the symbol θ' to mean the negation of θ (e.g., if θ is ">", then θ' is "≤")—the expressions NOT (C θ D) and (C θ' D) aren't equivalent, in general!

Of course, if we limit our attention for the moment to composite columns C and D with just two components each, the problem of assigning a meaning to the comparison "C θ D" is exactly the same as the problem of assigning a meaning to the comparison "$z1 \theta z2$" where $z1$ and $z2$ are complex numbers—and, of course, this latter comparison is defined only when θ is "equals" or "not equals." Moreover, in the case of "not equals" in particular, the comparison $z1 \neq z2$ where $z1$ and $z2$ are complex numbers is most certainly not evaluated in accordance with Codd's bizarre definition.

In any case, as I've argued elsewhere [16],[31] I don't believe composite domains and composite columns, as such, should be supported at all—the problem that's purportedly solved by such support can be solved much more simply and cleanly by means of proper data type support (including support for user defined types in particular).

Data Types (Class T)

RM/V2 requires certain specific "extended" data types (though oddly enough no specific *basic* data types?) to be built into the DBMS, viz., calendar dates, clock times, and decimal currency.[32] It also requires support for user defined "extended" types.

Curiously enough, the discussion of data types under class T nowhere mentions the necessary associated operators. Instead, these are discussed elsewhere (under Class F, functions), in a very divorced kind of manner. But a type has no meaning without operators! For instance, the only significant distinction I can see between "decimal currency" (which RM/V2 requires to be built into the DBM as an "extended" data type) and "decimal numbers" (which almost certainly would also be built into the DBMS as a "basic" data type, despite the

---

[31] *Note added in this rewrite:* I beefed up those arguments in an extended article titled "We Don't Need Composite Columns" (published under the title "Say No to Composite Columns" in *Database Programming & Design 8*, No. 5, May 1995, and republished in my book *Relational Database Writings 1994-1997*, Addison-Wesley, 1998). See also Chapter 3 of the present book.

[32] I note in passing that RM/V2 actually requires decimal currency values to be represented as nonnegative integers. Why integers?—surely "correct to two decimal places" would make more sense. And why nonnegative?—account balances, for example, might easily be negative (as I'm sorry to say I know from personal experience).

fact that reference [2] doesn't actually say as much) is that certain operators, such as multiply, might make sense for the latter but not for the former.[33] And a user defined type makes no sense *at all* without a corresponding set of user defined operators.

Class T also includes two rather strange—though, I suppose, well intentioned—operators called "FAO commands" (FAO standing for "find all occurrences"). Here's an example from the RM/V2 book, page 56 (very lightly edited here):

> Find all occurrences of all city names that exist anywhere in the database ... The result is a relation CITY_DOM, with columns RELNAME, COLNAME, PK, and VALUE.

> Column COLNAME of relation RELNAME is a column that contains city names; PK identifies a row of relation RELNAME by its primary key value; and VALUE contains the city name appearing in that row. *Some questions:* What's the primary key for CITY_DOM? What's the data type of column PK? How does the user access column PK, given that (in general) it's composite, with an unknown (and varying) number of components, with unknown (and varying) names? What about the case where column PK doesn't have any components at all (i.e., if the relation identified by RELNAME has an empty primary key [26])? Could the FAO command be used to find all occurrences of "null"? If so, how? Etc., etc.

Views (Class V)

RM/V2 requires proper support for views, including support for all retrieval operations and all theoretically possible update operations. The book gives some informal algorithms for the updating case.[34] I support these requirements, as far as they go; my only comment (already mentioned earlier in this chapter) is that there's almost no acknowledgment, except for a couple of throwaway remarks, of the huge amount of work done in this area by other researchers.

Distributed Database Management (Class X)

There seems to be little new here, although, again, there's very little acknowledgment of prior work, except for occasional scanty references to the IBM prototype R* (pronounced "R star"). But the tone once again is much too prescriptive: A particular approach to the distributed

---

[33] *Note added in this rewrite:* This criticism is a little too glib. In particular, decimal currency involves the interesting question of units (U.S. dollars? U.K. sterling? other?), while decimal numbers don't. See Chapter 4 of the present book for a brief discussion of this issue.

[34] Reference [2] does include at least one oddity regarding view updatability: In a discussion of the need to retain the primary key of the underlying relation in a projection view if that view is to be updatable, it says it would be possible to retain a candidate key other than the primary key but that RM/V2 doesn't allow for this case, "partly because the class of updatable views would not be significantly enlarged in this way [*sic!*], and partly because *RM/V1 and RM/V2 do not require all of the candidate keys for every base relation to be recorded in the catalog*" (my italics). *Note added in this rewrite:* In any case, I don't believe it's always necessary for a projection view to retain a key at all in order for that view to be updatable. My book (previously mentioned in footnote 6) *View Updating and Relational Theory: Solving the View Update Problem* (O'Reilly, 2013) elaborates on this point, as well as numerous others.

database problem is *required*, one that's at least partly debatable and is at least partly specified at the wrong level of abstraction. And there are a few curious, and/or contentious, remarks and claims. Here are some examples: "[It] is a simple task to extend a local-only optimizer to handle the distributed case"; "all of the data residing at any site X ... can be treated by the users at site X in exactly the same way as if it were ... isolated from the rest of the network" (this objective is not fully achievable [14]); "adoption of this assumption [of uniform value distributions in columns] is a significant step in the right direction" (i.e., toward getting good statistics based optimization); "there is every reason to believe that the naming rules introduced here [for the distributed database environment] actually work and would satisfy most users' needs."

Advanced Operators (Class Z)

Here's a brief summary of the operators in this class:

1. *FRAME:* FRAME is basically an attack on the problem addressed in SQL by GROUP BY; however, the result of FRAME is another relation, instead of the (conceptual) "set of relations" produced by SQL's GROUP BY. However, I see little need to apply FRAME without then immediately applying some further operator (probably an aggregate operator) to the result. So I'd like to see support for a SUMMARIZE operator along the lines sketched in reference [28]—or better still, support for an EXTEND operator (see the next point below), ideally together with support for image relations.[35]

2. *EXTEND:* An ad hoc, incomplete, nonorthogonal approach to dynamically adding columns to a relation. I'd prefer support for an EXTEND operator along the lines sketched in reference [28].

3. *SEMIJOIN:* The semijoin of *A* with *B* is the regular (inner) join of *A* and *B*, projected back on to the columns of *A*. While this operator can sometimes be useful internally, I see no need to expose it to the user, or to include it in any version of the relational model.[36]

---

[35] *Note added in this rewrite:* See my book *SQL and Relational Theory: How to Write Accurate SQL Code* (3rd edition, O'Reilly, 2015) regarding the use of EXTEND with image relations. As for seeing "little need to apply FRAME without then immediately applying some further operator": I still subscribe to this opinion as stated, but that fact shouldn't be construed as meaning I don't think FRAME or something like it should be supported. In fact **Tutorial D** does support an operator called GROUP, which addresses the same kind of problem as FRAME does (though I think it does so more elegantly).

[36] *Note added in this rewrite:* Wash my mouth out with soap! SEMIJOIN as defined here is very useful! I think I must have been confusing it with another operator of the same name, one that is indeed primarily of use internally (see Frank P. Palermo, "A Data Base Search Problem," in Julius T. Tou (ed.), *Information Systems: COINS IV*, Plenum Press, 1974). However, if SEMIJOIN is supported, then I think SEMIMINUS should be supported as well. I've written about both of these operators elsewhere—e.g., in the book mentioned in the previous footnote, *SQL and Relational Theory: How to Write Accurate SQL Code* (3rd edition, O'Reilly, 2015)—under the names MATCHING and NOT MATCHING, respectively. See also Chapter 1 of the present book.

4. *OUTER JOIN:* I assume you're familiar with this operator, at least in broad outline. I remark, however, that RM/V2 doesn't address the (very difficult) question of what *kinds* of "nulls" (or "marks") should be generated in the result. It does, however, address the baroque question of the interaction between "outer" and "maybe" operations; in fact, the "maybe" qualifier is *first discussed* in the context of the "outer" operators (reference [2], page 110), nearly 100 pages before it's explained.

5. *OUTER UNION, OUTER INTERSECTION, OUTER DIFFERENCE:* The definitions of these operators have been silently changed, but they're still—in my opinion—completely bizarre. I won't bother to give the new definitions here, which are in any case quite complex. For details, I refer you to the book.

6. *T-JOIN:* "[The] expected use of [this operator]" is "for generating schedules" [2]. The operator is very complex, and I won't try to explain it here—Codd's explanation takes over 13 pages of his book—except to note that it basically seems to be a specific application of the new comparison operators "least greater than," etc., which I've already commented on in this chapter. Once again, for details I refer you to the book.

7. *User defined SELECT and JOIN:* The "descriptive tag" here is inappropriate, and indeed misleading. What's really being proposed is the ability for users to define their own truth valued operators. Orthogonality, if available, would then take care of the rest.

8. *Recursive JOIN:* Given a relation that represents an acyclic directed graph, this operator computes the transitive closure of that graph (slightly simplified explanation). The intent is to provide a basis for an attack on the "bill of materials" problem. Here I'll only remark that, while this operator is clearly necessary (and desirable), there's a lot more that needs to be done to address the bill of materials requirement fully [21].[37]

As already mentioned, Codd's class of "advanced operators" doesn't include either SUMMARIZE or a proper EXTEND; nor does it include any kind of generalized DIVIDE operator, nor a proper column RENAME operator [28].[38] I note also that Codd doesn't seem to give relational calculus versions or definitions for any of the new RM/V2 operators; in fact, reference [2] says very little about the relational calculus at all, in any context—except for Feature RL-9, which as previously noted (and with little by way of justification) requires the user's language to be "more closely related to the relational calculus ... than to the relational algebra" (!).

---

[37] *Note added in this rewrite:* Incidentally, it's not clear why Codd chose to rename the operator. *Transitive closure* is well known and well understood. *Recursive join* suggests that something new is being proposed, which isn't really the case.

[38] *Note added in this rewrite:* Feature RE-11 does define a column rename operator, but it's not the operator I mean when I talk about "a proper column RENAME operator." See Chapter 1 for an example of this latter, also my book *SQL and Relational Theory: How to Write Accurate SQL Code*, 3rd edition (O'Reilly, 2015) for further details.

Summary

The only idea in all of the foregoing that seems to me both (a) genuinely new, in the sense that I've never seen it discussed before in the literature, and (b) possibly worthwhile, appears to be the new comparison operators ("least greater than," etc.). I really think that's it. And even here, I find matters somewhat confused—first, because a comparison involving such an operator isn't a proper restriction condition, as already pointed out; second, because there's a lack of orthogonality in the treatment of those operators; and third, because Codd himself says the operators aren't new anyway but "well known"! (reference [2], page 123).

If you disagree with the foregoing assessment, then I challenge you to point to a significant feature of RM/V2—one that's worthwhile, I mean—that hasn't already been described in some previously published book or paper.

By contrast, I do find numerous ideas in RM/V2 that aren't new, or are muddled, or are just plain bad. Some major cases in point are articulated in the section immediately following.

MAJOR AREAS OF CONCERN

In this section I'll briefly consider what I regard as some of the most serious problems with RM/V2. Space precludes discussion of all of my concerns in detail; in most cases, therefore, I'll simply state my overriding objections to the aspect in question and give references to other publications that describe alternative approaches.

Naming

Codd's proposed column naming scheme is extremely ad hoc (to say the least), involves a number of arbitrary and dogmatic judgments, and includes some suggestions that are plainly wrong. To be more specific:

■ The suggestion for naming columns in the result of a union, intersection, or difference operation (based on alphabetical ordering of names of operand columns) is weak—not to mention the fact that it might even be implementation dependent, depending as it does on the particular alphabet in use.[39]

---

[39] *Note added in this rewrite:* I'm not sure this latter criticism is entirely valid as stated. In fact, after a careful rereading of reference [2], I've come to the conclusion that—believe it or not—RM/V2 has *no rules at all* regarding names of columns in the result of a union, intersection, or difference, except inasmuch as it does require in the first two cases that operator commutativity not be impaired (Feature RN-7). Now, you might expect such rules to be given in Feature RN-6 ("Naming of Columns Involved in the Union Class of Operators"), which is part of Section 6.2 ("Naming Columns in Intermediate and Final Results")—which title, by the way, would be just "Naming of Columns in Results," or even just "Naming of Columns," if the features of RM/V2 were stated more orthogonally—but you won't find any such rules there. Which is rather odd, considering that other features in that section do spell out the rules for other operators, such as join: though the rules in question are unfortunately all very bad.

■ The suggestion for naming columns in the result of a join or division operation is very bad (among other things, it violates closure).

■ The suggestion for naming "computed columns" is grotesque; if taken literally, it would give the name "+.A", or possibly "+.A+", or possibly even "+.A+B", to a column whose values are computed by evaluating the expression A+B! Furthermore, which of these various possibilities is actually assigned in any given situation is unpredictable, in general. You might like to meditate on the case of, e.g., a union of two relations each involving such computed columns.

■ And there are further problems having to do with columns that are derived from literals (Codd's scheme does not address them), and with name uniqueness (Codd's scheme does not guarantee it), and with predictability (Codd's scheme does not guarantee it), and with "composite columns" (see earlier), and with the distributed database environment.

A naming scheme that's far superior to Codd's—one that's closed, systematic, comprehensive, not ad hoc, etc.—is sketched in reference [27].[40]

Data Types

I've explained elsewhere [10] what I think proper data type support should consist of. Codd's approach is again very ad hoc. A few quotes:

■ "For each composite domain, of course, the sequence in which the [component] domains are specified is a vital part of the definition." (I love that "of course"!)

■ "Note that a composite column is restricted to combining simple columns ... I fail to see the practical need for [composite columns defined on composite columns]." So a composite column isn't really a column, because it can't be a component of another such (another composite column, that is).[41]

---

[40] *Note added in this rewrite:* I've belatedly noticed that Codd not only fails to adopt that superior scheme, he goes out of his way to attack it. Feature RN-5 reads as follows: "Success of the DBMS in executing any [operation] that involves comparing database values from distinct columns must not depend on those columns having identical column names." To rub salt into the wound, the name of this feature is "Naming Freedom"! PS: Also, Feature RN-4 says "The syntax of [the user language] must avoid separating column names from relation names." So what happens if the relation in question is an intermediate result and thus has no name of its own?

[41] *Note added in this rewrite* (repeated from Chapter 3): As Jim Gray once said to me, anything in computer science that's not recursive is no good.

■ (From a discussion of Class I, integrity:) "One reason that [column integrity] is part of the relational model is that it makes it possible to avoid the needless complexities and proliferations of domains that are subsets of other domains."[42]

■ "When comparing (1) a computed value with a database value or (2) one computed value with another computed value ... the DBMS merely checks that the basic data types are the same." Well, I've pointed out elsewhere—see, e.g., reference [10]—that this rule implies among many other things that the two logically equivalent expressions

```
WEIGHT > QTY
```

and

```
WEIGHT - QTY > 0
```

have different semantics, which can't be correct, or acceptable.

■ "[The] basic data type [*i.e., the data type of the underlying representation*] indicates whether arithmetic operators are applicable" (in the discussion of Feature RE-3, CREATE DOMAIN). So the expression

```
WEIGHT * WEIGHT
```

is legal? Square weights?

Also, despite Codd's remarks on the subject (reference [2], page 44), I still don't understand the real difference between "basic" and "extended" data types. Nor do I think there is any—at least from the point of view of the user who merely makes use of the type in question, as opposed to the agency (system or human) that's responsible for actually defining that type.[43] See reference [11] for further discussion of this issue.

While I'm on this subject, I note too that the book includes a couple of rather fundamental questions for the reader—"What is the precise definition of a domain in the relational model?" (Exercise 2.2) and "Define the candidate key concept" (Exercise 2.5)—to neither of which, so far as I can tell, does the book provide any good answer. And Exercise 2.12 says: "Supply two reasons why the DBA should always control the introduction of new [data] types ... to ensure that [their] values are atomic in meaning as well as atomic with respect to the DBMS." I would be very hard pressed to say exactly

---

[42] *Note added in this rewrite:* Quite apart from the fact that I find this "justification" bizarre in the extreme, it turns out that allowing domains to be subsets of other domains is exactly what Hugh Darwen and I require as a basis for our model of type inheritance. See my book *Type Inheritance and Relational Theory: Subtypes, Supertypes, and Substitutability* (O'Reilly, 2016).

[43] Though a fruitful analogy *might* be drawn between the system vs. user defined types distinction, on the one hand, and the system vs. user defined relvars distinction on the other—where by "system defined relations" I basically mean the relvars in the catalog. But do note that I refer explicitly here to "system vs. user defined" types, not "basic vs. extended" types.

what this means, but the general intent seems to be that user defined data types shouldn't be allowed to be "of arbitrary complexity," a position I most certainly don't agree with [10].[44]

Finally, I categorically reject the "domain check override" idea, for reasons explained in detail in reference [10].

Operators

I have no objection (of course) to extending the relational model to include new operators such as (e.g.) T-joins and recursive joins (though I reserve judgment on these particular operators as such). But I do think it's important to get the basic operators right first, and I don't think RM/V2 has done that yet. See reference [17] for a discussion of what I would regard as a preferable set of basic operators.

Missing Information Support

I find everything to do with three- and four-valued logic support fundamentally misguided, and I categorically reject it [13]. Moreover, the chapter in Codd's book titled "Response to Technical Criticisms Regarding Missing Information" doesn't respond properly to *any* of the really serious questions raised in reference [13]. (Incidentally, that chapter in Codd's book mentions "[Date 1986]" as a paper that criticizes the three-valued logic approach, but omits that paper from the book's list of references—which makes it a little difficult for readers to study the arguments for themselves! For the record, "[Date 1986]" is reference [8] in the present chapter. But in any case, I now think the questions raised in reference [13] are much more serious.)

Orthogonality

I've mentioned my concerns in this area a couple of times already, and I won't repeat the details here. But I'll offer this thought: If the principle of orthogonality had been applied to the statement of requirements in RM/V2, would there really have been a need for 333 distinct features?

Distributed Database Support

Again, I've already stated my overall objection in this area: namely, the insistence that a certain possibly controversial approach to the problem be the one that must be followed. Codd ignores much of the work that has already been done elsewhere on distributed databases in general, and his proposals are sometimes at the wrong level of abstraction. For instance:

---

[44] *Note added in this rewrite:* Also, Exercise 3.3 begins thus: "A critic has stated that basic data types and extended data types are really built in and user defined, respectively ... ." I wonder who that critic could have been.

- *Feature RX-4:* The network [must contain] N copies ($N > 1$) of the global catalog, in the form of N small databases at N distinct sites.

- *Feature RX-29:* The DBMS [must detect] intersite deadlocks.

- *From reference [2], page 397:* The source code of application programs can contain local names, but these are converted by the DBMS ... into global names ... It is this *globalized source code* that is retained in the system and remains unaffected by redeployment of the data, partly because it contains no local names.

MISCELLANEOUS COMMENTS

In this section, I'd like to offer a few miscellaneous comments—comments, that is, that don't properly belong in any of the previous sections of this review and yet I feel ought not to be lost entirely.

- First, regarding the question (already touched on several times) of levels of abstraction: It seems to me that there are quite a few features of RM/V2 that simply have no place in an abstract model. For example:

    a. As mentioned in passing earlier, there's much talk of indexes of various kinds.

    b. There's a requirement (Feature RD-15, also mentioned in passing earlier) that the system "avoid generating cartesian products."

    c. There are requirements, also mentioned earlier, for (a) compilation as opposed to interpretation and (b) an embedded sublanguage approach.

    d. There's a requirement that deleted data be archived "for seven days" (no more and no less).

    e. There's a requirement that data of type TIME be accurate to the second (no more and no less).

    f. The example of "several relations sharing a primary key" (reference [2], top of page 26) is surely of *stored* relations or relvars, rather), not of relations or relvars that are visible to the user.

    g. The explanation of Feature RS-13 (reference [2], page 39) talks about "bit boundaries."

Many more examples could be given.

■ There are several very strange remarks in the book regarding join dependencies and fifth normal form [4]. First of all, Feature RI-30 talks about join dependencies, and introduces a notation for them, in a way that simply makes no sense so far as I can see:

Column A is join dependent on columns B and C: R.A = R.B * R.C.

This is the text of Feature RI-30 in its entirety! And in any case, in what sense exactly is this a *feature* of the model?[45]

Codd then requires the catalog for a distributed database (but not, apparently, for a nondistributed database?) to describe the total database "as if" (?) the user relations—really relvars—were *in fifth normal form* (my italics). Just what this means isn't entirely clear; but if it means the base relvars are all supposed to be in 5NF, then the requirement is unenforceable.[46] Of course, RM/V2 could prohibit the specification of integrity constraints that happened to be join dependencies not implied by candidate keys (though I suspect that even that prohibition might be hard to enforce, given the multiplicity of syntactic ways in which such a constraint might be formulated). But:

a. The objectives of Boyce/Codd normal form and "independent projections" can be in conflict (see Chapter 5), and so Boyce/Codd normal form—and hence, a fortiori, fifth normal form—is sometimes not even desirable.

b. In any case, prohibiting such specifications doesn't mean such constraints don't exist. And if they do but the DBMS isn't told about them, then they're going to have to be enforced by the user.

■ Reference [2] gives an example (page 270) that "clearly indicate[s] the need for the host language to be usable in programming the triggered action" (i.e., the action to be taken if an integrity constraint is violated—what I've referred to elsewhere as the *violation response* [12]). I would argue rather that what the example "clearly indicates" is that it was a mistake to separate the host language and the database language in the first place.

■ In a very strange subsection (17.5.2) titled "Relating View Updatability to Normalization," we find the following: "[If] a base relation T is the outer equijoin of two relations R and S

---

[45] Comments and questions analogous to those of this paragraph apply to Features RI-28 and RI-29 as well, which have to do with functional and multivalued dependencies, respectively. Also, Feature RI-28 says "the DBMS assumes that all columns ... are functionally dependent on the primary key, *unless otherwise declared*" (emphasis added). This remark is quite puzzling, given that (of course) *all* columns of *any* relvar are functionally dependent on *every* key of that relvar, always.

[46] Especially since, as noted earlier in this chapter, "RM/V2 [does] not require all of the candidate keys for every base [relvar] to be recorded in the catalog"!

that are more fundamental than T, but are not base relations themselves, R and S should nevertheless be described in the catalog ... Such relations are ... called *conceptual relations.*" I believe there's some confusion here, though I can't rightly say just what it is.

■ "Some excellent work on this transformation [*i.e., of SQL expressions involving "nested subqueries" to expressions involving joins*] has been done (Kim 1982, Ganski and Wong 1987)" (reference [2], page 380). While not at all wishing to disparage or discredit the referenced work, of course, I do feel bound to point out that it contains a number of errors, many of them having to do with nulls and three-valued logic. See references [3] and [15] for further discussion of this point.

■ Reference [2] claims (page 81) that the union of two relations having "the same" primary key also has "the same" primary key. This claim is easily seen to be false.

■ Reference [2], page 183, first paragraph, apparently (and incredibly) suggests that it is acceptable to build logical inconsistencies into our databases and DBMSs!

CONCLUDING REMARKS

In the body of this review, I've necessarily had to concentrate on what seem to me to be the major problems with RM/V2. It's my opinion that a number of those problems are very significant indeed, though of course I'm open to discussion on such issues. But I certainly don't want you to think the list of problems I've mentioned is exhaustive; there are numerous additional items in reference [2] that give me cause for concern. Some of them are merely typographical (e.g., "L<=" instead of "L>=" on page 485 and elsewhere), but they could cause confusion; some are more serious (e.g., silent—and occasionally incompatible—changes in the definitions of DIVIDE, duplicates, outer union, entity integrity, and many other items); some are inconsistencies or contradictions (e.g., pages 247 and 248 contradict each other on the timing of "type E" integrity constraints); and some are clearly wrong (e.g., page 212, paragraph beginning "If the comparator"). You have been warned.

REFERENCES AND BIBLIOGRAPHY

1. E. F. Codd: "Is Your DBMS Really Relational?" (*Computerworld*, October 14th, 1985); "Does Your DBMS Run by the Rules?" (*Computerworld*, October 21st, 1985). *Note added in this rewrite:* See also reference [18].

2. E. F. Codd: *The Relational Model for Database Management Version 2*. Reading, Mass.: Addison-Wesley (1990). Also available online at *https://codeblab.com/wp-content/uploads/2009/12/rmdb-codd.pdf*.

3. C. J. Date: "Query Optimization," Chapter 18 of C. J. Date, *An Introduction to Database Systems: Volume I* (5th edition, Addison-Wesley, 1990). *Note added in this rewrite:* This book is now in its eighth edition, where the title of the pertinent chapter—still Chapter 18, as it happens—has been simplified to the more appropriate "Optimization."

4. C. J. Date: "Further Normalization," Chapter 21 of C. J. Date, *An Introduction to Database Systems: Volume I* (5th edition, Addison-Wesley, 1990). *Note added in this rewrite:* A more recent and appropriate reference here is C. J. Date, *Database Design and Relational Theory: Normal Forms and All That Jazz* (O'Reilly, 2012).

5. C. J. Date: "Referential Integrity," Proc. 7th International Conference on Very Large Data Bases, Cannes, France (September 1981). Republished in slightly revised form in C. J. Date, *Relational Database: Selected Writings* (Addison-Wesley, 1986). *Note added in this rewrite:* A more recent and appropriate reference here is C. J. Date, "Inclusion Dependencies and Foreign Keys," in C. J. Date and Hugh Darwen, *Database Explorations: Essays on The Third Manifesto and Related Topics* (Trafford, 2010).

6. C. J. Date: "An Introduction to the Unified Database Language (UDL)," in C. J. Date, *Relational Database: Selected Writings* (Addison-Wesley, 1986).

7. C. J. Date: "Some Principles of Good Language Design," in C. J. Date, *Relational Database: Selected Writings* (Addison-Wesley, 1986).

8. C. J. Date: "Null Values in Database Management," in C. J. Date, *Relational Database: Selected Writings* (Addison-Wesley, 1986).

9. C. J. Date: "Updating Views," in C. J. Date, *Relational Database: Selected Writings* (Addison-Wesley, 1986). *Note added in this rewrite:* A more recent and appropriate reference here is C. J. Date, *View Updating and Relational Theory: Solving the View Update Problem* (O'Reilly, 2013).

10. C. J. Date: "What Is a Domain?", in C. J. Date, *Relational Database Writings 1985-1989* (Addison-Wesley, 1990). *Note added in this rewrite:* A more up to date overview of domains (in other words, types) as I now see them is given in Chapter 2 of my book *Type Inheritance and Relational Theory: Subtypes, Supertypes, and Substitutability* (O'Reilly, 2016).

11. C. J. Date: "User Defined vs. Extended Data Types," Appendix A to reference [10].

12. C. J. Date: "A Contribution to the Study of Database Integrity," in C. J. Date, *Relational Database Writings 1985-1989* (Addison-Wesley, 1990). *Note added in this rewrite:* A more up to date overview of integrity as I now see it is given in Chapter 8 of my book *SQL and Relational Theory: How to Write Accurate SQL Code* (3rd edition, O'Reilly, 2015).

13. C. J. Date: "NOT Is Not "Not"! (Notes on Three-Valued Logic and Related Matters)," in C. J. Date, *Relational Database Writings 1985-1989* (Addison-Wesley, 1990).

14. C. J. Date: "What Is a Distributed Database System?", in C. J. Date, *Relational Database Writings 1985-1989* (Addison-Wesley, 1990).

15. C. J. Date: "EXISTS Is Not "Exists"! (Some Logical Flaws in SQL)," in C. J. Date, *Relational Database Writings 1985-1989* (Addison-Wesley, 1990).

16. C. J. Date: "What Is a Relation?", in C. J. Date and Hugh Darwen, *Relational Database Writings 1989-1991* (Addison-Wesley, 1992). *Note added in this rewrite:* A more up to date overview of relations as I now see them is given in Chapter 3 of my book *SQL and Relational Theory: How to Write Accurate SQL Code* (3rd edition, O'Reilly, 2015).

17. C. J. Date: "Notes Toward a Reconstituted Definition of the Relational Model Version 1 (RM/V1)," in C. J. Date and Hugh Darwen, *Relational Database Writings 1989-1991* (Addison-Wesley, 1992). *Note added in this rewrite:* I've recently rewritten this paper to bring it more into line with my current thinking . The new version, with the revised title "The Relational Model Version 1," is included in the present book as Chapter 7.

18. C. J. Date: "An Assessment of Codd's Evaluation Scheme," Appendix D to reference [17]. *Note added in this rewrite:* This assessment has been updated and is included (under a different title) as an appendix to Chapter 7 of the present book.

19. Umeshwar Dayal and Philip A. Bernstein: "On the Correct Translation of Update Operations on Relational Views," *ACM Transactions on Database Systems 7*, No. 3 (September 1982).

20. K. P. Eswaran and D. D. Chamberlin: "Functional Specifications of a Subsystem for Data Base Integrity," Proc. 1st International Conference on Very Large Data Bases, Framingham, Mass. (September 1975).

21. Nathan Goodman: "Bill of Materials in Relational Database," *InfoDB 5*, No. 1 (Spring / Summer 1990).

22. P. A. V. Hall: "Optimisation of a Single Relational Expression in a Relational Data Base System," *IBM Journal of Research and Development 20*, No. 3 (May 1976).

23. Arthur M. Keller: "Algorithms for Translating View Updates to Database Updates for Views Involving Selections, Projections, and Joins," Proc. 4th ACM SIGACT-SIGMOD Symposium on Principles of Database Systems, Portland, Ore. (March 1985).

24. David McGoveran: "A Long Time Coming," *Database Programming & Design 3*, No. 9 (September 1990).

25. J. B. Rothnie Jr. and N. Goodman: "A Survey of Research and Development in Distributed Database Management," Proc. 3rd International Conference on Very Large Data Bases, Tokyo, Japan (October 1977).

26. Hugh Darwen (writing as Andrew Warden): "Table_Dee and Table_Dum," in C. J. Date, *Relational Database Writings 1985-1989*. Reading, Mass.: Addison-Wesley (1990).

27. Hugh Darwen (writing as Andrew Warden): "The Naming of Columns," in C. J. Date, *Relational Database Writings 1985-1989*. Reading, Mass.: Addison-Wesley (1990).

28. Hugh Darwen (writing as Andrew Warden): "Adventures in Relationland," in C. J. Date, *Relational Database Writings 1985-1989*. Reading, Mass.: Addison-Wesley (1990).

POSTSCRIPT

Now I turn to material that was omitted from my original review. (Actually the material in question was included in the first draft of that review, but I decided for various reasons to omit it from the published version.) I'll begin with a few general remarks. First of all, the book—reference [2], that is—is *not* well organized. A couple of examples:

- Fig. 4.1 is referenced on page 67 but doesn't appear until page 78.

- As noted earlier, the MAYBE qualifier is first discussed in the context of a discussion of outer join (page 111), and isn't defined until almost 100 pages later.[47]

The book is also highly repetitive, a state of affairs that would be amusing if it weren't so annoying, given that—as also mentioned earlier, in a footnote—we're told over and over again,

---

[47] By the way, neither *outer join* nor *outer natural join* appears in the index. However, *outer equi-join* does; in fact, it appears twice—once out of alphabetical order.

in effect, not to say the same thing twice. For example, the identical list of "ten [scalar] comparators" appears on pages 70, 74, 104, 123, and possibly elsewhere as well. The continual harping on the "domain safety feature" is also very annoying—it's mentioned in at least ten different places by my count[48]—especially as the feature in question represents a totally ad hoc, and in fact incorrect, "solution" to a problem for which a correct solution was not only already available but widely understood at the time. Overall, I believe that with (a) a good deal of technical editing, (b) a more orthogonal approach to stating requirements, and (c) last but not least, a systematic, canonical, universally used example, the book could have been reduced in size by at least 50%—and that's without eliminating the bad ideas, of which there are many.

One obvious question that springs to mind is this: What exactly does Codd mean by the term *model*, anyway? At least in its original incarnation (i.e., in 1969-1970), RM/V1 was comparatively well defined, well thought out, well integrated, and at a uniform level of abstraction. RM/V2 is none of these things. In fact, it's not even clear what the problem is that it's attempting to solve.

The remaining subsections in this postscript deal with a variety of more specific and more detailed issues.

Serious Flaws in SQL

"Serious Flaws in SQL" is the title of Chapter 23 of reference [2]. To quote from that chapter:

> The flaws [in question] are serious enough to justify immediate action by vendors to remove them, and by users to avoid the consequences of the flaws as far as possible.

I certainly agree with the general intent of these remarks. But Codd then goes on to ask "What ... are the flaws in SQL that have such grave consequences?"—and then he describes just three specific flaws, suggesting rather strongly that he regards those three as the most serious (in fact he goes on to say as much). The three in question are as follows (quoting):

1. SQL permits duplicate rows in relations.

2. [SQL] supports an inadequately defined kind of nesting of a query within a query.[49]

3. [SQL] does not adequately support three-valued logic, let alone four-valued logic.

---

[48] Be aware, however, that (as I discovered the hard way) it's indexed under *safety feature*, not *domain safety feature*.

[49] The kind of nesting Codd is referring to here isn't nesting in general but is, rather, SQL's "IN *subquery*" construct specifically—the construct that was the original justification for that *Structured* in the name "Structured Query Language," incidentally. PS: I note in passing that Codd is unfortunately adopting the common usage here (which in Chapter 7 of this book I described as "deprecated") according to which a relational expression is called a query. To repeat my rhetorical question from that chapter, if we call an expression a query, what do we call a query?

Well, I agree with Codd on Point 1 here, but not on Points 2 and 3.[50] Regarding Point 2, I don't agree that the kind of nesting he refers to is "inadequately defined" (I don't much like it, and as a matter of fact I believe it could be dropped without any serious loss of functionality, but that's a separate matter). The truth is, Codd's detailed criticisms on this issue seem to be either muddled or wrong—but maybe that's beside the point, because I hardly think it reasonable in any case to consider the issue one of SQL's "three most serious flaws."

As for Point 3, like most other serious students of database technology I regard Codd's insistence on support for three- and four-valued logic as a mistake. Not to mention that Codd's own definitions of those logics kept on changing, and in fact were never complete anyway.[51]

References and Credits

Codd's list of references (pages 505-510 of his book) seems to me to be notable in large part for what it omits. The omissions are of two kinds. First, there are references cited in the body of the text but omitted from the list; examples include [IBM 1972], cited on page 12, and [GOOD], cited on page 103. Second and perhaps more important, there are numerous cases where work by some other researcher really ought to be referenced but isn't. In particular—please forgive me if you see this as just special pleading on my part—there are only two references to publications of my own, and rather odd ones at that (I follow Codd's own reference style here):

- Date, C. J. (1984) "Why Is It So Difficult to Provide a Relational Interface to IMS?" *InfoIMS* 4:4.

- Date, C. J. (1987) "Where SQL Falls Short" (abridged). *Datamation*, May 1. Unabridged version, *What Is Wrong with SQL*, available from The Relational Institute, San Jose.

I observe, incidentally, that Codd fails to mention here the books in which these two papers were republished (books that might be a little easier to track down than the original sources), but let that pass. More to the point, I can think of quite a few other papers (and books) of mine that I would have thought much more worthy of inclusion in Codd's list than the two items referenced above. I see I also get no mention in the preface (none in the acknowledgments on page ix in particular). Frankly, I find these omissions a little hard, considering the huge amount of support I gave Codd throughout the period 1970-1990 (especially during the early and mid 1970s, when he was almost literally a voice crying in the wilderness)—not to mention my assistance with, and

---

[50] In fact, Codd's Chapter 23 goes on to say: "Criticisms of SQL have been plentiful ... See, for example, [Date 1987] ... Date's article, however, does not deal with [these] three most serious flaws." I have two responses to these remarks. First, this is one of the very few explicit references to myself in the entire book (see my remarks on such matters in the next subsection), and it appears to be included purely to allow Codd to indulge in a sideswipe. Second, that sideswipe is unjustified; my article does at least touch on the first two of Codd's alleged "serious flaws" (agreeing with Codd on the first but not on the second). It's true it doesn't have anything to say about the third, but that's because, although I agree with Codd that SQL's support for 3VL is defective, I don't believe it should be beefed up and "corrected"—rather, I believe it should be dropped.

[51] See "Why Three- and Four-Valued Logic Don't Work," in my book *Date on Database: Writings 2000-2006* (Apress, 2006), for some elaboration on these two points.

comments on, various iterations of earlier drafts of his writings on RM/V2 and other matters. By way of illustration, I list below the numbers of pages in the book where I feel it might have been charitable to include some reference to myself, accompanied in each case with a brief explanation of why I feel such a reference might have been included. Of course, you can skip directly to the next subsection (which starts on page 239) if you think what follows is all just me being upset over my own hurt feelings.

7 "*N* types of objects require *N* sets of operators ... *N* = 1 is the minimum" (paraphrasing). This point was first articulated, documented, and highlighted by me, in the fourth edition of my book in *An Introduction to Database Systems* (1986) and elsewhere.

18 Discusses the fact that an earlier version of the relational model allowed duplicates to appear in derived relations. I was the one who persuaded Codd that such a state of affairs made no sense (i.e., that duplicates should be prohibited in all cases).

21 "I ... proved that [the relational algebra and the relational calculus] had equal expressive power." First, it turned out that Codd's algebra and calculus weren't equally expressive; his proof showed only that his algebra is at least as expressive as his calculus, not the converse, and in fact the converse is false. Second, that proof had and still has at least one bug in it, having to do with prenex normal form; I pointed some of these bugs out to Codd at the time, and wrote them up in a couple of papers subsequently. See Chapter 3 in the present book for further explanation.

25 "Method 1 is the approach now adopted in the relational model"—but only after I pointed out that the suggested alternative ("Method 2") made no sense.

33 "I believe the idea [of a three-schema architecture] had already been conceived and published as part of the relational model"—yes, by me, in the first edition of *An Introduction to Database Systems*, written in 1972—"and as part of the System R architecture." My book predated System R by several years.

51 "... without [treating] dates and date intervals as distinct data types": I was the one who pointed out to Codd that dates could be treated as intervals. (I must make it clear, however, that I disagree with Codd here, in that I don't believe such treatment is desirable.)

78 Fig. 14.1 is heavily based, without acknowledgment, on one previously appearing in several of my books.

91 "Such an expression takes about three pages of commands": The three pages of code (not *commands*) Codd is referring to here were written by me. What's more, they don't support the argument Codd is trying to make!—viz., that "[this complexity] is just one of the severe

penalties stemming from the failure of SQL to support domains as extended data types." What they do show is the difficulty involved if the user and not the system has to be responsible for maintaining referential integrity.

106   The distributed database example is essentially the same as one previously given by me in my book *An Introduction to Database Systems: Volume II* (Addison-Wesley, 1983).

137   Feature RZ-38: The three components were identified and originally defined by me.

177   The three possibilities listed at the top of the page were originally identified and described by me (albeit in a different context, viz., one where they made sense, which here they don't, not quite).

223   Feature RJ-2: The definition of the result of dividing by an empty relation is due to me (Codd's original definition was wrong).

232   "... in RM/V2 no relation, whether base or derived, is allowed to have duplicate rows": See comment re page 18.

239   "... it is preferable that the traversal be executed using the [host language]": The fact that SQL-style cursors aren't the only way to do it was drawn to Codd's attention by me.

256   "... at least one alternative algorithm": I showed Codd how to do this.

257   Exercise 13.6: See my various writings on foreign keys.

260   Feature RI-23: The idea of a "violation procedure" was first described by me in my book *An Introduction to Database Systems: Volume II* (1983).

295   "One of the reviewers for this book stated that [two papers] reported independent work on view updatability that is somewhat similar to the approach [described] in this chapter. I regret that, at the time of writing this book, I was unaware of this work and still have not seen the papers." But Codd was quite definitely aware of my own paper on the subject (which also reported on a similar approach) but chose not to reference it; moreover, my paper references the papers he says he wasn't aware of, as well as several others.

322   "This is known as *logical data independence*." Yes, it is, and the term was first used in a 1971 paper by Paul Hopewell and myself (and the term was in fact coined by me, for what it's worth).

338   I was the one who explained to Codd the difference between scalar and aggregate operators ("functions"). In fact I strongly suspect that the reason Codd uses the term *scalar* here at all is because of me. It would have made a lot of sense in connection with his discussions of "atomic data values," too—in fact, I believe it would greatly have clarified those discussions—but as far as I'm aware he never used it in that context.

341   I'm pretty sure Codd got most of the specifics of "user defined functions" from a paper I wrote while I was still in IBM ("Extending SQL to Support User Defined Functions: A Discussion and Some Proposals," IBM internal memo, November 12th, 1981).

352   "... a recent release of a well known relational DBMS product, marketed by a vendor with an excellent reputation, fails under certain conditions to yield x from the expression $x + y - y$ when x happens to be a date and y happens to be a date interval." The product in question is IBM's DB2, and I was the one who pointed out this anomaly and many others like it (in my paper "Dates and Times in IBM SQL: Some Technical Criticisms," which Codd was certainly aware of).[52]

354   "Any coupling of one feature with another in the design of a DBMS must be justified by some clearly stated, unemotional, logically defensible reason." This would be funny if it weren't so sad ... Codd is asking here for orthogonality, something I'd tried for years to persuade him was important, and something his definition of RM/V2 so signally lacks.

363   "Frequently, a language is designed as a source language only. However, almost every source language [eventually] becomes a target language": Another point I'd been making for years (including in writing).

364   Feature RL-8: Same comment as for page 354, mutatis mutandis.

366   Feature RL-13: This whole process had been described and elaborated by me in *An Introduction to Database Systems* (several editions over the years). Of course, I certainly don't claim I invented this conceptual breakdown into a sequence of steps, but I do believe I was the one who explained it to Codd.

368   Feature RL-17 and subsequent discussion: Orthogonality again (incidentally, having several distinct "orthogonality features" is itself very unorthogonal). The specific SQL issues called out in the discussion had previously been documented by me and were explicitly pointed out to Codd by me.

---

[52] But RM/V2 suffers from a very similar problem!—see footnote 15. (Actually, so does RM/V1.)

382   The discussion of SQL's nested SQL subqueries and optimization derives heavily from writings of my own.

391   This chapter and the next (regarding distributed database) both appear to owe a great deal to my prior writings on the topic.

401   Codd's "reversibility" is just the familiar notion of nonloss decomposition by another name, and is discussed in my prior writings on distributed database.

418   The example on this page and the next two is essentially lifted from, or at the very least heavily based on, my own writings.

424   The various kinds of independence (or the first four, at least) were previously identified as requirements by me.

428   Exercise 25.2: Same comment as for page 418, mutatis mutandis.

464   The bugs in the CODASYL machine shop example—see Chapter 6 of the present book—that Codd says were found by "someone" were in fact found (and documented) by me.

465   Re files being better than cursors: Same comment as for page 239, mutatis mutandis.

And here are a few further issues I helped Codd sort out his ideas on during the gestation of his book:

- Nulls and three-valued logic (I still have major reservations here, of course, but I did provide comments that I believe were helpful on earlier drafts in this connection)

- Primary keys (I persuaded Codd that if the concept makes sense at all, then it has to make sense for all relations)

- Foreign keys (I helped Codd sort out his numerous conflicting definitions of this concept)

- Domains vs. data types (Codd and I never did fully agree on this issue, but in the course of numerous discussions I did get him to move a little closer to the correct position, viz., that domains and data types are the same thing)

- Nested transactions

- Outer join (difficulties over tuples in which "every attribute is null")

■ "Composite domains" and "composite attributes"

■ Outer union etc. (I drew Codd's attention to inconsistencies among existing definitions)

■ "Domain integrity" (see the subsection "Revised Definitions," later)

■ CREATE and DROP CONSTRAINT

■ Single- vs. multi-variable constraints

■ Use of dates and times in authorization, constraints, etc. (orthogonality!)

■ Names of view attributes

■ Operators for decimal currency

■ Aggregate operator result if the argument is empty

And here's a list of topics I explicitly disagreed with Codd on (and discussed with him at the time):

■ Relations of degree zero

■ Keys of degree zero

■ Primary vs. candidate keys

■ Composite foreign keys and nulls

■ Composite keys and composite columns in general

■ Integrity classification scheme in general

■ "User defined" integrity in particular

■ Column integrity rules in particular

■ Integrity "metarules"

■ EXTEND

- SUMMARIZE

- Generalized DIVIDE

- Foreign keys with two or more targets

- Overlapping keys

- Three- and four-valued logic

- Outer operators

- Type inheritance

- "Basic vs. extended" data types

- "Domain check override," type conversion, and coercions

- Clean treatment of aggregate operators

- DOD qualifier

- Orthogonality

- Distributed database—level of abstraction

- Fragmentation

- Global catalog

- Reversible derivability

- Column naming in derived relations

- Naming in distributed database

- Name based operators

- Outlawing cartesian product

- "Weak identifiers" (another concept defined by Codd in different ways in different writings, incidentally)

- Join dependence (at least as "defined" in Codd's book)

It also seems to me that Codd's knowledge of certain topics was less extensive than it might have been (and should have been, if he wanted to be in a position to be able to justify some of the remarks he makes regarding those matters in his text). Among the topics in question I would include:

- Specifics of relational or would-be relational support in various products (e.g., DB2, INGRES)

- Existing relational or would-be relational prototypes

- Object orientation

- Various research issues, including type inheritance, temporal data, logic databases, "NF squared relations," etc.

Inappropriate Remarks

In my opinion, the book contains far too many remarks of an inappropriate nature—even an unprofessional or ad hominem nature, in certain cases—remarks that (again in my opinion) have no place in a book of the kind the RM/V2 book is surely intended to be. Here are some examples, with page numbers:

vii "... many lecturers and consultants in relational database management have failed to see [the] importance [of domains, primary keys, and foreign keys]."

4 "... AI researchers write their programs solely for other AI researchers to comprehend."

10 "Occasionally, support for some basic [relational] feature has been omitted due to [its] being assessed as useless."

18 "This fundamental property [*i.e., unique identification*] ... is not enforced by any other approach to database management."

23 "This detail is not supported in many current DBMS products, even when the vendors claim that their products support referential integrity." (The reason might be that, at least as stated, the detail in question doesn't really make sense.)

27 "Designers of the relational DBMS products of many vendors appear to be ignorant of these facts or to have ignored them."

33 "[ANSI/SPARC] announced *with great fanfare* something called the three-schema architecture" (my italics—and I might also have italicized "something called").

43 "It has become clear that domains as data types go beyond what is normally understood by data types in today's programming languages." I would say rather that what has become clear is that Codd has no knowledge of data types as they've been understood in the programming language context since at least the early 1970s, and probably earlier than that.

46 "... the usual [*sic*] result was that no two currency declarations were in precise agreement, placing an immense and unnecessary burden on the DBA and on the community of users." *Note: Currency* here refers to monetary units—e.g., euros or U.S. dollars—not to the "current position" notion supported in SQL by cursors, and supported also by various nonrelational DBMSs.

58 "Frequently, people get confused about [*two very obviously distinct issues, having to do with possible vs. actual values*]."

72 "The vendor falsely advertised that the product was a relational DBMS." If Codd is going to say this kind of thing, I think he should name names.

76 "Users who are wedded to the approaches of the past often think that the only kind of join in the relational model is either the equijoin or the natural join ... and that the only comparand columns allowed are primary keys or foreign keys ... This *tunnel vision* ... etc." (my italics).

88 "... relational assignment is beyond the capability of most programming languages." If by "beyond the capability" Codd means the languages in question don't support the operator (i.e., relational assignment), the claim is trivially and obviously true, because they don't support relations. If he means they can't support it, it's trivially and obviously false.

110 "... in certain circumstances, the outer equijoin is clearly superior as a view to its inner counterpart. I am confident that this use of the outer equijoin was not conceived when the operator was invented." Well, I was present (as Codd was not) when Ian Heath invented the operator, and I wouldn't be so bold as to make such a claim. And I dispute the alleged superiority in any case.

111 "... a DBMS that has only two truth values ... may be unable to determine in a nonguessing mode the truth value of a truth valued expression." This remark is simply fatuous.

140 "It has been asserted in a public forum that the relational algebra is incapable of recursive join. In fact, such an assertion is astonishingly erroneous." (I strongly suspect I'm the person Codd is referring to here. If so, however, he's either misquoting me or quoting me out of context. Be that as it may, claims to the effect that "It has been asserted" surely cry out for a concrete reference.) In any case, the assertion in question was certainly true of RM/V1, and RM/V1 was equally certainly what the assertion in question was referring to. *Note:* See also my comments later in this subsection regarding page 450.

165 "... tables [from nonrelational sources] are likely to contain duplicate rows." I think "are likely to" should be replaced by "might." Incidentally, the lengthy discussion following the quoted remark is extraordinarily confused.

184 "I fail to see any problem ... because the use of truth valued conditions involving ordering when applying a relational data sublanguage is at a higher level of abstraction than the use of the ordering of marks relative to values in the ORDER BY clause." Well, maybe so; but Codd gives absolutely no justification for the rather highhanded claim he's making here.

186 "... alert the user to his or her folly." In my opinion, the "folly" is in either the example or 4VL, and very likely both.

189 "... derived relations (often loosely called tables) ..." Is Codd suggesting that base relations should *not* be "loosely called tables"? Also, that parenthetical remark seems meant to be taken as pejorative. If so, who introduced the tabular terminology, anyway?

190 "I fail to see any problem ... because the semantic notions of equality are applicable at a higher level of abstraction than the symbolic equality involved in removal of duplicate rows." Well, maybe so; but again Codd gives no justification for the rather highhanded claim he's making.

197 "Some of this criticism has been directed by mistake at the relational model." The criticism referred to was mine, and "by mistake" is incorrect—it was deliberate.

197 "... technical criticisms have strayed across the boundary [between model and products] without proper justification." The criticisms referred to were mine, and the comment is incorrect—there was justification.

202 "In nonIBM products, even the representation aspects have gone astray. In several of these products, the DBMS designer has misinterpreted nulls as [values]." Well, the IBM

products do this too (in fact the SQL language does so). Praising one particular vendor is inappropriate, regardless of whether the praise is explicit or implicit—and doubly so if it's undeserved, as in the case at hand.

230 "[The relational model] does not require any associative addressing hardware, even though the need for such hardware was once frequently claimed by opponents of the relational model." Really? Can we see some references?

231 "... until [a logic as powerful and rigorous as predicate logic] is developed, which could take another two millennia."

232 "The following misinterpretations [of the relational model] are common": The first is that the relational language can't support any operators not part of the model as currently defined. Really? Who says so? The second is that a derived relation must have a primary key (Codd says a derived relation doesn't have to have a primary key—though if it doesn't, it must at least have a "weak identifier").

240 "... in the mid 1970s ANSI/SPARC [advocated] 42 distinct interfaces and (potentially) 42 distinct languages ... Fortunately, that idea seems to have been abandoned."

257 "When I introduced the domain concept into database management 20 years ago ... it was regarded by almost all of my IBM colleagues as a purely academic exercise."

295 "Part of the problem ... was and is their incredible lack of support for primary keys, foreign keys, and domains—incredible because I made it clear to the designers well in advance that it was important not to omit these particular features."

327 "In nonrelational DBMS[s], the approach to authorization was (and is) often negative—that is, based on explicit denial of access."

355 "So far, the only relational DBMS I have encountered with a domain-based index is one developed at the University of Nice."

361 "Experience in dealing with the standards committees for [Fortran, COBOL, and PL/I] had convinced me that the members were not very interested in technical issues of any depth." (This remark is pretty offensive. The offense is compounded by the fact that Codd seems to pay no attention whatsoever to matters, regarding data types in particular, that the languages world got right but he himself got wrong. In fact Codd seems himself to be "not very interested" in the languages world in general, let alone in "any depth.")

372   "[IBM's DB2 and SQL/DS] are good products when compared with other products on the market today." See my comment regarding page 202.

383   "DB2 is one of the few relational DBMS products that *represents* missing information independently of the type of data that is missing." See my comment regarding page 202. In any case, Codd's claim is incorrect, since any product that supports SQL does the same thing as DB2 does in this connection.

427   "This ease of redistribution is an important requirement ... that [customers] often overlook."

444   "Today's leader in general fault tolerance, including DBMS fault tolerance, is Tandem ... ." See my comment regarding page 202.

450   "... many people were glibly and falsely claiming that the relational model was incapable of solving [the bill of materials problem]." Again I strongly suspect that I'm one of the people Codd is referring to here; if so, then I reject the accusation. Interestingly, just four pages later, on page 454, Codd himself says "It was clear at least 10 years ago ... that *extensions to the relational model* would be required to handle" such problems (my italics). There seems to be some contradiction here.[53] *Note:* See also my comments earlier in this subsection regarding page 140.

Revised Definitions

Here now is a short and almost certainly incomplete list, with relevant page numbers, of concepts whose definitions in reference [2] represent silent revisions of their definitions as given in earlier writings of Codd's:

23   composite foreign keys

46   domain integrity[54]

61   relational algebra (i.e., the totality thereof, as defined in the chapter beginning on that page)

---

[53] Indeed, Chapter 28 of reference [2], which is all about the bill of materials problem, is called "Extending the Relational Model" [*sic*]. PS: Here'a quote from that chapter: "I claim to have a solution to [this] problem, one that is very concise ... [It] will, of course, be published later." But it wasn't.

[54] For a discussion of what I think domain integrity ought to be, see Chapter 7 of the present book. But this is what page 46 of reference [2] actually has to say about the matter: "Domain integrity consists of those constraints that are shared by all the columns that draw their values from that domain. Three kinds of domain integrity constraints that are frequently encountered are (1) regular data type (?!?), (2) ranges of values permitted, and (3) whether or not the ordering comparators greater than (>) and less than (<) are applicable to those values." I believe there's some serious confusion here.

70 legal "scalar" comparison operators

84 DIVIDE

111 names of truth values

116 "outer" operators

176 entity integrity

189 duplicates (!)

200 functional dependency

306 candidate key

Miscellaneous Issues

A few further quotes and comments:

v "I believe that this is the first book to deal exclusively with the relational approach."
   Except, of course, for the books by Delobel and Adiba (1982); Maier (1983); Gray (1984);
   Merrett (1984); Alagić (1986); Yang (1986); Miranda (1988); Gardarin and Valduriez
   (1989); and very likely others. *Note:* The foregoing list covers just books in my own
   personal library, and doesn't include books by myself.

v "All the ideas in the relational model described in this book are mine, except in cases where
   I explicitly credit someone else."

vi "In developing the relational model, I have tried to follow Einstein's advice, *Make it as
   simple as possible, but no simpler*." The advice is good (and I was the one who drew
   Codd's attention to it, incidentally), but I hardly think RM/V2 can be said to abide by it.

vii "... the new definitions [of entity and referential integrity, in 1988] were available to
   DBMS vendors well before their first attempts to implement referential integrity." I don't
   believe this claim is correct.

13 "QUEL ... was invented by Held and Stonebraker." Actually the original paper on QUEL
   was by Held, Stonebraker, and Wong, and I'm quite sure that Wong deserves at least as
   much of the credit for the invention (and perhaps more) as do the other two.

17   "I consider it extremely misleading to use the term *array* to describe the structuring of data in the relational model." I couldn't agree more. However, I note that it was Codd himself who introduced the array terminology, and used it extensively, in his first two papers (see Chapter 2 of the present book).

17   Definition of "base relation" isn't very precise, and in fact is seriously misleading.

20   Degree zero should be legal.

22   Empty keys should be legal.

26   The terms introduced in Section 1.9 don't seem to be used anywhere. In fact, the corresponding index entries all point to this section and nowhere else!

29   I very much doubt whether the first paragraph of Section 2.1 will be understood by most readers. "As explained in Chapter 1": No, it wasn't.

30   Feature RS-1: The remark re ordering in derived relations is mysterious at best, but more likely just plain wrong.

31   The argument concerning repeating groups and positioning is specious.

44   Table 3.1 doesn't seem to make a lot of sense, and at least in some respects is clearly wrong. *Note:* A table essentially identical to Table 3.1 is shown and briefly criticized in Chapter 2 of the present book (see page 38).

49   The definition of "primary domain" is just slipped in, and in any case is at least arguably unnecessary.

51   Regarding point 4.3, I would add that pseudovariable functionality is desirable too.

53   Feature RT-6: What's a composite data type? (RM/V2 does have composite domains, but Codd insists that domains and data types are different things.)

69   The discussion of projection on this page displays ignorance of how programming language constructs are bound to their run time counterparts—in particular, ignorance of the mechanism needed to achieve true data independence.

72   Feature RB-13 ("The Boolean Extension of Theta Select"): Doesn't define the operator!

75   Actually it's *always* possible to join a relation with itself. That is (and contrary to what Codd is saying here), it's not necessary for the relation in question to have "two or more [distinct] columns on a common domain."

75   The example at the bottom of the page shows clearly why an attribute RENAME operator is needed, but Codd seems not to recognize that need. Instead, he introduces another piece of adhocery, as well as what I'm very tempted to describe as a spot of *deus ex machina*.

76   Feature RB-24 ("The Boolean Extension of Theta Join"): Doesn't define the operator!

78   The figure should be on page 67, where it's first referenced.

79   The explanation of union is unnecessarily complicated, extremely longwinded, and not even correct.

80   "The simplest approach appears to be ...": The approach described is in fact a very long way from being "the simplest."

81   "The following special case is noteworthy." I wouldn't say it's noteworthy, I'd say it's extremely muddled, and wrong.

82   The text on this page and the next is highly and unnecessarily repetitious, as well as being wrong.

86   The explanation of the quantifiers—viz., "[EXISTS] corresponds to the theta-join operators ... [FORALL] corresponds to relational division"—is inadequate at best.

93   "... usually referential integrity is not fully checked until the end of a transaction." *What?* Really? I've explained elsewhere—see, e.g., my book *SQL and Relational Theory: How to Write Accurate SQL Code* (3rd edition, O'Reilly, 2015)—why all constraints, referential constraints in particular, need to be checked at statement boundaries. (The point is mentioned in Chapter 1 of the present book also, where it's referred to as **The Golden Rule**.)

94   "If the command participates in a transaction ...": But don't "commands" always "participate in transactions"?

98   Re FRAME: Far too much adhocery. And what if "<" isn't a defined operator for the domain underlying column C?

106   "The following example shows the semijoin operator in action"—but it doesn't!

115   "... outer natural join is not necessarily a projection of outer equijoin—a fact that may decrease the usefulness of outer natural join." The first part of this sentence is correct (and was pointed out to Codd by me in 1983), but I don't see how the second part follows, and I don't agree with it.

115   "[Union] is applied exclusively to a pair of relations of precisely the same type": But Codd doesn't really *have* a concept of relations being of a type. (His text continues "In other words," but what follows that phrase is hardly a definition of such a concept.)

117   "The close-counterpart concept ... is used instead of row equality to remove duplicate rows": So "union" isn't union.

137   Feature RZ-38 ("User Defined Select"): Doesn't define the operator!

140   "Recursive join" is not a good name. In fact, why was it necessary to invent a new name at all, since (as noted in footnote 37) the operation is in fact nothing but the well known operation of transitive closure?

143   I note in passing that the person to person example isn't transitive (if person *A* knows person *B* and person *B* knows person *C*, it doesn't follow that person *A* knows person *C*), so performing a "recursive join" could lead to a "connection trap" mistake[55]—quite possibly a rather serious one, given the suggested application ("recording contacts between criminals and suspects in a database for use by the police").

151   Feature RN-9: "The column names and sequencing of such names in the result of a project operator ... ." *Sequencing*? Relational attributes have a left to right *sequence*?

161   DROP COLUMN can produce a result of degree zero! Also, the details of this feature are inappropriate for an abstract model.

163   CREATE SNAPSHOT but no CREATE VIEW? (Also, Codd's CREATE SNAPSHOT—see page 405—provides no way of naming the snapshot in question.) *Note:* Features RV-1 and RV-3 (pages 285, 288) have to do with a hypothetical CREATE VIEW, of course, but why the asymmetry of treatment? And in any case, Features RV-1 and RV-3 suffer from certain weirdnesses of their own. (Actually, so does Feature RV-2.)

---

[55] See Chapter 2 of the present book for an explanation of the connection trap.

166 "... a derived relation may consist of any combination of rows, providing they are all of the same extended data type." Codd is attempting to grapple here with the notion that relations and tuples have types, but not making a very good job of it.

186 I don't think the final paragraph addresses the problem raised—or if it does, it does so in a very muddled way.

192 "One user friendly solution that is *not* being advocated is [as follows] ... ": Most of the rest of the page then consists of a detailed example of what's not being advocated. Given also the fact that the solution not being advocated is described as "user friendly," the reader could be forgiven for being a little confused as to what exactly *is* being advocated.

205 "The reader will undoubtedly agree ..."—a rather strong claim, in this reader's opinion.

207 A truth valued MAYBE operator would be much better than a MAYBE qualifier (if you believe in this 3VL and 4VL stuff at all, that is, which of course I don't).

221 A lot of prescriptive adhocery (at the wrong level of abstraction, too, in my opinion) regarding the setting of indicators.

233 "The System R terms are adopted"—but the terms Codd uses aren't the System R terms.

234 Feature RM-7: "Immediately before encountering [an END CAT command], the DBMS [carries out certain actions]." That's very clever! How is the DBMS supposed to know that it's going to encounter such a "command" *before it actually does so*?

237 Very convoluted justification for applying MAYBE to partial conditions.

238 "... it is not easy to [determine] the ... data type of such function-generated values." This remark is one of many in the book that (as previously noted) display ignorance of data types as they've been understood in the programming language context since at least the early 1970s, and probably earlier than that.

239 Ad hoc nonsense at the top of the page.

240 Feature RM-19: I thought RM/V2 was supposed to be at a high level of abstraction?

243 "... incorrect data can lead to incorrect business decisions." True enough—but incorrect data is exactly what three- and four-valued logic in particular are likely to produce.

249 Sentence beginning "Consequently, when a vendor" is hard to construe.

249   Feature RI-11, line 5: For "program" read "transaction."

251   Feature RI-14 is nonsense for at least two different reasons.

251   Final sentence is incorrect. Suppose the projection of the parts relation over the COLOR attribute contains just one tuple, and the COLOR value is "marked" in that tuple.[56] The interpretation is: "There exists at least one part, but no part with a known color."[57] Contrary to Codd's claim, that interpretation is clearly not "devoid of information."

255   Contrary to what Codd claims on this page, System R didn't invent the transaction concept.

260   Feature RI-24 requires integrity constraints to be checked on read-only as well as update operations. Why?

268   Regarding "symbols for marks": This is the second time Codd has said this, but he doesn't use the scheme himself.

274   Feature RI-34 ("The MARK Command"): Doesn't define the operator!

279   "Domains, relations, views, [and] integrity constraints ... are each described separately [in the catalog] because, to a large extent, they are objects whose existence is mutually independent." No, the reason they're described separately is because, to a large extent, the relationship between the objects in question is many to many. In fact, and contrary to what Codd states, the existence of several of these objects depends quite explicitly on the existence of others. Also, note the deprecated use of the term *relations* here to mean base relations specifically.

280   "For each view, the catalog contains ... (4) for each column, the name of an already declared domain (unless the column is not directly derived from a single base column), ... (7) whether insertions of new rows are permitted by the DBMS" [etc., etc.]: There are so many things wrong with these "requirements," I don't know where to begin.

281   "The domains ... of computationally derived columns can be difficult to determine": Nonsense. "Present day host languages normally do not deal with this problem": Well,

---

[56] I apologize for spouting such nonsense, but it's impossible to talk about this stuff without spouting nonsense in one way or another. To be specific in the case at hand, a "tuple" in which some value—or (perhaps a trifle more sensibly) some attribute position, rather—is "marked" simply isn't a tuple in the first place, by definition.

[57] If (a) tuples containing nothing but nulls are automatically removed from the result of a projection, as Codd is presumably suggesting, and (b) the result of projecting the parts relation over the COLOR attribute is empty, then (c) the interpretation of that empty result would be the logically different proposition "There exists no part with a known color" (meaning among other things that there might exist no parts at all).

languages that support a proper type system do, and have done for many years. "Hence, determining the domains of computationally derived columns is not a requirement at this time": Guarantees future compatibility problems.

291   Bottom of page: Define "computationally derived."

302   "It is the responsibility of the DBA to declare for each base relation and view whether it is or not fully normalized." What *does* this mean?

303   (Top of page) Should discuss what happens if "#" is (e.g.) "least greater than."

303   Why are INSERT and UPDATE treated differently? In any case, view updatability surely isn't something to be determined by the DBA.

308   What about updating a join column?

323   "The situation is very similar ... ." Actually it's completely different.

328   I'm sorry, but the discussion on this page and the next is really nonsense.

329   Feature RA-3 seems to be a major complication. Levels of abstraction again?

330   "2. delete the data later"? Either "delete" means "delete" or it doesn't. Clarify.

331   Feature RA-6: "Seven days"? Why not 4 days 3 hours 6 minutes 27.503 seconds?

334   "Compatible with government-type security"? No, it's a totally different concept.

336   The last sentence above the exercises is surely incorrect.

337   Line 3, "relation name" should be "range variable name."

338   The syntax is a mess (in the same way that SQL is, incidentally). The term "target list" is redefined (compare the definition on the previous page). "This query could not be expressed as simply in SQL": Far be it from me to defend SQL, but this is a contentious and debatable claim.

342   "The relational model supports at least [Fortran, COBOL, and PL/I] as languages with which the principal relational language can communicate." What on earth does the relational model have to do with these specific languages, or vice versa?

348 The claim concerning products that support Feature RP-4 is false.

355 Feature RD-7: Blessing a particular implementation style? Levels of abstraction?

357 Feature RD-15: Seems completely inappropriate. Levels of abstraction?

365 Feature RL-10: I believe this feature contains the sole mention in the entire book of the important idea that the set comparison operators "=", "≠", "⊆", "⊂", "⊇", and "⊃"(or relational analogs of those operators, rather) need to be supported. Moreover, the associated explanatory text is seriously inadequate, reading as it does in its entirety thus:

> [The relational language] also includes set comparators such as SET INCLUSION. These comparators must be defined, at least in technical papers available to the public, in terms of the predicate logic supported in [the relational language].

365 Feature RL-11: Is very odd in several different ways—not least in the topics addressed, which seem to have little or nothing to do with each other.

387 First mention of "appending," at least in the sense intended (?).

392 The condition in paragraph 4 isn't achievable (consider fragments and replicas).

397 GC2 isn't always desirable.

397 Feature RX-4: Presupposes a specific implementation.

398 "... every reason to believe ..."—another very strong claim, in my opinion.

399 Feature RX-6 ("Unique Names for Sites"): Wrong name for the feature; and items 4 and 5 aren't components of the said "unique name"; and further down the page an additional (sixth) "component" [*sic*], viz., "current site name," is mentioned too.

402 INGRES/STAR was a product, not a prototype. Also, contrary to Codd's assertion, it didn't support fragmentation.

408 Section 24.8 (and elsewhere): What's a site?

409 "... invented by the R* team, then located at the IBM research laboratory in San Jose (most team members are now located at the IBM Almaden Research Center)": Is it likely that the reader would really have any interest in these details regarding life at IBM?

421   "In early versions of relational DB2 products": Freudian slip? I think Codd meant to say either "In early versions of relational products" or "In early versions of DB2," with the latter probably being the more appropriate.

423   Feature RX-29: Requiring deadlock detection is too strong. For absorbing read aborting.

451   Section 28.3 totally ignores the vast amount of work that had already been done on this problem by many other people.

461   Point 6 is too dogmatic (end users might well require a still higher level).

462   Regarding point 7, I'd like to see how "least greater than," "T-join," etc., can be explained without descending to a lower level of abstraction.

508   [Codd 1988a] has the wrong title!

The foregoing list is by no means exhaustive.

Concluding Remarks

Well, that's it, I'm done. Of course, I seriously doubt whether many people apart from myself will ever read this expanded review in its entirety, but that's OK; I wanted to get it all down in writing anyway, if only to support certain claims and assertions made by me in Chapter 22, "A Very Sorry Saga," of my 2018 book *Uncommitted Crimes*.[58] Of course, I realize that in some ways I'm just beating a dead horse—Codd's RM/V2 has had essentially no impact on the database field whatsoever (and I frankly think that's a very good thing); moreover, the book is so bad that I can quite literally find something to criticize on every single page. On the other hand, as noted earlier in this chapter, bad ideas do have a way of surfacing again later, even long after they've been thoroughly debunked, and so it might prove useful, some day, to allow this expanded review to surface as well.

APPENDIX: THE FUNDAMENTAL LAWS OF DATABASE MANAGEMENT

In Chapter 29 of his book, Codd introduces "some 20 principles with which *any* approach to database management should comply," and goes on to claim that "[these] fundamental laws are principles to which the relational model adheres." Now, I don't think Codd is suggesting here that the laws in question were developed before the relational model itself was developed; certainly I never saw them in print before the publication of reference [2]. Indeed, I think it

---

[58] Privately published, and subject to limited distribution.

might be argued that those "laws" represent, as much as anything, features that happen to *characterize* the relational approach, rather than a set of formal underpinnings on the basis of which that approach was developed. But the idea of trying to identify such a set of laws, even if after the fact, is certainly an interesting one, and I'd like to examine it briefly in this appendix.

As soon as Codd's book suggested the idea to me, I took a few minutes to jot down what seemed to me might be a reasonable set of such "fundamental laws." Here's the list I came up with:

- The DBMS mustn't forget anything it has been told to remember (i.e., data mustn't be lost).

- The DBMS must function from the user's point of view as an abstract machine.

- That abstract machine must (of course) be formally and precisely defined.

- Two specific corollaries of the previous point are that the behavior of the DBMS must be *predictable* and *repeatable*.

- The higher the level of abstraction, the better (broadly speaking).

- It mustn't be necessary to go to a lower level of abstraction in order to explain the functioning of that abstract machine.

- That abstract machine must possess certain specific properties, including:

  a. Parsimony (in particular, no unnecessary complexity)

  b. Orthogonality

  c. Closure (algebraic)

  d. Identifiability (distinct objects must be distinguishable)

  e. Integrity is a property of the data, not an application responsibility

  f. Isolation (users can behave as if the database were private)

  g. Ownership (each piece of data belongs to some specific user)

Now, this list is certainly incomplete: It's the result of perhaps fifteen minutes' thought, and I make no great claims for it. Though it did occur to me as I was compiling it that many of the points applied equally well to programming languages, and that a study of the design of a well designed programming language would probably turn up a few more "fundamental laws."

Here by contrast are the laws that Codd gives (with a few words of explanation in those cases that seem to warrant it):

1. Object identification

2. Objects identified in one way

3. Unrelated portions of a database ("if the database can be split into ... unrelated parts without loss of information, ... there [must exist] a simple and general algorithm ... to make this split")

4. Community issues ("all database issues of concern to the community of users ... should be ... explicitly declared ... and managed by the DBMS")

5. Three levels of concepts (logical, physical, and "psychological" issues should not be confused)

6. Same logical level of abstraction for all users

7. Self-contained logical level of abstraction (this is the same as my point that it shouldn't be necessary to go to a lower level of abstraction in order to explain anything; however, I think Codd violates this law himself in several places in RM/V2—e.g., in his explanation of T-joins)

8. Sharp separation (between logical and physical)

9. No iterative or recursive loops

10. Parts of the database interrelated by value comparing

11. Dynamic approach ("dynamic data definition," etc.)

12. Extent to which data should be typed ("types should be strict enough to capture some of the meaning of the data, but not so strict as to make the initially planned uses and applications the only viable ones")

13. Creating and dropping performance oriented structures

14. Adjustments in the content of performance oriented structures

15. Reexecutable commands

16. Prohibition of cursors *within the database* (italics in the original)

17. Protection against integrity loss

18. Recovery of integrity

19. Redistribution of data without damaging application programs

20. Semantic distinctiveness ("semantically distinct observations ... must be represented distinctly to the users")[59]

Comparing the two lists, it seems to me that they're really at two different levels, with the first being the more abstract. Furthermore, it seems to me that the second isn't even at a uniform level of abstraction. But I'll stop here and let you be the judge.

---

[59] I'm not really sure what this means, but Codd goes on to say that "The crucial question is: If the data were removed, would information be lost?"—suggesting, I think, that this law has something to do with the important notion of *essentiality* (see Chapter 6 of the present book).

APPENDIXES

There are three appendixes. Appendix A is the piece I wrote for Codd for the Turing Award winners section of the ACM website (*amturing.acm.org*). Appendix B gives some formal definitions. Appendix C provides a consolidated list of references for the entire book.

Appendix A

The Turing Award Website Piece

This is the piece I wrote for Codd for the Turing Award winners section of the ACM website (amturing.acm.org). It was originally written, by request, in August 2011. As you'll quickly realize, it was required to conform to a rather rigorous template.

NAME

Edgar Frank ("Ted") Codd.

CITATION

For his invention of the relational model of data and his fundamental and extensive contributions to the theory and practice of database management systems.

MAJOR CONTENT ESSAY

Please see attachment.

CAPSULE BIOGRAPHICAL INFORMATION ITEMS

Biography: Born August 19th, 1923, Isle of Portland, England; died April 18th, 2003, Williams Island, Florida.

Education: Poole Grammar School, Poole, England (1930s); honours degree in mathematics (B.A., subsequently M.A.), Exeter College, Oxford University, England (1941-1942 and 1946-1948); M.Sc. and Ph.D., computer and communication sciences, University of Michigan, Ann Arbor, Michigan (1961-1965).

Experience: Flight lieutenant, Royal Air Force (1942-1946); lecturer in mathematics, University of Tennessee (1949); programming mathematician and computer scientist, IBM

(1949-1953 and 1957-1984); head of data processing, Computing Devices of Canada (1953-1957); chief scientist, The Relational Institute (1985-1994).

Major Awards and Honors:

■ Fellow, British Computer Society (1974)

■ IBM Fellow (1976)

■ ACM Turing Award (1981)

■ Elected member, National Academy of Engineering (1981)

■ IDUG First Annual Achievement Award (1986)

■ ACM Fellow (1994)

■ Elected member, American Academy of Arts and Sciences (1994)

■ IEEE Computer Pioneer Award (1996)

■ DAMA International Achievement Award (2001)

■ Inductee, Computing Industry Hall of Fame (2004, post.)

■ Member, Phi Beta Kappa and Sigma Xi

Note: In 2004, the ACM Special Interest Group on Management of Data (SIGMOD), with the unanimous approval of ACM Council, decided to change the name of its annual innovations award to the "SIGMOD Edgar F. Codd Innovations Award" to honor Codd "who invented the relational model and was responsible for the significant development of the database field as a scientific discipline." SIGMOD, now one of the largest of the ACM Special Interest Groups, had its origins in an earlier ACM organization called SICFIDET (Special Interest Committee on File Definition and Translation), which was founded by Codd himself in 1970.

Codd was also active at various times on various editorial boards, including those of the IBM Systems Programming Series of books, *IEEE Transactions on Software Engineering*, *ACM Transactions on Database Systems*, and the *Journal of Information Systems*.

ANNOTATED BIBLIOGRAPHY

Codd wrote some 60 technical articles and papers and two books and made valuable contributions in several distinct areas, including multiprogramming, natural language processing, and others. The following very short list concentrates on the papers in which he laid the groundwork for his most famous contribution, the relational model of data.

E. F. Codd: "A Relational Model of Data for Large Shared Data Banks," *Communications of the ACM 13*, No. 6 (June 1970); reprinted in *Milestones of Research—Selected Papers 1958-1982 (Communications of the ACM 25th Anniversary Issue)*, *Communications of the ACM 26*, No. 1 (January 1983). See also the earlier version "Derivability, Redundancy, and Consistency of Relations Stored in Large Data Banks," IBM Research Report RJ599 (August 19th, 1969); reprinted in *ACM SIGMOD Record 38*, No. 1 (May 2009).

> *The 1969 paper was Codd's very first paper on the relational model; the much more widely read (and referenced) 1970 paper, which is generally credited with being the seminal paper in the field, was essentially a revised version of that earlier paper.*

E. F. Codd: "A Data Base Sublanguage Founded on the Relational Calculus," Proc. 1971 ACM SIGFIDET Workshop on Data Description, Access and Control, San Diego, Calif. (November 11th-12th, 1971).

> *This paper gave a concrete example of how concepts from predicate logic could be used as the basis for the design of a very high level database language. The ideas in this paper had a major influence on numerous commercially available languages, including QUEL, Query-By-Example, and (to a lesser extent) SQL.*

E. F. Codd: "Further Normalization of the Data Base Relational Model," in Randall J. Rustin (ed.), *Data Base Systems: Courant Computer Science Symposia Series 6*. Englewood Cliffs, N.J.: Prentice-Hall (1972).

> *This is the paper that introduced the basic ideas of relational normalization (including functional dependencies and the first three normal forms), thereby laying the groundwork for research into database design. Database design theory has since become a major field of study in its own right.*

E. F. Codd: "Relational Completeness of Data Base Sublanguages," in Randall J. Rustin (ed.), *Data Base Systems: Courant Computer Science Symposia Series 6*. Englewood Cliffs, N.J.: Prentice-Hall (1972).

In this important paper, Codd (a) defined a formal relational calculus, (b) defined a formal relational algebra, and (c) proved, by exhibiting an algorithm for converting an arbitrary calculus expression into a semantically equivalent algebraic expression, that the algebra was at least as expressive as the calculus and was therefore "relationally complete."[1]

E. F. Codd: "Interactive Support for Nonprogrammers: The Relational and Network Approaches," Proc. ACM SIGMOD Workshop on Data Description, Access, and Control, Vol. II, Ann Arbor, Michigan (May 1974).

A debate raged throughout the 1970s on the relative merits of Codd's relational approach and various nonrelational approaches, including the so called network approach in particular. This paper contains Codd's typically enlightening thoughts on the matter.

ATTACHMENT

Edgar Frank Codd, the youngest of seven children, was born August 19th, 1923, on the Isle of Portland in the county of Dorset on the south coast of England. His father was a leather manufacturer and his mother a schoolteacher. During the 1930s he attended Poole Grammar School in Dorset. He was awarded a full scholarship to Oxford University (Exeter College), where he initially read chemistry (1941-1942). In 1942—despite the fact that he was eligible for a deferment because of his studies— he volunteered for active duty and became a flight lieutenant in the Royal Air Force Coastal Command, flying Sunderlands. After the war he returned to Oxford to complete his studies, switching to mathematics and obtaining his degree in 1948.

As part of his service in the RAF, Codd was sent to the United States for aviation training. That experience led to a lifelong love of recreational flying, also to a recognition that the United States had a great deal to offer for someone of a creative bent like himself. As a consequence, he emigrated to the United States soon after graduating in 1948. After a brief period with Macy's in New York City, working as a sales clerk in the men's sportswear department, he found a job as a mathematics lecturer at the University of Tennessee in Knoxville, where he taught for six months.

Codd's computing career began in 1949, when he joined IBM in New York City as a programming mathematician, developing programs for the Selective Sequence Electronic Calculator (IBM's first electronic—or at least electromechanical—computer, a huge and noisy vacuum tube machine). He also lived for a brief period in Washington, DC, where he worked on IBM's Card Programmed Electronic Calculator. In the early 1950s, he became involved in the design and development of IBM's 701 computer. (The 701, originally known as the Defense

---

[1] This summary is oversimplified. See Chapter 3 of this book for a more comprehensive look at the situation.

Calculator, was IBM's first commercially available computer for scientific processing; it was announced in 1952 and formally unveiled in 1953.)

In 1953, Codd left the United States (and IBM) in protest against Senator Joseph McCarthy's witchhunting and moved to Ottawa, Canada, where he ran the data processing department for Computing Devices of Canada Limited (which was involved in the development of the Canadian guided missile program). A chance meeting with his old IBM manager led to his return to the U.S. in 1957, when he rejoined IBM. Now based in Poughkeepsie, New York, he worked on the design of STRETCH (i.e., the IBM 7030, which subsequently led to IBM's 7090 mainframe technology); in particular, he led the team that developed the world's first multiprogramming system. ("Multiprogramming" refers to the ability of programs that have been developed independently of one another to execute concurrently. The basic idea is that while one program is waiting for some event to occur, such as the completion of a read or write operation, another program can be allowed to make use of the computer's central processing unit. Multiprogramming is now standard on essentially all computer systems except for the smallest personal computers.) In 1961, on an IBM scholarship, he moved to Ann Arbor, Michigan, where he attended the University of Michigan and obtained an M.Sc. and Ph.D. in communication sciences (1965). His thesis—which was published by Academic Press in 1968 under the title *Cellular Automata*—represented a continuation and simplification of von Neumann's work on self-reproducing automata; in it, Codd showed that the 29 states required by von Neumann's scheme could be reduced to just eight.

During this period Codd also became a U.S. citizen—though he never lost his British accent, his British sense of humor, or his British love for a good cup of tea.

Codd then returned to IBM Poughkeepsie, where he worked on high level techniques for software specification. He then turned his attention to database issues and in 1968 transferred to the IBM Research Laboratory in San Jose, California. (He subsequently claimed that what initially motivated him in his database research was a presentation by a representative from a database company who seemed—incredibly, so far as Codd was concerned—to have no knowledge or understanding of predicate logic.) Several database products did indeed exist at that time; however, they were without exception ad hoc, cumbersome, and difficult to use—they could really only be used by people having highly specialized technical skills—and they rested on no solid theoretical foundation. Codd recognized the need for such a foundation and, applying his knowledge of mathematical logic, was able to provide one by creating the invention with which his name will forever be associated: **the relational model of data** (see sidebar).

The relational model is widely recognized as one of the great technical achievements of the 20th century. It revolutionized the way databases were perceived; indeed, it transformed the entire database field—which previously consisted of little more than a collection of ad hoc products, proposals, and techniques—into a respectable scientific (and academic) discipline. More specifically, it provided a theoretical framework within which a variety of important database problems could be attacked in a scientific manner. As a consequence, it is no exaggeration to say that essentially all databases in use or under development today are based on

Codd's ideas. Whenever anyone uses an ATM machine, or purchases an airline ticket, or uses a credit card, he or she is effectively relying on Codd's invention.

Codd described his model further and explored its implications in a series of research papers, staggering in their originality, that he published over the next several years (see annotated bibliography). Throughout this period, he was helpful and supportive to all who approached him—the author of these notes included— with a serious interest in learning more or with a view to helping disseminate, and perhaps elaborate on, his ideas. At the same time, he was steadfast and unyielding in defending those same ideas from adverse criticism.

It should be noted, incidentally, that the relational model was in fact the very first abstract database model to be defined. Thus, Codd not only invented the relational model in particular, he actually invented the data model concept in general.

During the 1970s Codd also explored the possibility of constructing a natural language question and answer application on top of a relational database system, leading a small team that built a prototype of such an application, called Rendezvous. Rendezvous allowed a user with no knowledge of database systems (and with, perhaps, only limited knowledge of the exact content of the database) to engage in a dialog with the system, starting with a would-be query expressed in possibly not very precise form and winding up with a precise query and corresponding answer, where the entire dialog was conducted in natural language (English, in the case of the prototype).

Throughout this time, Codd continued to be employed by IBM. Perhaps because it was heavily invested in its existing nonrelational database product IMS and was anxious to preserve the revenue from that product, however, IBM itself was initially quite unreceptive (not to say hostile) to Codd's relational ideas. As a consequence, other vendors, including Relational Software Inc. (later renamed Oracle Corporation) and Relational Technology Inc. (later renamed Ingres Corporation), were able to steal a march on IBM and bring products to market well before IBM did. Seeing the way the winds were blowing, senior IBM management decided in the late 1970s that IBM should build a relational product of its own. That decision resulted in the announcement of SQL/DS for the VSE environment in 1981 and DB2 for the MVS environment in 1983.

In Codd's opinion, however, those IBM products, though clearly superior to their nonrelational predecessors, were less than fully satisfactory because their support for the relational model was incomplete (and in places incorrect). Partly for that reason, Codd resigned from IBM in 1984. After a year or so working as an independent consultant, in 1985 he formed, along with colleagues Sharon Weinberg (later Sharon Codd) and Chris Date, two companies— The Relational Institute and Codd & Date Consulting Group—specializing in all aspects of relational database management, relational database design, and database product evaluation. (C&DCG subsequently grew into a family of related companies, including a parent company called Codd & Date International and a European subsidiary called Codd & Date Limited.)

Over the next several years, Codd saw the relational database industry grow and flourish, to the point where it was—and continues to be—worth many tens of billions of dollars a year (though he himself never benefited directly from that huge financial growth). Throughout that period, and indeed for the remainder of his professional life, he worked tirelessly to encourage vendors to develop fully relational products and to educate users, vendors, and standards organizations regarding the services such a product would provide and why users need such services. He was also interested in the possibility of extending his relational ideas to support complex data analysis, coining the term OLAP (On Line Analytical Processing) as a convenient label for such activities. At the time of his death, he was investigating the possibility of applying his ideas to the problem of general business automation.

Codd died April 18th, 2003, in Williams Island, Florida. He is survived by his wife Sharon; his first wife Libby; a daughter, Katherine; three sons, Ronald, Frank, and David; and several grandchildren.

SIDEBAR

Alan M. Turing Award

Edgar Frank Codd (1981)

The Relational Model of Data

The relational model of data is, in essence, a formal and rigorous definition of what the data in a database should look like to the user; i.e., it is a (somewhat abstract) specification of the user interface to a database system. In other words, a database system is relational if and only if the user interface it supports is a faithful implementation of the relational model—meaning that, as far as the user of such a system is concerned, (a) the data looks relational, and (b) relational operators such as *join* are available for operating on data in that relational form.

Data Looks Relational

Relations can be depicted on paper as simple tables of rows and columns. Loosely, therefore, we can say the user sees the data in the form of such tables.

Relational Operators Are Available

Relational operators are operators that derive further relations from given relations. Since relations can be thought of (loosely) as tables, therefore, we can think of those operators as "cut and paste" operators for tables. For example, given a table of employee information, the *restrict* operator will let us "cut out" just the rows for employees with a certain salary. And if we are also given a table of department information, the *join* operator will then let us "paste on" to those employee rows department information for the employees in question.

Implementation

Since the user interface in a relational system is so radically different from (and of course so much simpler than) the way data is physically stored and manipulated inside the system, there are some significant implementation challenges to be faced. Researchers began to investigate this problem early in the 1970s, soon after the publication of Codd's original papers, and numerous prototypes were built throughout the 1970s. The first commercial products began to appear toward the end of that decade. And while it is unfortunately still true, even today, that none of those products is entirely faithful to Codd's original vision, they quickly came to dominate the marketplace. The relational model—thanks to its solid foundation in set theory and formal logic—is here to stay. It will stand the test of time.

Appendix B

Formal Definitions

And then the justice ...
With eyes severe, and beard of formal cut,
Full of wise saws and modern instances

—William Shakespeare:
As You Like It (1599-1600)

This appendix provides reasonably formal and precise definitions of various fundamental aspects of the relational model and related matters. They're based on definitions given in my book *The New Relational Database Dictionary* (O'Reilly Media, 2016), but for the most part are slightly simplified or otherwise revised here.

attribute renaming Let relation r have an attribute called A and no attribute called B. Then the operation of renaming A as B in r returns the relation with heading identical to that of r except that attribute A in that heading is renamed B, and body identical to that of r except that all references to A in that body are replaced by references to B.

body Given a heading H, a body B conforming to H is a set of m tuples ($m \geq 0$), each with heading H. The value m is the *cardinality* of B.

Boyce/Codd normal form Relvar R is in Boyce/Codd normal form, BCNF, if and only if, for every nontrivial FD $X \rightarrow Y$ that holds in R, X is a superkey for R.

constraint An integrity constraint (unless the context demands otherwise).

database constraint Any integrity constraint that isn't a type constraint.

difference Let relations $r1$ and $r2$ be of the same type T. Then the difference between $r1$ and $r2$ (in that order) is the relation of type T with body the set of all tuples t such that t appears in $r1$ and not in $r2$.

first normal form Relation r is in first normal form, 1NF, if and only if every tuple in r contains exactly one value (of the appropriate type) for each of its attributes. *Note:* Since every relation satisfies this condition by definition, it follows that every relation, and hence every relvar, is in 1NF. Equivalently, every relation, and hence every relvar, is normalized. Normalized and 1NF mean exactly the same thing.

foreign key   Let *R1* and *R2* be relvars, not necessarily distinct, and let *K* be a key for *R1*. Let *FK* be a subset of the heading of *R2* such that there exists a possibly empty set of attribute renamings on *R1* that maps *K* into *K'*, say, where *K'* and *FK* contain exactly the same attributes (in other words, *K'* and *FK* are in fact one and the same). Further, let *R1* and *R2* be subject to the constraint that, at all times, every tuple *t2* in *R2* has an *FK* value that's the *K'* value for some necessarily unique tuple *t1* in *R1* at the time in question. Then *FK* is a foreign key, the associated constraint is a foreign key constraint (or referential constraint), and *R2* and *R1* are the referencing relvar and the corresponding referenced relvar (or target relvar), respectively, for that constraint. Also, *K*—not *K'*—is referred to, sometimes, as the referenced key or target key.

functional dependency   Let *H* be a heading; then a functional dependency (FD) with respect to *H* is an expression of the form $X \rightarrow Y$, where *X* (the determinant) and *Y* (the dependant) are both subsets of *H*. (The qualifying phrase "with respect to *H*" can be omitted if *H* is understood.) The expression $X \rightarrow Y$ is read as "*Y* is functionally dependent on *X*," or "*X* functionally determines *Y*," or, more simply, just "*X* arrow *Y*."

Let relation *r* have heading *H*, and let $X \rightarrow Y$ be an FD, *F* say, with respect to *H*. If all pairs of tuples *t1* and *t2* of *r* are such that whenever (a) the projections of *t1* and *t2* on *X* are equal then (b) the projections of *t1* and *t2* on *Y* are also equal, then (c) *r* satisfies *F*; otherwise *r* violates *F*.

Let relvar *R* have heading *H*. Then the FD *F* holds in *R*—equivalently, *R* is subject to the FD *F*—if and only if every relation *r* that can successfully be assigned to *R* satisfies that FD *F*. The FDs that hold in relvar *R* are the FDs of *R*, and they serve as integrity constraints on *R*.

heading   A heading *H* is a set, the elements of which are *attributes*. Let *H* have cardinality *n* ($n \geq 0$); then the value *n* is the *degree* of *H*. A heading of degree zero is *nullary*, a heading of degree one is *unary*, a heading of degree two is *binary*, ..., and more generally a heading of degree *n* is *n-ary*. Each attribute in *H* is of the form $<Aj,Tj>$, where *Aj* is the *attribute name* and *Tj* is the corresponding *type name* ($0 < j \leq n$), and the attribute names *Aj* are all distinct.

integrity constraint   A boolean expression, or something equivalent to such an expression, that's required to be satisfied—i.e., to evaluate to TRUE—at all times, where "at all times" effectively means at statement boundaries (or, loosely, "at semicolons"), not merely at transaction boundaries. There are two basic kinds, database constraints and type constraints; however, the term *integrity constraint* (constraint for short) is usually taken to mean a database constraint specifically, unless the context demands otherwise. The DBMS will reject any attempt to perform an update that would otherwise cause some integrity constraint to be violated (i.e., to evaluate to FALSE).

intersection   Let relations *r1* and *r2* be of the same type *T*. Then the intersection of *r1* and *r2* is the relation of type *T* with body the set of all tuples *t* such that *t* appears in both *r1* and *r2*.

join   Let relations *r1* and *r2* be such that attributes with the same name are of the same type. Then the join of *r1* and *r2* is the relation with heading the set theory union of the headings of *r1* and *r2* and body the set of all tuples *t* such that *t* is the set theory union of a tuple from *r1* and a tuple from *r2*.

key   Let *K* be a subset of the heading of relvar *R*; then *K* is a key for, or of, *R* if and only if (a) no possible value for *R* contains two distinct tuples with the same value for *K* (the uniqueness property), while (b) the same can't be said for any proper subset of *K* (the irreducibility property).

normalized   (*Of a relation or relvar*) First normal form.

product   Let relations *r1* and *r2* have no attribute names in common. Then the product of *r1* and *r2* is the relation with heading the set theory union of the headings of *r1* and *r2* and body the set of all tuples *t* such that *t* is the set theory union of a tuple from *r1* and a tuple from *r2*.

projection   Let relation *r* have attributes called *A1, A2, ..., An* (and possibly others). Then the projection of *r* on {*A1, A2, ..., An*} is the relation with heading {*A1,A2,...,An*} and body consisting of all tuples *t* such that there exists a tuple in *r* that has the same value for each of attributes *A1, A2, ..., An* as *t* does.

relation   Let *H* be a heading, and let *B* be a body conforming to *H*. The pair <*H,B*>—call it *r*— is a *relation value* (or just a *relation* for short) over the attributes of *H*. *H* is the *relation heading* (or just the heading for short) for *r*, and the degree and attributes of *H* and the cardinality of *B* are, respectively, the degree, attributes, and cardinality of *r*.

relation type   For each heading *H*, there exists exactly one relation type *T* with the same degree and attributes as *H*, and every relation and every relvar with heading *H* is of that type *T*. Conversely, for each relation type *T*, there exists exactly one heading with the same degree and attributes as *T*.

relation variable   A variable whose type is some relation type. Let relation variable *R* be of type *T*; then *R* has the same heading (and therefore the same attributes and degree) as type *T* does. Let the value of *R* at some given time be *r*; then *R* has the same body and cardinality at that time as *r* does.

relational algebra   An open ended collection of read-only operators on relations, each of which takes one or more relations as operands and produces a relation as a result. Exactly which operators are included is somewhat arbitrary, but the collection overall is required to be at least relationally complete.

relational assignment   An operation that assigns a relation value of type T to a relation variable of that same type T. *Note:* The operations INSERT, DELETE, and UPDATE are all special cases; in fact, every invocation of one of these operators is logically equivalent to some invocation of the explicit relational assignment operation (":=") as such. Fundamentally, therefore, relational assignment is the only relational update operator logically required.

relational calculus   An applied form of predicate calculus, tailored to operating on relations, with the property that every relational calculus expression is semantically equivalent to some relational algebra expression.

relational comparison   A boolean expression of the form $r1 \; \theta \; r2$, where $r1$ and $r2$ are relations of the same type and θ is any comparison operator that makes sense for relations ("=", "$\neq$", "$\subseteq$", etc.). *Note:* Since all possible relational comparisons can be defined in terms of the relational inclusion operator "$\subseteq$", relational inclusion is the only relational comparison operator logically required.

relational completeness   A language is relationally complete if and only if it's at least as expressive as relational calculus, meaning that any relation definable by some relational calculus expression is also definable by some expression of the language in question.

relational model   The formal theory or foundation on which relational databases in particular and relational technology in general are based. It consists of five components:[1] (a) an open ended collection of types, including in particular the scalar type BOOLEAN; (b) a relation type generator and an intended interpretation for relations of types generated thereby; (c) facilities for defining relation variables of such generated relation types; (d) a relational assignment operator; and (e) a relationally complete but otherwise open ended collection of generic read-only operators, based on relational algebra or relational calculus or something logically equivalent, for deriving relations from relations. *Note:* For an extended explanation of this definition, see either Chapter 1 of the present book or my book *SQL and Relational Theory: How to Write Accurate SQL Code* (3rd edition, O'Reilly, 2015).

relvar   Short for relation variable.

renaming   Attribute renaming (unless the context demands otherwise).

---

[1] Not three, as in Codd's RM/V1 (see Chapter 7), and not 18, as in his RM/V2 (see Chapter 8).

restriction   Let r be a relation and let bx be a restriction condition on r. Then the restriction of r according to bx is the relation with heading the same as that of r and body consisting of all and only those tuples of r for which bx evaluates to TRUE.

restriction condition   Let r be a relation; then a restriction condition on r is a boolean expression in which every attribute reference is a reference to some attribute of r and there are no relvar references. Observe, therefore, that a restriction condition on r can be evaluated (to yield either TRUE or FALSE) for a given tuple t of r by examining just tuple t in isolation.

second normal form   Relvar R is in second normal form, 2NF, if and only if, for every nontrivial FD $X \rightarrow Y$ that holds in R, (a) X is a superkey or (b) Y is a subkey or (c) X isn't a subkey.

subkey   Let X be a subset of the heading of relvar R; then X is a subkey for, or of, R if and only if there exists some key K for R such that X is a subset of K.

superkey   Let X be a subset of the heading of relvar R; then X is a superkey for, or of, R if and only if there exists some key K for R such that X is a superset of K.

third normal form   Relvar R is in third normal form, 3NF, if and only if, for every nontrivial FD $X \rightarrow Y$ that holds in R, (a) X is a superkey or (b) Y is a subkey.

trivial FD   The FD $X \rightarrow Y$ is trivial if and only if Y is a subset of X.

tuple   Let heading H be of degree n. For each attribute $<Aj,Tj>$ in H, define a *component* of the form $<Aj,Tj,vj>$, where the *attribute value vj* is a value of type Tj. The set—call it t—of all n components so defined is a *tuple value* (or just a *tuple* for short) over the attributes of H. H is the *tuple heading* (or just the heading for short) for t, and the degree and attributes of H are, respectively, the degree and attributes of t.

tuple join   Same as tuple union.

tuple projection   Let tuple t have attributes called $A1, A2, ..., An$ (and possibly others). Then the projection of t on $\{A1, A2, ..., An\}$ is the tuple obtained by removing from t all components other than those corresponding to attributes $A1, A2, ..., An$.

tuple type   For each heading H, there exists exactly one tuple type T with the same degree and attributes as H, and every tuple and every tuplevar[2] with heading H is of that type T. Conversely, for each tuple type T, there exists exactly one heading with the same degree and attributes as T.

---

[2] Further specifics regarding tuplevars (i.e., tuple variables) are beyond the scope of this appendix, and indeed this book.

tuple union   Let tuples *t1* and *t2* be such that attributes with the same name are of the same type and have the same value. Then the union of *t1* and *t2* is the tuple that's the set theory union of *t1* and *t2*.

type   A named (and in practice finite) set of values; not to be confused with the internal or physical representation of the values in question, which is an implementation issue. Every value, every variable, every attribute, every read-only operator, every parameter, and every expression is of some type. Types can be either scalar or nonscalar; as a consequence, attributes of relations in particular can also be either scalar or nonscalar. Types can also be either system defined (i.e., built in) or user defined. They can also be generated.

type constraint   A definition of the set of values that make up a given type.

union   Let relations *r1* and *r2* be of the same type *T*. Then the union of *r1* and *r2* is the relation of type *T* with body the set of all tuples *t* such that *t* appears in *r1* or *r2* or both.

Appendix C

Consolidated List of References

At least avoid all citations from poets

—Hippocrates:
Precepts (c. 400 BCE)

W. W. Armstrong: "Dependency Structures of Data Base Relationships," Proc. IFIP Congress, Stockholm, Sweden (August 5th-10th, 1974).

Charles W. Bachman: "The Programmer as Navigator," *Communications of the ACM 16*, No. 11 (November 1973).

D. Bjørner, E. F. Codd, K. L. Deckert, and I. L. Traiger: "The GAMMA-0 *N*-ary Relational Data Base Interface: Specifications of Objects and Operations," IBM Research Report RJ1200 (April 11th, 1973).

D. Cantor, B. Dimsdale, and A. Hurwitz: "Query Language One (QL/1) Users Manual," IBM Scientific Center Report 320-2627, Los Angeles, Calif. (June 1969).

Luca Cardelli and Peter Wegner: "On Understanding Types, Data Abstraction, and Polymorphism," *ACM Computing Surveys 17*, No. 4 (December 1985).

E. F. Codd: "Derivability, Redundancy, and Consistency of Relations Stored in Large Data Banks," IBM Research Report RJ599 (August 19th, 1969). Republished in *ACM SIGMOD Record 38*, No. 1 (March 2009).

E. F. Codd: "A Relational Model of Data for Large Shared Data Banks," *Communications of the ACM 13*, No. 6 (June 1970). Republished in *Milestones of Research—Selected Papers 1958-1982 (Communications of the ACM 25th Anniversary Issue), Communications of the ACM 26*, No. 1 (January 1983). Also republished in Phillip LaPlante, *Great Papers in Computer Science* (West Publishing, 1996) and elsewhere.

E. F. Codd: "Access Control Principles for Security and Privacy in Integrated Data Banks," IBM internal memo (July 1970).

E. F. Codd: "A Data Base Sublanguage Founded on the Relational Calculus," IBM Research Report RJ893 (July 26th, 1971). Republished in Proc. 1971 ACM SIGFIDET Workshop on Data Description, Access and Control, San Diego, Calif. (November 1971).

E. F. Codd: "Further Normalization of the Data Base Relational Model" (presented at Courant Computer Science Symposia Series 6, "Data Base Systems," New York City, N.Y., May 24th-25th, 1971), IBM Research Report RJ909 (August 31st, 1971). Republished in Randall J. Rustin (ed.), *Data Base Systems: Courant Computer Science Symposia Series 6* (Prentice-Hall, 1972).

E. F. Codd: "Normalized Data Base Structure: A Brief Tutorial," Proc. 1971 ACM SIGFIDET Workshop on Data Description, Access, and Control, San Diego, Calif. (November 11th-12th, 1971).

E. F. Codd: "Relational Completeness of Data Base Sublanguages" (presented at Courant Computer Science Symposia Series 6, "Data Base Systems," New York City, N.Y., May 24th-25th, 1971), IBM Research Report RJ987 (March 6th, 1972). Republished in Randall J. Rustin (ed.), *Data Base Systems: Courant Computer Science Symposia Series 6* (Prentice-Hall, 1972).

E. F. Codd: "Seven Steps to Rendezvous with the Casual User," IBM Research Report RJ1333 (January 7th, 1974). Republished in J. W. Klimbie and K. L. Koffeman (eds.), *Data Base Management*, Proc. IFIP TC-2 Working Conference on Data Base Management (North-Holland, 1974).

E. F. Codd: "Recent Investigations into Relational Data Base Systems," Proc. IFIP Congress, Stockholm, Sweden (August 5th-10th, 1974).

E. F. Codd: "Extending the Database Relational Model to Capture More Meaning," IBM Research Report RJ2599 (August 6th, 1979). Republished in *ACM Transactions on Database Systems 4*, No. 4 (December 1979).

E. F. Codd: "Data Models in Database Management," in Michael L. Brodie and Stephen N. Zilles (eds.), Proc. Workshop on Data Abstraction, Databases, and Conceptual Modelling, Pingree Park, Colo. (June 1980), Joint Issue, *ACM SIGART Newsletter* No. 74 (January 1981); *ACM SIGPLAN Notices 16*, No. 1 (January 1981); *ACM SIGMOD Record 11*, No. 2 (February 1981).

E. F. Codd: "Relational Database: A Practical Foundation for Productivity," *Communications of the ACM 25*, No. 2 (February 1982).

E. F. Codd: "Is Your DBMS Really Relational?" (*Computerworld*, October 14th, 1985); "Does Your DBMS Run By The Rules?" (*Computerworld*, October 21st, 1985).

E. F. Codd: "Domains, Keys, and Referential Integrity in Relational Databases," *InfoDB 3*, No. 1 (Spring 1988).

E. F. Codd: *The Relational Model for Database Management Version 2*. Reading, Mass.: Addison-Wesley (1990). Available online at *https://codeblab.com/wp-content/uploads/2009/12/rmdb-codd.pdf*.

E. F. Codd and C. J. Date: "Interactive Support for Nonprogrammers: The Relational and Network Approaches," IBM Research Report RJ1400 (June 6th, 1974). Republished in Randall J. Rustin (ed.), Proc. ACM SIGMOD Workshop on Data Description, Access, and Control, Vol. II, Ann Arbor, Michigan (May 1974), also in C. J. Date, *Relational Database: Selected Writings* (Addison-Wesley, 1986).

Hugh Darwen (writing as Andrew Warden): "Adventures in Relationland," a series of articles in *The Relational Journal*, comprising "The Naming of Columns," Issue 3 (March 1988); "In Praise of Marriage," Issue 4 (August 1988); "The Keys of the Kingdom," Issue 5 (November 1988); "Chivalry," Issue 6 (March 1989); "A Constant Friend," Issue 7 (August 1988); "Table_Dee and Table_Dum," Issue 8 (November 1988); "Into the Unknown," Issue 9 (March 1990). *Note: The Relational Journal* was a publication of Codd & Date International. It and the company are both long since defunct. However, the Andrew Warden articles were republished in C. J. Date and Hugh Darwen, *Relational Database Writings 1985-1989* (Addison-Wesley, 1990).

Hugh Darwen: "Relation Valued Attributes, *or* Will the Real First Normal Form Please Stand Up?", in C. J. Date and Hugh Darwen, *Relational Database Writings 1989-1991* (Addison-Wesley, 1992).

Hugh Darwen: "The Role of Functional Dependence in Query Decomposition," in C. J. Date and Hugh Darwen, *Relational Database Writings 1989-1991* (Addison-Wesley, 1992).

Hugh Darwen and C. J. Date: "An Overview and Analysis of Proposals Based on the TSQL2 Approach," in C. J. Date, *Date on Database: Writings 2000-2006* (Apress, 2006).

Data Base Task Group of CODASYL Programming Language Committee: *Report* (April 1971).

C. J. Date: "An Introduction to the Unified Database Language (UDL)," Proc. 6th International Conference on Very Large Data Bases, Montreal, Canada (September/October 1980). Republished (in considerably revised form) in C. J. Date, *Relational Database: Selected Writings* (Addison-Wesley, 1986).

C. J. Date: "Some Principles of Good Language Design," *ACM SIGMOD Record 14*, No. 3 (November 1984). Republished in C. J. Date, *Relational Database: Selected Writings* (Addison-Wesley, 1986).

C. J. Date: "Null Values in Database Management," Proc. 2nd British National Conference (Bristol, England, July 1982). Republished in C. J. Date, *Relational Database: Selected Writings* (Addison-Wesley, 1986). *Note:* An earlier version of this paper appeared in somewhat different form in C. J. Date, *An Introduction to Database Systems: Volume II* (Addison-Wesley, 1983).

C. J. Date: "Dates and Times in IBM SQL: Some Technical Criticisms," *InfoDB 3*, No. 1 (Spring 1988). Republished in C. J. Date, *Relational Database Writings 1985-1989* (Addison-Wesley, 1990).

C. J. Date: "What Is a Domain?", in C. J. Date, *Relational Database Writings 1985-1989* (Addison-Wesley, 1990).

C. J. Date: "Referential Integrity and Foreign Keys Part I: Basic Concepts," in C. J. Date, *Relational Database Writings 1985-1989* (Addison-Wesley, 1990).

C. J. Date: "The Default Values Approach to Missing Information," in C. J. Date, *Relational Database Writings 1985-1989* (Addison-Wesley, 1990).

C. J. Date: "NOT Is Not "Not"! (Notes on Three-Valued Logic and Related Matters)," in C. J. Date, *Relational Database Writings 1985-1989* (Addison-Wesley, 1990).

C. J. Date: "EXISTS Is Not "Exists"! (Some Logical Flaws in SQL)," in C. J. Date, *Relational Database Writings 1985-1989* (Addison-Wesley, 1990).

C. J. Date: "What Is a Distributed Database System?", in C. J. Date, *Relational Database Writings 1985-1989* (Addison-Wesley, 1990).

C. J. Date: "What Is a Relation?", in C. J. Date, *Relational Database Writings 1989-1991* (Addison-Wesley, 1992).

C. J. Date: "A Note on the Relational Calculus," *ACM SIGMOD Record 18*, No. 4 (December 1989). Republished as "An Anomaly in Codd's Reduction Algorithm" in C. J. Date, *Relational Database Writings 1989-1991* (Addison-Wesley, 1992).

C. J. Date: "We Don't Need Composite Columns," in C. J. Date, Hugh Darwen, and David McGoveran, *Relational Database Writings 1994-1997* (Addison-Wesley, 1998).

C. J. Date: *The Database Relational Model: A Retrospective Review and Analysis.* Reading, Mass.: Addison-Wesley (2001).

C. J. Date: *Go Faster! The TransRelational*^{TM} *Approach to DBMS Implementation.* Frederiksberg, Denmark: Ventus Publishing (*http://bookboon.com/en/textbooks/it-programming/go-faster*, 2002, 2011).

C. J. Date: *An Introduction to Database Systems* (8th edition). Boston, Mass.: Addison-Wesley (2004).

C. J. Date: "Optimization," Chapter 18 of C. J. Date, *An Introduction to Database Systems* (8th edition, Addison-Wesley, 2004).

C. J. Date: "What First Normal Form Really Means," in C. J. Date, *Date on Database: Writings 2000-2006* (Apress, 2006).

C. J. Date: "A Sweet Disorder," in C. J. Date, *Date on Database: Writings 2000-2006* (Apress, 2006).

C. J. Date: "Why Three- and Four-Valued Logic Don't Work," in C. J. Date, *Date on Database: Writings-2000-2006* (Apress, 2006).

C. J. Date: "Why Is It Called Relational Algebra?", in C. J. Date, *Logic and Databases: The Roots of Relational Theory*(Trafford Publishing, 2007).

C. J. Date: "Inclusion Dependencies and Foreign Keys," in C. J. Date and Hugh Darwen, *Database Explorations: Essays on The Third Manifesto and Related Topics* (Trafford, 2010).

C. J. Date: "A Brief History of the Relational Divide Operator," in C. J. Date and Hugh Darwen, *Database Explorations: Essays on The Third Manifesto and Related Topics* (Trafford, 2010).

C. J. Date: "A Remark on Prenex Normal Form," in C. J. Date and Hugh Darwen, *Database Explorations: Essays on The Third Manifesto and Related Topics* (Trafford, 2010).

C. J. Date: *Database Design and Relational Theory: Normal Forms and All That Jazz.* Sebastopol, Calif.: O'Reilly (2012).

C. J. Date: "Primary Keys Are Nice but Not Essential," Appendix A of C. J. Date, *Database Design and Relational Theory: Normal Forms and All That Jazz* (O'Reilly, 2012).

C. J. Date: *SQL and Relational Theory: How to Write Accurate SQL Code* (3rd edition). Sebastopol, Calif.: O'Reilly (2015).

C. J. Date: *View Updating and Relational Theory: Solving the View Update Problem* (O'Reilly, 2013).

C. J. Date: *Type Inheritance and Relational Theory: Subtypes, Supertypes, and Substitutability.* Sebastopol, Calif.: O'Reilly (2016).

C. J. Date: *The New Relational Database Dictionary.* Sebastopol, Calif.: O'Reilly (2016).

C. J. Date and E. F. Codd: "The Relational and Network Approaches: Comparison of the Application Programming Interfaces," IBM Research Report RJ1401 (June 6th, 1974). Republished in Randall J. Rustin (ed.), Proc. ACM SIGMOD Workshop on Data Description, Access, and Control, Vol. II, Ann Arbor, Michigan (May 1974), also in C. J. Date, *Relational Database: Selected Writings* (Addison-Wesley, 1986).

C. J. Date and Hugh Darwen: *Databases, Types, and the Relational Model: The Third Manifesto* (3rd edition). Reading, Mass.: Addison-Wesley (2007). See also *www.thethirdmanifesto.com*.

C. J. Date, Hugh Darwen, and Nikos A. Lorentzos: *Time and Relational Theory: Temporal Data in the Relational Model and SQL.* San Francisco, Calif.: Morgan Kaufmann (2014).

Umeshwar Dayal and Philip A. Bernstein: "On the Correct Translation of Update Operations on Relational Views," *ACM Transactions on Database Systems 7*, No. 3 (September 1982).

K. P. Eswaran and D. D. Chamberlin: "Functional Specifications of a Subsystem for Data Base Integrity," Proc. 1st International Conference on Very Large Data Bases, Framingham, Mass. (September 1975).

R. L. Frank and E. H. Sibley: "The Data Base Task Group Report: An Illustrative Example," ISDOS Working Paper No. 71, U.S. National Technical Information Service Document AD-759-267 (February 1973).

Nathan Goodman: "Bill of Materials in Relational Database," *InfoDB 5*, No. 1 (Spring / Summer 1990).

P. A. V. Hall, P. Hitchcock, and S. J. P. Todd: "An Algebra of Relations for Machine Computation," Conference Record of the 2nd ACM Symposium on Principles of Programming Languages, Palo Alto, Calif. (January 1975).

P. A. V. Hall: "Optimisation of a Single Relational Expression in a Relational Data Base System," *IBM Journal of Research and Development 20*, No. 3 (May 1976).

I. J. Heath: "Unacceptable File Operations in a Relational Database," Proc. 1971 ACM SIGFIDET Workshop on Data Description, Access, and Control, San Diego, Calif. (November 11th-12th, 1971).

Arthur M. Keller: "Algorithms for Translating View Updates to Database Updates for Views Involving Selections, Projections, and Joins," Proc. 4th ACM SIGACT-SIGMOD Symposium on Principles of Database Systems, Portland, Ore. (March 1985).

Anthony Klug: "Equivalence of Relational Algebra and Relational Calculus Query Languages Having Aggregate Functions," *Journal of the ACM 29*, No. 3 (July 1982).

David McGoveran: "A Long Time Coming," *Database Programming & Design 3*, No. 9 (September 1990).

Frank P. Palermo: "A Data Base Search Problem," IBM Research Report RJ1072 (July 27th, 1972). Republished in Julius T. Tou (ed.), *Information Systems: COINS IV* (Plenum Press, 1974).

J. B. Rothnie Jr. and N. Goodman: "A Survey of Research and Development in Distributed Database Management," Proc. 3rd International Conference on Very Large Data Bases, Tokyo, Japan (October 1977).

Joachim W. Schmidt: "Some High Level Language Constructs for Data of Type Relation," *ACM Transactions on Database Systems 2*, No. 3 (September 1977).

S. J. P. Todd: "The Peterlee Relational Test Vehicle—A System Overview," *IBM Systems Journal 15*, No. 4 (1976).

I n d e x

For alphabetization purposes, (a) differences in fonts and case are ignored; (b) quotation marks are ignored; (c) other punctuation symbols—hyphens, underscores, parentheses, etc.—are treated as blanks; (d) numerals precede letters; (e) blanks precede everything else.

www.ingramcontent.com/pod-product-compliance
Lightning Source LLC
Chambersburg PA
CBHW062111050326
40690CB00016B/3286